D1374017

GUESTWORKERS IN THE GERMAN *REICH:*
A POLISH COMMUNITY IN WILHELMIAN GERMANY

Richard Charles Murphy

EAST EUROPEAN MONOGRAPHS, BOULDER
DISTRIBUTED BY COLUMBIA UNIVERSITY PRESS, NEW YORK
1983

EAST EUROPEAN MONOGRAPHS, NO. CXLIII

ACKNOWLEDGEMENTS

The subject of Polish migration into the Ruhrgebiet was first suggested to me as a dissertation topic by Professor David Schoenbaum. His interest, advice, and encouragement have continued far beyond the completion of that thesis and are gratefully, if inadequately, acknowledged here. It was, in large part, through his efforts that I was able to secure a stipend from the *Deutscher Akademische Austauschdienst.* That grant enabled me to spend two years in Germany completing the research on which this work is based. During that time I profited from the extensive knowledge of sources and materials of Professor Hans Mommsen who gave freely of time and advice.

Much of my time was spent in Bottrop where I was not only welcomed but given every possible assistance. The then director of the municipal archives, *Herr Oberbibliothekrat* Dr. Rudolf Schetter, gave both personal assistance and free access to the archival material. Herr Schmidt and Frau Müller of the *Einwohnermeldeamt* and Frau Schmiedgen of the *Standesamt* tolerated my presence in their busy offices for long months and answered my appeals for help whenever possible. A special thanks must go to Herr Joachim Geisler whos generousity provided me with office space. He also sought out for me many an obscure source and explained—more than once—the intricacies of the municipal system. In addition, much of the material on which this study is based was gleaned from the holdings of the *Staatsarchiv* in Münster. The staff of that institution was cooperative and helpful in every way.

A large part of the analysis in this study was completed with the aid of a computer. Mr. John Kolp of the Laboratory for Political Research at the University of Iowa patiently instructed me in the mysteries of the operation of the machine. His advice on problems of statistical analysis was frequently sought and gratefully accepted. Professor William Welsh, now of the University of Arizona, offered comment in that respect which has served to prevent many egregious errors from being presented in the text. Those that remain are, of course, the responsibility of the author.

iii

Finally, Joyce Morrison typed and proofread the greatest part of the text. Those services, however, were the least of her contributions to the completion of this study. Her understanding that the work was important to me, her refusal to become disheartened at the seeming endlessness of it all and the support that flowed from those positions have created a debt that can never adequately be repaid.

TABLE OF CONTENTS

LIST OF TABLES

LIST OF MAPS

LIST OF FIGURES

ABBREVIATIONS

AbB	Adressbuch der Stadt Bottrop
AAB	Acta des Amtes Bottrop
AEB	Akten des Einwohnermeldeamtes Bottrop
ASB	Akten des Standesamtes Bottrop
AR	Amt Recklinghausen
DDR	Deutsche Demokratische Republik
JSB	Jahrbuch der Stadt Bottrop
PSL	Preussisches Statistisches Landesamt
RA	Regierung Arnsberg
RD	Regierung Düsseldorf
RM	Regierung Münster
SDR	Statistik des Deutschen Reichs
SJDR	Statistisches Jahrbuch für das Deutsche Reich
SR	Statistisches Reichsamt
VSDR	Vierteljahrsheft zur Statistik des Deutschen Reichs
ZKPSB	Zeitschrift des Königlichen Preussischen Statistischen Bureaus
ZKPSL	Zeitschrift des Königlich Preussischen Statistischen Landesamts
ZZP	Zjednoczenie Zawodowe Polskie (the Polish Trade Union)

INTRODUCTION

In the second half of the nineteenth century Germany underwent an economic transformation that left the unified *Reich* the leading continental European industrial power. By the eve of the First World War German industrial production had surpassed that of Great Britain and stood second in the world only to the output of the United States. That German metamorphosis from an agricultural into an industrial form, compressed as it was into the space of two generations, may truly be called an industrial revolution. As is always the case with revolutions its effects were difficult to constrain and impossible to predict. Many expected that social modernization and political democratization would be logical, even necessary, consequences. In fact, the *Reich*— and especially its dominant member, Prussia—resisted the pressures for social and political change with remarkable success. However, even that aggressively authoritarian state could not prevent the social mutations that were directly attendant to the process of industrialization, a process it had itself encouraged. In particular, the development of an industrial economy required the concentration of an ever larger part of the population. That is, it led to the growth of cities, cities far different in size and function from the old Hanseatic and Free Imperial cities. An urban society with its implications of heterogenity, social and spatial mobility and loss of authority by an hereditary, landowning aristocracy was antithetical to the Prussian tradition. Yet these manifestations of an industrial society could not be repelled.

Those industrial cities grew primarily by means of a great internal migration. The large-scale emigration of Germans to America, so characteristic of the early and middle years of the nineteenth century, had by the closing years of that century been largely replaced by a mass movement of the rural poor to industrial centers. Thus, a village might have grown to a factory town by drawing on the surplus labor of its environs. As its industries prospered and expanded, however, the increasing work force was likely attracted from diverse and more distant regions. In the end, the large industrial city would contain a population with discordant customs, religions and even languages. The Catholic Rhinelander and the Evangelical Saxon who worked side by side in the factory might find the marriage or burial ceremony of the other as grotesque as his speech was incomprehensible. The translation of peasants into mill hands might, in short, produce a meeting of xenophobes.

Nor was cultural conflict the only product of mass migration to urban centers. The traditional forces—psychological if not legal—which bound a person to place in a rural, agricultural setting were largely obviated in an industrial city. Thus, it is unsurprising to note that they changed rapidly in content as well as in form. Many, perhaps most, of the persons who comprised the population of a city in any given year were very likely not the same persons who had populated it a decade or even a year before. The countless thousands who left the rural areas to join the migration to the growing industrial cities formed an unstable urban population. Once in the cities and perhaps dissatisfied with housing, wages or companions, unsuccessful in the industrial milieu or simply bored, many rural migrants moved on. Cities then did not simply receive and absorb migrants, they also acted as way stations for thousands of them and, as a result, held populations which were constantly in flux.

Implicit in the migration of the rural thousands to cities was another problem—the creation of an industrial working class. The strictures of a job in a foundry or mine differ in many and obvious ways from those of an agricultural occupation or a handicraft and need not be explicated here. However, the emerging urban work force was not only compelled to learn and accept a new industrial labor discipline, it was also afforded new opportunities. Socio-economic mobility—if not into the bourgeoisie at least into the ranks of skilled workmen—became a real possibility. No such opportunity existed on the farm, and the chances that an artisan might become master declined steadily throughout the nineteenth century. A young foundry worker, on the other hand, might well become a machinist. Beyond the chance for individual success an urban worker had an opportunity to affect his economic life in a significant way. Labor organization, unionization, gave the industrial working class the strength to fight for the improvement of wages, hours and conditions of employment. Industrialization then created not only a new social class but also new social conventions.

These threads of German social history—urbanization, mass internal migration and the creation of an industrial working class—were woven together in a most conspicuous manner in the Ruhrgebiet. If the word "Ruhrgebiet" invites any associations, they would most likely center on coal and steel. In historical perspective, however, such associations would only be valid for the most recent times. Well into the nineteenth century it remained a lightly populated, agricultural area. After 1850 the cities which make up the modern-day Ruhrgebiet expanded rapidly from villages and market towns into industrial giants. Their populations, very largely the products of internal migration, were culturally diverse and spatially mobile, and faced all the problems of transition from preindustrial to industrial and rural to urban social patterns. The work force that manned the foundries and mines organized itself in the final decade of the nineteenth century and pursued its interests with vigor. The social tensions thus engendered were further exacerbated by the ethnic factor. For in addition to the varieties of German migrants, the Ruhrgebiet attracted hundreds of thousands of Poles, *Reich* subjects, native to the eastern provinces of Prussia.

It is with these Poles in the context of the industrial Ruhrgebiet that this study is concerned. In conjunction with the other elements of instability present in the urbanizing Ruhrgebiet the influx of large numbers of ethnically foreign migrants intensified the threat of dangerous social disruption. The bitter and protracted struggle between German and Pole in the German East indicated the potential for such ethnic contention.[1] Yet the Ruhrgebiet did not become a battleground of ethnic warfare. Equally, the evidence shows that the Poles were not immediately absorbed into the German population. As late as 1933 representatives of the Polish Party were successful in local elections in the Ruhrgebiet.[2] The assumption must be then that the Poles managed—and were allowed— to fit into the social structure of the region. This study is an attempt to discover and explicate the means and extent of that social accommodation.

The Polish question arose for the German nation in January 1871 with the foundation of the *Reich.* Until the destruction of the Holy Roman Empire in 1806 Germany had been a supernational entity. The German Confederation, that pale heir to empire, was composed of a wholly German constituency. However, its two most important members, Prussia and Austria, were both possessed of significant territories that stood outside the Confederation and were populated, very largely, by non-Germans. Still the dynastic principle of statehood allowed for such machinations. During the course of the nineteenth century, however, the spirit of nationalism grew ever increasingly stronger, and under the leadership of Prussia the *Reich* was created in response to its pressure. This, new, avowedly national state—the political and geographical manifestation of a specifically German culture—had then to face the problem of the several million Poles who were included within its borders. If it was to be truly a national state, how should it deal with that large non-German minority?

In the German East the answer was a policy of Germanization. This was begun during the *Kulturkampf* with an attack on the schools. Authority over them was taken from ecclesiastical hands (largely Polish) and transferred to the Prussian state. Polish was then excluded as a language of instruction in favor of German. It soon followed that Polish was no longer deemed a necessary subject for study, and thus the schools were—or would become in time—effectively Germanized. For a time Polish was permitted as the language of instruction in classes for religious education. However, that privilege too was eventually withdrawn. In 1886 thousands of Poles who did not hold Prussian citizenship were expelled from the eastern provinces. Soon afterward Bismarck effected the expropriation of large Polish landowners on the theory that only the nobility were infected with the virus of Polish nationalism. In these and other ways the Prussian state sought to transform its Polish subjects into Germans.

With the mass migration of Poles to the Ruhrgebiet the Polish question was extended to western Germany. That fact has not escaped the notice of historians. The most assiduous historian of the Ruhrgebiet, Wilhelm Brepohl, has asserted a different end to the story of German-Polish relations there. He has advanced the theory that an entirely new cultural group has emerged in that industrial region.[3] It was formed, to a certain extent, by the exigencies of the urban, industrial setting. More important, however, was the amalgamation of the various cultural groups which originated in East and West Prussia, Posen and Silesia with the Germans of the West, including those native to the Ruhrgebiet. That mixture has produced a Ruhr type which is distinctive in his behavior, speech and mentality. The characteristics displayed by the majority of immigrants have contributed most to the formation of the new culture, while those of the smaller groups have disappeared. ("So haben alle Völkerschaften vieles von dem verloren, was ihnen ursprünglich als Wesenmerkmal anhaftete. Geblieben sind die grossen Grundzüge des Wesens . . . .")[4] What he proposes is, no more and no less, a German melting pot.

However, Brepohl appears to be unique in his view of German-Polish relations in the Ruhrgebiet. Most historians agree that the Ruhrgebiet was a repetition of the East. Thus, Hans-Ulrich Wehler, a perceptive student of minorities in Germany, has seen evidence of the same policy of Germanization. For example, in 1899 a language decree was issued by government mining authorities with jurisdiction over the Ruhrgebiet which was aimed at curtailing the use of Polish in the mines. This was reinforced in 1908 by the Reich Law Concerning Organizations (*Reichsvereinsgesetz*) which forbad the use of Polish in public assemblies. It was viewed by Wehler as the capstone of the Prussian language and nationalities policy.[5] Of course, the same strictures regarding education which applied in the East were also in force in the West.

It is readily admitted that many of the actions taken by the authorities were clumsy and served largely to engender a heightened national sense on the part of the Poles.[6] That the Ruhrgebiet Poles should have been Germanized, however, is generally accepted as both desirable and inevitable. It was desirable because the *Reich* was, after all, a German national state. But that attitude may also reflect a belief—perhaps unconscious—in Polish cultural inferiority. Politically united the *Reich* may have been, but it was far from being a cultural entity. The heterogeneity of Germans in Wilhelmian Gemany was accepted, if not applauded, and Saxons, Bavarians and Rhinelanders strove to maintain the differences of dialect, regional dress and customs. The federal system itself was a manifestation of German diversity. It was not adopted, it need scarcely be said, in an attempt to foster democracy in the *Reich*. Rather it was a necessary concession that made it possible for the constituent members—not least Prussia—to preserve their traditional institutions and regional or tribal identities within the politically unified state. Since it is acknowledged that a variety of distinctive German types were accommodated fairly harmoniously in the *Reich,* why was it impossible to accept a similar accommodation involving Germans and Poles in the Ruhrgebiet? It is true that there were differences of language and custom between them, but were they that much greater than those between Bavarian mountaineer and Friesian peasant?

No doubt the belief in the inevitability of Germanization is partly a function of the acceptance of its desirability. It may also be the result of a touching confidence in the effectiveness of authoritarian government. As has been pointed out, confronted with the problem of Poles in the Ruhrgebiet the Prussian authorities did indeed move energetically to Germanize them. Decrees were promulgaged, laws passed and policy publicty stated. There was even created a special section in the police department (in the headquarters, in Bochum) to deal with the Poles. But has it occurred to anyone to ask if this labor had issue? Where the Ruhrgebiet Poles in fact Germanized? By consensus the answer seems to be yes. However, that answer is less rooted in a careful examination and objective interpretation of the facts than in a belief that whatever the government set out to accomplish it did accomplish—the examples of the anti-socialist laws, the *Kulturkampf* and even the Germanization of the Poles in the East notwithstanding.

In fact, the government failed in the Ruhrgebiet. The Poles there successfully resisted Gemanization and created a vital Polish community. The network of Polish social and religious organizations, the success of the Polish labor union and, eventually, the entrance of Polish representatives into local governments all bear witness to this. These manifestations of a Polish national (or ethnic) sensibility have long been recognized and duly noted. However, they have always been interpreted as a Polish response to Germanization. That is, Polish organization in the West was merely a reaction to the policy of the Prussian government. Only recently have the efforts of the Poles been viewed as positive steps in the formation of the new urban society in the Ruhrgebiet.[7] The Poles did not confuse the preservation of a distinct ethnic community with the creation of an autonomous "Little Poland." They were participants in varied and important areas of public life. They very organizations that traditionally have been seen as separating Polish Ruhrgebieters from the German fellows served, to the contrary, to secure them a place in the larger society. Intimate and personal relationships, on the other hand, were considered the proper reserve of ethnic attention. In short, what the Polish migrants in the Ruhrgebiet succeeded in creating was a German version of the plural society.

That contention is supported in this work by means of a case study. Its venue is Bottrop, a city in the Emscher zone, which was as representative or as exceptional as any city of the Ruhrgebiet. Moreover, it offers two important advantages. First, throughout the period covered by the study the city's boundaries remained almost unchanged. Thus the analysis was of a consistent unit whose inhabitants could be studied over time with relative ease. Second, Bottrop's municipal archives survived the destruction of the Second World War largely intact. Among them are the records of the City Clerk's Office (*Standesamt*) and the Registration Office (*Einwohnermelde-amt*). The latter are of particular importance in the study of immigrants. Every adult or head of household who entered the city—indeed, each native upon reaching fourteen years of age—was required to complete a form which demanded extensive bibliographical information. The data and place of birth, community of previous residence and marital and occupational status are examples of the information which new arrivals had to provide. The forms completed by migrants who entered the city from 1891 through 1920 are separated from the active records and were available for research purposes. It was during that period that Bottrop received most of its Polish migrants. The preservation and availability of the registration forms offered a unique opportunity to examine important aspects of Bottrop's Polish community with some precision.

Limitations other than the spatial must be defined. The work presented here is not, and makes no claims to be, a comparative study. However, at any point where it appeared useful reference has been made to the wider Ruhrgebiet. One chapter does juxtapose Bottrop and two American cities, a comparison made for the specific purpose of gaining perspective on the dimensions of socio-economic mobility. No attempt is made to trace the course of German-Polish relations in the East. Nor is the discovery of the grounds for the Polish migration a subject of examination here. The temporal boundaries encompass a little more than a generation—1891 to 1933. It begins at a point when Polish migration rose dramatically, though the urbanization of the Ruhrgebiet was already well underway. It carries through a period of war and political and economic crisis, and ends at a turning point in German history.

A particularly troublesome problem was encountered with regard to ethnic classification. As a result it was decided to use the word "Pole" in a limited fashion here. At the beginning of the period that is under examination there was no Poland. From the time of the third Polish Partition in 1795 until the end of World War I that territory inhabited primarily by Poles was divided among the sovereignties of Prussia—later the *Reich*—Russia and the Habsburg Empire. Most of the migrants from that territory who entered Bottrop were, in law, Prussian subjects, although there were some of Russian legal nationality and a few Habsburg subjects. It is those Prussian subjects of Polish ethnicity who are referred to in the following pages as Poles. The others are contained in the category of "foreigners." In the few cases that Russian and Habsburg Poles are combined with Prussian Poles that grouping will be specified.

The problem of ethnic classification was compounded by differing methods of official record-keeping. The Prussian Census Bureau reported regularly on the numbers of Poles in the various cities of the Ruhrgebiet, and it differentiated between Prussian and foreign Poles. The municipal Registration Office also noted legal nationality. However, it listed Poles native to the German East as "Prussians." Since it was necessary to separate Poles from Germans for the purposes of analysis a method has to be found to identify the Poles who registered in the city. At length only one solution to the problem proved practical. All registrants who were native to the heavily Polish eastern provinces of Prussia were assumed to be Poles. The system is obviously far from perfect, and there is little doubt that some Gemans were included within that group. On the other hand, it is possible that a few Poles, children of very early migrants, were noted as natives of western Prussia. A close study of the avaiable records, however, convinces me that the number of misclassifications is minimal.

Another term which must be defined is "persistence." It describes a simple absence of physical movement. To speak of the persistence of the Poles in Bottrop is only to say that they remained in the city. It is flexible as to its reference. That is, it can be used to describe a residence period of one, five or ten years—or for that matter, any length of time. The only requirement is that the period be specifically stated. In addition, persistence may be analyzed on two levels. The rates of persistence of individual persons can be noted and analyzed in relationship to other phenomena. But one might also speak of group persistence. Thus, in Bottrop a large number of Poles were resident throughout the period under examination, although the persons who comprised that group—or many of them—were inhabitants of the city for only a short time. The concept of group persistence is of particular importance here since the emphasis of this study is on the organization of the Polish community and its intercourse with German society rather than on the biographies of certain of its members.

A word is also in order concerning sources. The registration forms referred to above contained much information that was invaluable to the description and analysis of the Polish community in Bottrop. In fact so much information was available that it could not be exploited in whole. The sheer numbers of completed forms—more than 200,000 for the years from 1891 through 1920—made it impossible to make use of the entire group. An acceptable alternative was to obtain a sample of the forms.[8] The data gained from the sample were subjected to statistical analysis with the aid of a computer.[9] The inevitable problems which arose with regard to classification and interpretation have been resolved, or at least delineated, in the appropriate palces in the text and footnotes. Extensive use has also been made here of archival holdings, newspapers, monographs and other traditional sources of historical research. At times the two varieties of source material complement each other and strengthen the force of an argument. On occasion one or the other must support a position alone. It is hoped that judicious use of varying forms of material and analysis has resulted in a contribution to the understanding of a society which is as of compelling an interest to its historians as it was to its contemporaries.

CHAPTER I

THE RUHRGEBIET AND BOTTROP IN
HISTORICAL PERSPECTIVE

In order to understand what the Ruhrgebiet became one must understand what it was. As a first step it is necessary to determine where it is; not so easy a task as it might seem. It may be true that natives of the Ruhrgebiet have a fine sense of exactly what does and what does not belong to it.[1] The outsider, however, has no such instinctive advantage. The Ruhrgebiet has a certain economic unity and at least partial geographic definition, but it has never been a political entity. From the widest perspective the Ruhrgebiet is part of an international belt that reaches across northern Europe from France to Poland and is distinguished by dense population, a high level of industrialization and rich coal deposits.[2] More narrowly, it is the industrial core of the *Land* Nordrhein-Westfalen of the Federal Republic of Germany, located in the west-central part of that *Land*. Even within these relatively narrow limits its boundaries are subject to varying definition. The expression "Ruhrgebiet" is itself somewhat misleading, since it refers to an area almost entirely north of the river Ruhr. It is possible, and certainly not extravagant, to define a "Greater" Ruhrgebiet which would include the industrial cities of Wesel, north of the river Lippe; Hamm, on its eastern end; Krefeld, west of the Rhine; and Wuppertal, south of the Ruhr.[3] A more restricted view would limit it to the territory east of the Rhine and between the Lippe and the Ruhr. For the purposes of this study the Ruhrgebiet will be defined in this final sense.

MAP I-1

THE RHINE-RUHR REGION

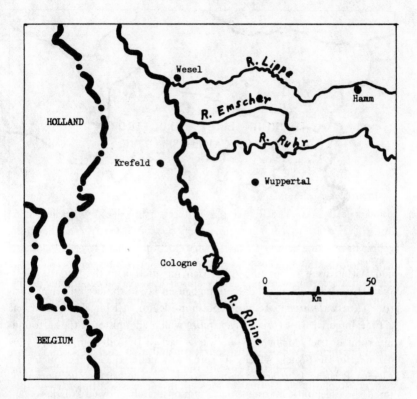

Most specifically, it is comprised of fifteen cities (*Stadtkreise*) which lie within this territory.[4]

The area occupied by the Ruhrgebiet is small. It is little more than thirty miles from Duisburg, at its western end, to Dortmund, at its eastern limit. From north to south it measures less than half that distance. Yet even within this small area the tangled history of German political geography is evident. Today, although it lies wholly inside Nordrhein-Westfalen, the Ruhrgebiet is still divided among three administrative districts—the *Regierungsbezirke* Arnsberg, Düsseldorf and Münster. At the end of the eighteenth century it was divided among a variety of sovereignties. Bochum

MAP I-2

CITIES OF THE RUHRGEBIET

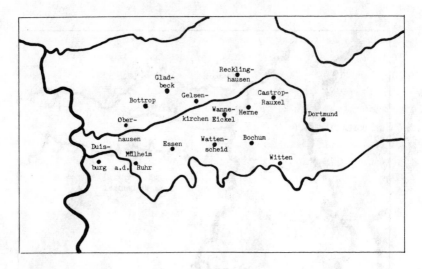

and Witten were towns under Prussian jurisdiction in the County (*Grafschaft*) of Mark. Essen and Recklinghausen lay in the ecclesiastical territory (*Kurfürstentum*) of the Archbishop-Elector of Köln. Dortmund was a Free Imperial City (*Freie Reichstadt*) which administered the surrounding rural district. Mülheim/Ruhr was a part of the sub-dominion (*Unterherrschaft*) of Broich which, in turn, was under the protection of the Elector Palatine (*Kurfürsten von der Pfalz*).[5] The Napoleonic Wars shattered the old political arrangements and ultimately allowed Prussia to gain control of the entire area. In 1802 and 1805 in compensation for French annexation of its possessions along the Rhine, Prussia received territories which included all the Ruhrgebiet except the Dortmund district. Following the defeat at Jena, however, the Hohenzollerns lost everything west of the Elbe. The entire Ruhrgebiet was then included within a French satellite known as the Grand Duchy (*Grossherzogtum*) of Berg. Prussia recovered the area at the Congress of Vienna, where she received all the territory between the river Weser and the western frontier. In the reconstituted Prussian state the Ruhrgebiet was again divided between two newly established provinces, Westfalen (*Regierungsbezirke* Arnsberg and Münster) and the Rheinprovinz (*Regierungsbezirk* Düsseldorf).

Although it continued to be politically dividied, the Ruhrgebiet was contained within a special administrative district—the Royal Mining Office at Dortmund (*das königliche Oberbergamt zu Dortmund*). This fact points to the source of its wealth and the basis of its growth—the mining of coal. Coal mining had been carried on in the Ruhr area since the Middle Ages. Documents refer to it from the beginning of the fourteenth century.[6] To the middle of the nineteenth century, however, coal was of secondary importance in the economic life of the region; agriculture remained dominant. Coal production was concentrated in the Ruhr valley where the seams lay close to the surface. There was no need for the sinking of deep shafts, the use of elaborate technology or the employment of skilled, professional miners. Minining was carried on as a part-time occupation by small numbers of peasants who dug coal for only a few hours a day.[7] Well into the nineteenth century the immense reserves which lay to the north were untapped and scarcely recognized. In 1754 an observer predicted that the future of Wattenscheid, later a coal mining center, lay forever in the direction of agriculture.[8] Even as the deep lying coal fields of the Ruhrgebiet began to be exploited the full potential was not imagined. As late as 1852 the German commissioners to the Crystal Palace Exposition pointed out that Germany's limited endowment of resources would never allow her to attain the English level of coal production.[9]

It was the development of more sophisticated techniques in the iron and steel industry which produced industrial growth in the Ruhrgebiet. For centuries the art of iron making had depended on the use of charcoal. It was thus tied timber producing areas. In the hills just south of the Ruhr abundant woodolands were to be found, and it was there, in the Siegerland and the Sauerland, that the German iron industry first emerged. A series of innovations in the eighteenth and nineteenth centuries—for the most part of British origin and later adapted to local German conditions —enabled the industry to convert to the use of coke.[10] The particular type of coal needed to produce coke is found north of the Ruhr valley. The immense deposits of bituminous coal (*Fettkohle*) not only established the Ruhrgebiet as a supplier of raw material, but they also decisively influenced the growth of the iron and steel industry there. Coal is necessary for the refining of iron ore both as a source of heat and, in its coke form, of carbon. During the refining process the entire weight of the coal is consumed. The less the full weight of the a raw material is incorporated into the final product, the less economical it is to transport it to the manufacturing center. Since coal represented more than a quarter of the cost of production of iron and steel, the shipment of iron ore to the source of coal supply entailed a considerable savings.[11]

In 1849 the first blast furnace in the Ruhrgebiet fired by coke, the *Friedrich-Wilhelms-Hütte,* was erected at Mülhein/Ruhr. Technical difficulties prevented it going into production until 1853, by which time a second one had been constructed at Bergeborbeck (near Essen).[12] By 1860 there were about thirty-two furnaces in the Ruhrgebiet.[13] Between 1854 and 1856 Henry Bessemer perfected a process which greatly increased the speed and scale of steel manufacture. German steel makers, howerver, did not immediately utilize the Bessemer converter because the type of iron ore most readily available to them was not suited to it. In May 1879, the Gilchrist-Thomas process for the production of basic steel was introduced. This made possible the profitable working of low grade, phosphoric ores which were mined in Lorraine and other parts of Germany. Together with the Bessemer process it provided the technological base for the rapid growth of the German steel industry. In September 1879, the first basic steel was produced simultaneously at opposite ends of the Ruhrgebiet— in Hörde and Ruhrort. Within five years Germany was making over half the basic steel of the world.[14]

The effects on caol mining of the developments in the steel industry can be seen in Table I-1. The small and crude anthracite mines of the Ruhr valley were nearing the end of their usefulness by 1880. The bituminous coal necessary for coking was found to the north. In 1837 in Essen, the first deep shaft was sunk through the overlying secondary beds.[15] The deep shaft mines moved steadily northward to Oberhausen, Herne and Gelsenkirchen. By 1900 almost 70 percent of the production of the Ruhr coal field (both the Ruhr valley and the Ruhrgebiet) came from mines on the southern side of the Emscher valley. To the north of the Emscher, mines which had not even been in existence in 1850 contributed another 20 percent of the total output.[16] The total number of mines in the coal field was not appreciably greater in 1910 than 1792. The increase in the number of mines until 1860 reflected the opening of the deep shaft mines of the Ruhrgebiet. The decrease thereafter was the result of mine closings in the Ruhr valley. Even as the total number of mines decreased, however, production rose—from 1792 to 1910 more than four hundredfold. The

TABLE I-1

Growth of Coal Mining in the Ruhr, 1792-1910

Year	No. of Mines	Production in Tons	No. of Miners
1792	154	176,676	1,357
1800	158	230,258	1,546
1850	198	1,665,662	12,741
1860	281	4,365,834	29,320
1870	220	11,812,528	51,391
1880	202	22,495,204	80,152
1890	177	35,469,290	127,794
1900	167	59,618,900	226,902
1910	165	86,864,594	345,136

Source: Max Jurgen Koch, *Die Bergarbeiterbewegung im Ruhrgebiet zur Zeit Wilhelms II., 1889-1914* (Dusseldorf, 1954), p. 139.

mines of the Ruhrgebiet were considerably larger and more efficient than those of the Ruhr valley. The average number of persons employed per mine had increased from about nine in 1792 to more than 2,090 in 1910. Production per employee had almost doubled despite the necessity imposed by the deep shaft mines to employ a large percentage of the work force in tasks ancillary to the actual cutting of coal.[17] As late as 1913 more than 97 percent of the cutting was still being done by hand.[18]

Bound up with the industrial and mining expansion was a population explosion. In 1800 the Ruhrgebiet had been primarily rural. Its cities, with the exception of Recklinghausen, were located along the Hellweg—the medieval trade route between Duisburg and Paderborn—and were little more than small towns. Essen had not expanded beyond its medieval walls, and contained only about 4,000 inhabitants. Dortmund had about the same number, and Bochum and Recklinghausen were only half that size.[19] Through the first half of the nineteenth century the Ruhrgebiet retained a rural cast. A topographical survey of the Rheinland and Westfalen, published by the Prussian government in 1842, described in detail the agricultural economy of the *Kreise* Dortmund and Bochum while mentioning the mining of coal only as an afterthought.[20] The cities along the Hellweg grew, but in 1850 only Duisburg held as many as 20,000 inhabitants. To the north the Emscher valley was still a thinly settled, forbidding fringe territory (ein *ödes siedlungsfeindliches Grenzgebiet*).[21] The second half of the century, particularly the last thirty years, saw a complete transformation of the Ruhrgebiet. The historic cities now counted their inhabitants in the scores and hundreds of thousands. Places such as Wattescheid and Castrop-Rauxel, which had been villages with only a few hundreds of population, were becoming major industrial cities.

In 1871 the population of the Ruhrgebiet numbered just over 605,000; in 1910 it was more than 2,800,000. Table I-2 shows its growth at intervals of ten years.

TABLE I-2

Population Growth in the Ruhrgebiet, 1871-1910
(Absolute Numbers in Thousands)

Year	Population	Increase	Percentage Increase	Percentage Increase over 1891
1891	605	--	--	--
1880	834	229	37.8	37.8
1890	1,116	282	33.8	84.4
1900	1,872	756	67.7	209.4
1910	2,801	929	49.6	362.9

Sources: For 1871 and 1880—ZKPSB 12. Jg., (1872) and 21 Jg. (1881). For 1890-1910—Robert Müller, *Die Bevolkerungsentwicklung des rheinisch-westfalischen Industriegebiets von 1895 bis 1919* (Dissertation, Münster, 1921). *Zahlentafeln* 12, 13 and 15.

This population explosion created severe physical pressures. Police and fire protection had to be expanded. Retail outlets for goods and food had to be established, and the goods and food transported into the Ruhrgebiet. A water supply both for private and industrial use had to be secured, and a sewage system constructed. The Ruhr itself was the most important source of water for the Ruhrgebiet. In 1893 more than 3.1 billion cubic feet of Ruhr water was used. Four years later the use had climbed to over 4.8 billion cubic feet, and by 1904 usage exceeded 7.5 billion cubic feet. The *Ruhrtalsperrenverein* was founded in 1898 to subsidize the building of reservoirs. In 1913 the *Ruhrverband* was created to regulate water use in the Ruhr valley.[22] The river Emscher was the natural drainage canal (*Vorfluter*) of the Ruhrgebiet. The encroachment of the coal mines had turned it and its tributaries into sewers of industrial waste (*Schmutzwassergräben*). The *Emschergenossenschaft* was established in 1899 to build water purification plants and drain the marshy ground along the banks of the Emscher.[23] Housing had to be built for the mushrooming population. In the incorporated cites of the Rurhgebiet alone[24] the number of dwellings rose from 37,512 in 1895 to 99,408 in 1910.[25] Schools provided for the education of more than 500,000 children under fourteen in 1895. Fifteen years later over one million children of school age lived in the Ruhrgebiet.[26] In brief, within the space of a single generation entire cities along with their service facilities had to be built.

Given time and organizational ability the problems of brick and mortar —of houses, schools and sewers—could be solved. Equally important, but less tangible, were the problems of creating the sense of place, community and shared institutions that permit living and working together in an atmosphere of social toleration if not total amity. The absence of historical urban centers in the Ruhrgebiet impeded such social evolution. Of the fifteen cities which make up the contemporary Ruhrgebiet only seven existed as cities in 1800, and these were ecclesiastical, administrative or market centers rather than modern urban complexes. Seven other were mere villages, and one—Oberhausen—was a solitary moor (*inmitten von Kiefen und Heide einsam gelegen*) not to be settled until the middle of the century.[27] Compounding the problem was the composition of the population. Tables I-3 and I-4 show clearly that the growth of the Ruhrgebiet was due largely to immigration, or more properly, to internal migration, since most of the migrants were subjects of the German *Reich*. Because the former term denotes entry from a foreign country, the more general "in-migration" will be used hereafter.

By 1900 migrants actually formed a majority of the population. In addition, it is to be remembered that a number of those included in the native population were children of migrants. Thus, the effect of in-migration on the population growth was even greater than shown in the tables.

TABLE I-3

Ruhrgebiet Population Born within the Census Kreis, 1880-1910
(Absolute Numbers in Thousands)

Year	Population	Increase	Percentage Increase	Percent of Total Percentage
1880	488	––	––	58.4
1890	596	108	22.2	53.4
1900	881	285	47.8	47.0
1910	1,302	421	47.8	46.5

Sources: For 1880—ZKPSB 21. Jg. (1881). For 1890-1910—Müller, *Die Bevolkerungsentwicklung, Zahlentafeln* 12, 13 and 15.

TABLE I-4

Ruhrgebiet Population Born Outside the Census Kreis, 1880-1910
(Absolute Numbers in Thousands)

Year	Population	Increase	Percentage Increase	Percent of Total Percentage
1880	346	––	––	41.6
1890	520	174	50.2	46.6
1900	981	471	90.6	53.0
1910	1,498	507	51.1	53.5

Sources: For 1880—ZKPSB 21. Jg. (1881). For 1890-1910—Müller, *Die Bevolkerungsentwicklung, Zahlentafeln* 12, 13 and 15.

The swell of in-migration was the result of the expansion of mining and manufacturing in the Ruhrgebiet. Until the 1840s the coal miners of the Ruhr valley were, for the most part, drawn from the local population. The occupation was often hereditary.[28] As mining pushed northward past the

schen Sprache mächtig)—almost doubled the number of Ruhrgebiet residents classified as not fully Polish.[41] Nor did language allow discrimination among the Poles themselves. The migrants included Masurians from East Prussia, Polish speaking Protestants loyal to the crown; Polish nationalists from Posen, veterans of the *Kulturkampf* and the *Hakatist* wars; and Upper Silesian peasants who spoke dialectical Polish (*Wasserpolnisch*) or even a variety of Czech (*Mährisch*).

Another index of ethnicity can be gained by means of an examination of statistics concerning the birthplaces of the Ruhrgebiet population. Of the population of the cities of the region in 1910 who were born outside the census district (*Kreis*), a little more than 30 percent (about 450,000) were born in the five eastern provinces.[42] This number almost certainly does not coincide with the number of Poles in the Ruhrgebiet, since some of those born in the East must have been ethnic Germans. On the other hand, a portion of the population born in the census district must have been children of Polish migrants. However, if 450,000 is accepted as the approximate number of Poles resident in the Ruhrgebiet, then the ethnically Polish population constituted about one-sixth of the whole. Even without an accurate count of Poles in the Ruhrgebiet it is evident that they were numerous, and thus were an important social factor.

The destination of thousands of the Polish migrants was the city of Bottrop in the Emscher zone. That area, the northern part of the Ruhrgebiet, developed later than the Hellweg.[43] The modern industrial cities of the latter grew out of historic towns which for centuries had ecclesiastical or administrative importance. With the exception of Recklinghausen the modern cities of the Emscher Zone remained simple market or church villages until late in the nineteenth century. Bottrop is typical of this development. It is located in the northwestern section of the Emscher Zone and is bounded by Oberhausen on the west, Essen on the south and Gladbeck on the east. As is the case with most of the Emscher Zone cities Bottrop has a long, but until recently, unexceptional history. It was the site of a prehistoric settlement and was peopled by various Teutonic tribes, falling finally under the hegemony of the Carolingian Empire.[44] The name is known from the eighth century, though some dispute exists as to its derivation.[45] Until the mining of coal began late in the nineteenth century the most noteworthy socio-economic events of Bottrop's history were the clearing of land for farming (*Hauptrodungszeit*) about the middle of the

eighth century and the introduction of copyhold and proprietary rights
(*Erb-und Markenköttern*) near the beginning of the thirteenth century.[46]
Fairly early on Bottrop became the center of local religious observance.
The Chapel of St. Cyriakus (*Cyriakus-Kapelle*) was mentioned in a document in 1160. It served as a focus for the surrounding farm communes
(*Bauernschaften*). In 1419 the chapel was expanded into a towered
church.[47] With the exception of brief interludes during the religious wars
of the sixteenth century Bottrop retained almost total Catholic homogeneity until the era of its industrial development when the Protestant
population became measurable.[48] Its political ties were for centuries
bound up with its religious subordination. Until the dissolution of ecclesiastical territories in 1803 Bottrop was under the sovereignty of the Archbishop-Elector of Köln. During the Napoleonic Wars it was subject to the
political shifts common to the German West.[49] At the conclusion of the
Wars it became part of the Prussian kingdom and was combined with Osterfeld as a single mayoralty district (*Bürgermeisterei*) in the *Landkries*
Recklinghausen. Only in 1891 did the two become separate.[50]

Bottrop's commonplace political history was matched, until the late
nineteenth century, by an equally placid demographic history. Figure I-1
shows its population growth since 1800. During the first sixty years of
the nineteenth century Bottrop's population doubled. Over the next thirty
years it tripled. The base, however, was small—a little less than 2,000 in
1800. In 1890 it still had a population of only 12,500. From that year for
the next twenty-five years the increase was spectacular. From 1890 to
1900 the population doubled. From 1900 to 1910 it doubled again, and
from 1910 until 1916, when the war began to play an increasingly dominant role, it increased a little more than 60 percent. The decline of the war
years was abruptly reversed after 1918. By 1921 the population has surpassed the 1916 level. During the next few years a slight decline occurred.
During the decade 1923 to 1933 the city gained about 10,000 inhabitants.
This pattern of population growth coincided with the development of coal
mining. During the years 1800 to 1875 the population increased from
1,989 to 6,567, an impressive 30 percent, but only 4,578 in absolute numbers. In 1875 the first mine in Bottrop began producing coal.[51] The next
fifteen years saw an increase of nearly 6,000 people. From 1891 to 1933
the growth in absolute numbers was more than 73,000.

It is clear that—with the best will in the world—natural increase could
not have accomplished these numbers, even though before the First World

FIGURE I-1

POPULATION GROWTH OF BOTTROP, 1800-1933
(In Thousands)

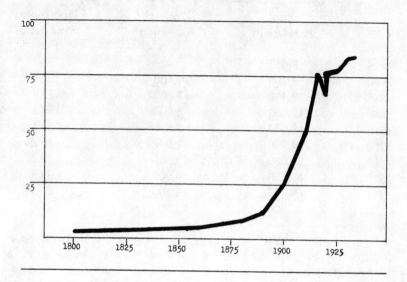

Sources: AbB—1911, 1920, 1930/31 and 1953.

War Bottrop, along with Zabrze in Upper Silesia, had the highest birth rate of all German cities.[52] Nor did Bottrop, unlike many cities of the Ruhrgebiet, gain much population by the process of annexation (*Eingemeindung*). Until 1929 it consisted of the historic central village and the surrounding *Bauernschaften* of Battenbrock, Boy, Eigen, Fuhlenbrock and Lehmkuhle. During a general reordering of city boundaries in that year Bottrop gained a small area to the south of the city, Ebel, and with it a little over 5,000 people.[53] The bulk of the population increase occurred through in-migration. Although the exact percentage of population increase due to net migration gains is not recorded until 1920—Bottrop gained municipal status (*kreisfreie Stadt*) only in 1921—a rough estimate can be made. By calculating a hypothetical population increase for the city with the use of published birth and death rates the comparison shown below in Table I-5 is achieved.

TABLE I-5

Actual and Projected Population Increase in Bottrop, 1875-1920

Year	Actual Population*	Projected Population*	Proj. Pop. as % of Actual
1875	6,600	—	—
1880	7,700	7,100	92.2
1885	9,300	7,800	83.8
1890	12,500	8,600	68.8
1895	18,000	9,800	54.4
1900	24,700	11,500	46.2
1905	34,000	13,500	39.7
1910	47,100	16,000	33.9
1915	69,000	18,300	26.5
1920	75,000	19,100	25.4

Sources: Birth and death rates 1875-1910: Chmielecki, *Die Bevolkerungs-Entwicklung im Stadt-und Landkreis Recklinghausen in den Jahren 1875 bis 1910* (Dissertation, Freiburg, 1914), p. 47 and p. 55; birth and death rates 1911-1920: Müller, *Die Bevolkerungsentwicklung, Zahlentafeln* 22 and 23; Bottrop's actual population: AbB, 1911 and 1920.

Note: The projected growth for the years 1875 to 1910 is based on the birth and death rates for the *Stadt-und Landkreis* Recklinghausen. The rates for the years 1911 to 1920 are for Bottrop. Since the death rates for the years 1915 to 1917 were not available the 1918 rate was used in the calculations for those years.

* To the nearest 100.

The projected growth by natural increase, while not to be accepted as exact, indicates by its deviation from the actual population figures the part played by in-migration in the population growth of Bottrop. In short, by 1920 it was possible that about 75 percent of Bottrop's population consisted of in-migrants and their children.[54] The post-war period from 1921 to 1933 shows a completely different picture. During that period

Bottrop grew by about 10,000 people. The figures for in- and out-migration, however, yield a net loss of over 11,000.[55] A little more than 5,000 of the difference was made up by the annexation of Ebel. Thus, it seems probable that during the post-war period the growth in population was due largely to natural increase.[56]

CHAPTER II

THE IN-MIGRANTS

Merely establishing the fact of mass in-migration contributes but little toward an understanding of its effect on the formation of Bottrop's urban society. A description and analysis of some of the demographic characteristics of the in-migrants can be useful in moving toward that end. The source for the information on which the following pages are based is the sample taken of the records of Bottrop's Registration Office (*Einwohnermeldeamt*) for the years 1891 to 1920.

Almost one in-migrant in five (see Table II-1) was of foreign birth. The majority of the foreign-born were Poles from Russian Poland and Slavic subjects of the Habsburg Empire. A smaller part of the foreign contingent was made up of Italians, and Holland contributed a tenth of the total. One of the sample group was a native of Mount Pleasant, New York. German nationals native to areas outside the East made up about 30 percent of all in-migrants.[1] Bottrop's nearest neighbors, the cities of the Ruhrgebiet, contributed relatively few in-migrants, less than 9 percent of the total. The great demand for labor throughout the Ruhrgebiet could have largely obviated the economic motive for migration within the region. Simple proximity and that same high labor demand, however, would have greatly facilitated movement for those determined on it. That these people came at all is evidence more of an increasing physical mobility than of the uniqueness of economic opportunity offered in Bottrop. The western German

TABLE II-1

Place of Birth of Bottrop's In-Migrants, 1891-1920

Place of Birth	Number	Percent*
Upper Silesia	75	23.2
Posen	42	13.0
Other East	46	14.3
Ruhrgebiet	28	8.7
Rhineprovince-Westphalia	35	10.8
Other West	37	11.4
Foreign	59	18.3
TOTAL	322	—

Source: AEB.
* Due to rounding percentages for this and subsequent tables may total less than 100 percent.

area immediately surrounding the Ruhrgebiet—the area that today is the *Land* Nordrhein-Westfalen—which might have been expected to be heavily represented, contributed about the same percentage of the in-migrants. The remainder of the western German in-migration came from places as widely separated as Hamburg and Bavaria, and Alsace-Lorraine and Frankfurt/Oder.

Easterners made up a bare majority of the in-migration. It is within this group that the Poles are contained. Although, as previously mentioned, there is no method of discerning exactly the percentage of the eastern in-migration that was ethnically Polish, it seems safe to assume that in-migrants from the heavily Polish areas of the German East were, for the most part, ethnic Poles. This assumption was certainly made by native Bottropers.[2] In particular, the in-migrants from Upper Silesia and Posen were almost surely Poles. Almost half of the Polish in-migration—about a quarter of the whole—consisted of natives of Upper Silesia. The Upper Silesians made their way to Bottrop earlier than any other groups of Poles, and they continued to come in larger numbers than any group—Pole, German or foreigner—until quite late in the era of mass in-migration. The natives of Posen represented the second largest geographically homogeneous group of

Poles. The migration of Poseners was influenced not only by the economic attraction of the Ruhrgebiet, but also by the government's anti-Polish policy in Posen. In an attempt to "Germanize" Posen a policy had been adopted in the latter years of the nineteenth century one of whose aims it was to prevent Poles from gaining control of the land. For example, an amendment of 1904 to the Settlement Law (*Ansiedlungsgesetz*) allowed Poles in Posen to acquire land but not to build on it. Although the anticipated results were not forthcoming, the legislation had by 1906 effected a rise in land prices of almost 250 percent over the level of 1888.[3] In 1908 a more drastic law was passed which provided for the expropriation of land for the purpose of ". . . the safeguarding of the jeopardized German nationality. . . ."[4] Poles from the four other eastern provinces together only slightly outnumbered the Poseners. In this group were to be found East and West Prussians—among them Masurians and Kasubians—a few Lower Silesians and the odd Pomeranian.

The disproportionate number of Upper Silesians among the Bottrop in-migrants requires some explanation, particularly since Upper Silesians made up only about 7 percent of all eastern in-migrants in the Ruhrgebiet.[5] The movement of migrants from particular areas to specific cities was not uncommon in the Ruhrgebiet. In fact, the tendency was all in that direction. Ruhrgebiet cities could be classified on the basis of their in-migrants' birth places. Masurians settled in Gelsenkirchen, Poseners in Oberhausen and Wanne-Eickel, West Prussians in Wattenscheid and Upper Silesians in Bottrop.[6] Even finer distinctions can be made. Eastern in-migrants in Ruhrgebiet cities often came from specific *Kreise*. For example, West Prussian migration into Wattenscheid was dominated by natives of the *Kreise* Stuhm and Strasburg.[7] A large majority of the Upper Silesians in Bottrop came from the *Kreise* Ratibor and Rybnik. The labor policy of the mines was initially responsible for this geographic pattern. The demand for labor in the coal mines of the Ruhrgebiet shortly out-stripped the available local supply. In order to meet demands companies were forced to recruit labor, often sending agents to the East, an area of a large and often poor rural population.[8] Once a settlement of Upper Silesians, Poseners or Masurians was made in a particular Ruhrgebiet city it served as a magnet for others from the same eastern *Kreise* if and when they considered migration.[9] This system did not, of course, exclude in-migrants from other areas, but it does explain the prevalence of geographic groupings.

Upper Silesian movement to Bottrop started in just this way, although it began not in Bottrop proper, but in Ebel. In January 1871 an agent for the mine Prosper I, located in Ebel and a part of the city after 1929, journeyed to the East in search of miners. He returned with twenty-five men from *Kreis* Rybnik. In May of the same year a foreman (*Steiger*) from Prosper I of Polish extraction, Karl Sliwki, retraced the route to Rybnik and recruited 400 men. The strike of 1872 sent most of them packing East again, but Sliwki returned to Rybnik and was able to secure 500 more workers. Again, most of them left as a result of the depression of 1873.[10] In 1875 another agent, Leopold Kowalik, himself an Upper Silesian from Pzów, was sent out recruiting. Perhaps the memories of the strike and the depression had an inhibiting effect, for he was only able to bring 200 men back with him. However, in 1875 a more important event in the history of Upper Silesian settlement in Bottrop occurred. Up to that time the men who had been recruited had either been single or had moved West without wives and families. They were fed and housed in barracks erected by the mining companies, and lived almost totally apart from the rest of the community. In 1875 Upper Silesian miners first began to bring their families with them. By the following year there were twenty Polish families living in Bottrop. Though the numbers of Poles in Bottrop waxed and waned in rhythm with the economic cycle the core of permanent Polish residents continued to grow.[11] By the early 1880s when Kowalik went again to Upper Silesia, there about about 2,000 Poles, mostly Upper Silesians, resident in Bottrop.[12] By the mid-1880s the local newspaper, the *Bottroper Volkszeitung,* began to take notice of the Poles. For the most part this consisted of specifying ethnic background whenever Poles were involved in court proceedings dealing with petty theft, public drunkenness and the like. However, their growing numbers were also taken into account in more practical ways. Local merchants, from time to time, placed Polish-language advertisements in the *Bottroper Volkszeitung,*[13] and many merchants hired at least one Polish-speaking cleark.[14] From the 1890s the movement of Poles into Bottrop became a flood.[15] So great were their numbers that in 1906, when Bottrop petitioned for a grant of municipal charter (*Stadtrecht*), the provincial government refused on the grounds that one third of the population was Polish.[16] By the beginning of World War I an estimated 24,000 Upper Silesian Poles alone, primarily natives of Ratibor and Rybnik had migrated into Bottrop.[17]

TABLE II-2

Five Characteristics of Bottrop's In-Migrants, 1891-1920

		Nr.	%
Date of	1891/1900	33	10.2
Registration	1901/1910	123	38.2
	1911/1920	166	51.6
Last	Kreis of Birth	131	49.8
Residence*	Other	132	50.2
Age at	−/20	85	26.4
Registration	21/25	92	28.6
	26/30	55	17.1
	31/35	31	9.6
	36/40	19	5.9
	41/−	39	12.1
Marital Status	Single	202	62.7
at	Married	40	12.4
Registration	Married with Children**	80	24.8
Religion	Catholic	241	74.8
	Protestant and Others***	81	25.2

N = 322
Source: AEB.
Note: The numbers in each section of the table may not total 322 due to
incomplete registration forms.
*   This information available for German-born only.
**   Includes one unmarried with children.
***   Others were less than one percent.

In-migration varied in size as well as ethnic and national composition
during the thirty year period. (See Table II-2.) The number of in-migrants
who moved into Bottrop during the last decade of the nineteenth century
was not negligible. These numbers, however, become less impressive when
compared with the flood of the succeeding twenty years. The probable

reasons for the acceleration were four: Rheinbaben, Prosper III, Arenberg Fortsetzung and Vereinigte Welheim. These four mines came into production in Bottrop between 1900 and 1914. Before the turn of the century Bottrop's attraction was based on Propser II which had begun producing in 1875. To a lesser extent Prosper I, in Ebel, immediately to the south of the city and productive since 1863, must have added to Bottrop's population.[18] The high point of in-migration was reached during the years from 1911 to 1915. Almost a third of the total in-migration occurred during those years. After 1915 the in-migration was reduced to below the pre-1910 level. The decrease of in-migration together with the increased flow of men into the armed services during the latter years of the war was reflected in the drop in population after 1915 which is shown in Figure I-1.

Foreigners were not numerous during the early part of the sample period. (See Appendix A for crosstabulations of demographic characteristics at registration with ethnicity/nationality.) Indeed, none were included in the sample, though a modest number, for the most part Netherlanders, had been migrating into Bottrop since the 1860s.[19] It was only after 1900 that foreigners formed an appreciable part of the in-migration. During the last decade, 1911-1920, they formed almost as large a part of the in-migration as either the Germans or the Poles. Germans also increased as a percentage of the whole, as well as in absolute numbers, over the thirty years. During the first decade of the sample period they formed only about a sixth of the total. In the years 1901 to 1910 that percentage doubled, and it remained almost unchanged until 1920. The Polish in-migration was more evenly spread across the period. It reached its peak during the years from 1901 to 1910. Thereafter it declined, although it remained higher than it had been in the nineteenth century. The decrease in Polish in-migration as a percentage of the whole after 1910 was due to a drop in the numbers of Upper Silesian in-migrants. Poseners increased in numbers every decade, while the other Poles maintained an almost constant percentage over the entire period.

Half of the German-born in-migrants came to Bottrop directly from the places of their birth. During the first decade of the sample period more than three-quarters were first time migrants. Thereafter the percentage dropped sharply, to just under 50 percent during the year 1901 to 1910 and 42 percent during the final ten year period. There was no significant difference between German and Pole in this respect. Within the Polish in-migration, however, the figures were strongly influenced by the Upper Silesians. Almost 70 percent of them moved into Bottrop from their *Kreis* of birth. More than six out of every ten Polish in-migrants—and four of ten of the total—who claimed their birth place as last residence on the registration form named a city or town in Upper Silesia. Apparently the effects of the labor recruiting of the nineteenth century lingered on well after the practice had been abandoned. Among Germans, the Upper Silesian percentage was approached both by Ruhrgebieters (61 percent) and natives of the rest of the Rhineprovince and Westphalia (54 percent). Their combined numbers, however, were only two-thirds those of the Upper Silesians. About 35 percent of in-migrants noted a city in the Ruhrgebiet as last residence. Of those who later migrated out of Bottrop almost 34 percent indicated another city in the Ruhrgebiet as their destination. Taken together with the rate of mine employee turnover previously mentioned, these statistics indicate that a highly mobile labor force was to be found within the Ruhrgebiet.

Perhaps not surprisingly the in-migrants were young. As a practical matter, for the young person of the rural East the acquisition of land was not easy. The situation in Posen has already been sketched. In Upper Silesia the problem was simply the lack of available land. Until after World War I the great estates of the landed nobility covered most of the area. In *Kreis* Rybnik, for example, only sixty of almost 8,000 landowners held about two-thirds of all farm land.[20] In such areas the out-migration was considerably greater than where small and medium sized farms were the rule.[21] However, a breakdown of the sample reveals that the age structures of all regional groups were very similar. Perhaps the explanation is simply that young people, with few responsibilities and a desire for novelty, are more disposed to migration. Overall, the median age was 25.1 years, and there was little difference in that figure over the years. Earlier it had been a little higher, 26.2, but in the last decade of the sample period it had slipped to 24.6 years. The only exception of any consequence was formed by Poles other than Upper Silesians and Poseners whose median age was over twenty-eight years. There is no ready explanation for this, and it may simply be the result of sample error.

Most of the in-migrants were single, and in that category men outnumbered women three to one. No regional group in in-migrants contained less than 54 percent of single people. At the other extreme, the highest percentage of unmarrieds was almost 72 percent. There was no significant difference between Germans and Poles. In temporal terms, however, a definite tendency was evident. Until 1900 married in-migrants made up a majority. Thereafter their relative numbers declined steadily, in the period 1911 to 1920 to just under a third of the total. A closer examination of the married group reveals a perhaps unexpected pattern. Married in-migrants with children outnumbered childless couples almost two to one. This relationship was true for all Poles. In the case of the foreign-born, childless couples and families were about equal in number. Ruhrgebieters also deviated from the average. No married native of the Ruhrgebiet encountered in the sample was without children. It is possible that an extraordinary fertility can account for this, but it may be more prudent to explain it in terms of sample error.

The in-migrants were overwhelmingly Catholic. In all, Catholics outnumbered Protestants by a ratio of three to one. Given the historic confessional structure of Bottrop this is not unexpected. Protestant in-migrants, however, increased both in numbers and as a percentage of the whole over the sample period. During the first decade more than 90 percent of the in-migrants were Catholic. By the end of the second decade of the sample period the Protestant population of Bottrop had risen to 12.8 percent of the city's total.[22] For the period 1911 to 1920 the Catholic portion of the in-migration dropped to just under 70 percent. By 1914 there were four Protestant (Lutheran) grade schools (*Volksschule*) in Bottrop.[23] Among Poles, the Upper Silesians and Poseners were almost uniformly Catholic. The remainder of the Poles showed a Protestant majority. These were, for the most part, the Masurians, Evangelical Poles of East Prussia. It is also possible that some ethnic Germans were among this group.

Of course not all the in-migrants remained in Bottrop to become permanent residents.[24] Granting the social ramifications of a large transient population, and more than half of all in-migrants had left Bottrop within five years of registration—a third by the end of one year, it is the permanent residents who determine the texture of the society. Transients, by definition, are never integrated into the social pattern. In-migrants who choose to remain may become an integral part of the city, or they may live on the margins. Thus, it is important to analyze the characteristics of the in-migrants who settled permanently in Bottrop.

The crucial question is whether or not these characteristics were important in determining either persistence or integration. The two concepts are clearly related, though they are not identical. It is certainly possible for a person to live a period of years in a particular area yet not participate fully in the social, economic and political life of the community. This single fact of continued residency defines persistence. It describes only physical immobility, and no proof of integration can necessarily be inferred from it. It is also, of course, blindingly obvious that unless an in-migrant remained, the chances for integration were nil. That is, persistence is a precondition for integration. Integration is a more complex process. It involves accommodation in the institutions that define and direct the social body. The demographic characteristics of the in-migrants may have influenced their intergration into Bottrop's social structure. For example, adherence to Catholicism could have led to membership in a particular parish or religiously oriented organization. Thus, institutional and possibly, personal bonds would have been created. The complexities of such institutionally cemented relationships, however, must be dealt with in succeeding chapters.

The relationship of persistence to those six demographic characteristics can be examined here. For the purposes of analysis persistence was divided into three categories—to one year, one year to ten years, and ten years and more. Its relationship to the demographic characteristics, individually and collectively, was then determined.[25] The summary statistics yielded by the analysis are presented below in Table II-3.

The table shows that about a third of the in-migrants remained in the city less than a year. Just under a quarter resided there between one and ten years, and 43 percent were long-term residents (ten years and more). This last category provides a foundation on which a discussion of the relationaship of the demographic characteristics to persistence can be based. Had one simply assigned all in-migrants to that group it would have been the correct choice in 43 percent of the cases. However, the use of the demographic variables increases predictive power. The multivariat Theta (Θ) shows that almost 58 percent of the in-migrants can be correctly classed with the aid of the information provided by the demographic variables as a group. The assocition between persistence and those variables collectively is expressed by R^2, the generalized squared multiple correlation. It may be interpreted, roughly, as the amount of variance explained (15.3 percent) in the dependent variable, persistence. The final

TABLE II-3

SUMMARY STATISTICS OF AN ANALYSIS OF THE RELATIONSHIP OF PERSISTENCE TO SIX DEMOGRAPHIC VARIABLES

	to 1 yr.	1-10 yrs.	10 yrs.
Over all %	33.02	23.99	42.99
R^2 = .153			
Θ = .579			
R-squared	.189	.018	.222
Marital Status			
η^2 = .080			
Θ = .517			
Eta-squared	.080	.012	.131
Ethnicity			
η^2 = .046			
Θ = .502			
Eta-squared	.076	.002	.051
Date of Registration			
η^2 = .034			
Θ = .482			
Eta-squared	.042	.001	.051
Age			
η^2 = .034			
Θ = .480			
Eta-squared	.042	.001	.052
Religion			
η^2 = .008			
Θ = .448			
Eta-squared	.010	.000	.012
Last residence			
η^2 = .006			
Θ = .429			
Eta-squared	.008	.000	.008
Total N = 321	N = 106	N = 77	N = 138

multivariate statistic, R-squared, is also of some interest. It shows that the category "ten years +" was best predicted. The transients were also placed in the appropriate category relatively frequently. The demographic variables, however, were useless in predicting the intermediate classifications.

Having considered the overall percentage distribution and the collective relationship one may now turn to an examination of the individual demographic variables. (Complete crosstrabulations between persistence and the demographic variables can be found in Appendix B.) It might have been expected that knowledge of the in-migrant's previous place of residence would have been of use in predicting persistence. The theory could be advanced, for example, that veteran migrants would be more likely to remain only briefly in the city while first-time migrants would pause for a while before moving on. However, on the basis of these statistics neither that nor any other theory can be supported. The association, the generalized eta squared, between last residence and persistence is very low ($\eta^2 = .006$). The category-specific eta squares are also valueless. With the help of this variable alone less than one percent of in-migrants could be correctly placed in the transient and long-term categories while none could be put in the intermediate. The bivariate theta (Θ) bears out the weakness of this variable. It shows that knowledge of the lsat residence of the in-migrant yields no improvement in predictive power over the simple expedient of placing all of them in the third category.

Neither does knowledge of the religion of the in-migrants add much to the power of prediction. The association between persistence and religion is also very weak ($\eta^2 = .008$), and the category specific eta squares are again very low. The percentage of in-migrants that can be correctly classed on the basis of their religion is just barely (1.9 percent) about the result that could be obtained by assignment of all to the modal category. It is perhaps surprising that religion is so weakly associated with persistence given the confessional makeup of Bottrop. However, it may be that in an urban environment a "correct" confessional stance did not have the social force that it might have held in a more homogeneous and socially conservative village.

Age at registration (dichotomized in the analysis—through twenty-five years and twenty-six and older) and persistence are mildly associated ($\eta^2 = .034$). It shows greatest predictive power among the long-time residents and a slightly lesser degree with respect to transients. Again, the intermediate group is almost wholly unpredictable. It may be, as previously mentioned, that the tendency of older in-migrants to remain in Bottrop for a longer time than younger in-migrants—55.6 percent to 32.8 percent respectively for a period of ten years or more—can be attributed to the restlessness of youth. A more compelling explanation may be sought in the relationship of age to marriage. More than 83 percent of older in-migrants were married at registration; only 22 percent of the twenty-five and under group were not single when they entered the city. Those figures yield a strong association (Phi = .592) between age and marital status.

The overall association and category specific associations for date of registration (here, 1891-1910 and 1911-1920) and persistence are almost identical with those shown between age and persistence. More than half of the in-migrants who entered the city by 1910 remained there for at least ten years while fewer than a third of the later arrivals did so. There is obviously nothing inherently more disadvantegeous in a registration date in the teens that one for the earlier period. It is possible, however, that as the number of in-migrants multiplied the later arrivals were less able to secure satisfactory employment and lodging. In addition, during the years after 1910 in-migrants were more likely to be single, foreign-born and young, characteristics which were also associated with transience. Not least, it would be well to keep in mind the disruptive effects of the war.

A stronger associatin was shown between ethnicity and persistence (η^2 = .046). Foreigners were less likely than German in-migrants to be long-time residents of Bottrop (18.6 percent to 39.0 percent). Thus, it may be hold that the cultural difference implicit in foreign birth proved an effective deterrent to permanent residence. However, German-born Poles, who were also culturally different, remained in Bottrop for a period of ten years of more at a much higher rate than ethnic Germans (54 percent to 39 percent). This fact points to a phenomenon that is crucial to this study—the existence in Bottrop of a settled Polish community or, in other terms, the group persistence of Poles. That group persistence is graphically displayed in Table II-4.

Since none of the sample group had left the city or died before 1901 the in-migrant population at the turn of the century coincides with the total in-migration at that time. It is highly unlikely that this was true among the whole population, but the sample finding does indicate that many of the early arrivals did remain in Bottrop for some time. At the end

TABLE II-4
BOTTROP'S IN-MIGRANT POPULATION AT FOUR TIME PERIODS

Years of Residence	Poles		Germans		Foreigners		Total	
	Nr.	%	Nr.	%	Nr.	%	Nr.	%
1900								
to ten yrs.	27	100	6	100	—	—	33	100
ten yrs. +	—	—	—	—	—	—	—	—
Total	27		6		—		33	
1910								
to ten yrs.	44	63.8	19	76.0	4	100	67	68.4
ten yrs. +	25	36.2	6	24.0	—	—	31	31.6
Total	69		25		4		98	
1920								
to ten yrs.	33	42.8	22	52.4	8	72.7	63	48.4
ten yrs. +	44	57.1	20	47.6	3	27.2	67	51.6
Total	77		42		11		130	
1933								
to ten yrs.	—	—	—	—	—	—	—	—
ten yrs. +	50	100	21	100	9	100	80	100
Total	50		21		9		80	

of the century the in-migrant population was overwhelmingly Polish. Since the in-migration had played such a large role in the population growth of the city the Poles not only dominated the ranks of the new-comers bu they also formed a large part, perhaps more than 40 percent, of the total population.[26] Most of the Poles were Upper Silesians, which, again, was not the result of chance, but of policy. The relatively small number of German in-migrants indicated by the sample does not repre-sent the full dimensions of the non-Polish in-migrant population. The earliest in-migration had been almost wholly German. Bottrop had first satisfied its demand for labor by tapping the immediately surrounding area of Münsterland. After that the Lower Rhineland and the rest of Westphalia contributed to the growing stream of in-migration. Still later Hesse, Thuringia and Saxony supplied additional miners to the expanding industry.[27] This in-migration, however, was small in comparison to the tens of thousands who poured into the city after 1890. Even the relatively modest numbers of Poles who had registered between 1891 and 1900 eclipsed the earlier German in-migration. An examination of the employee lists of Prosper I and Prosper II for the period from 1870 to 1899 showed that just under 65 percent of the people employed in the two mines during those years were Polish—almost half of them natives of Upper Silesia.[28]

Over the next thirty-three years the composition of Bottrop's in-migrant population changed, but the ordering of the ethnic groups remained the same. At each time shown in the table the Poles represented a majority of Bottrop's in-migrants. The most important figures in the table are those which show the percentages of long-time Polish residents in the city. In 1910 a little more than a third of the Poles had lived in Bottrop for ten years or more. By 1920 the percentage had climbed to just over 57 percent. The sample included no in-migrants who entered the city after 1920. However, since an independent Polish state had been formed after World War I, it is likely that few Poles migrated into Germany after that date and virtually the whole of Bottrop's Polish community was composed of long-time residents. The fact of a significant group persistence of the city's Poles is thus demonstrated.

To return to the analysis of individual persistence, Table II-3 shows that easily the strongest association was displayed between marital status at registration and persistence. More than 40 percent of single in-migrants stayed less than a year in Bottrop. The corresponding figure for in-migrants who were married at the time of registration was only 15 percent. After ten years just over 70 percent of in-migrants who were single at registration were gone. Two-thirds of the married ones remained in Bottrop. Almost 52 percent of in-migrants could be placed in the correct persistent category on the basis of knowledge of marital status alone.

This analysis of persistence has shown that some of the demographic characteristics displayed by the in-migrants at registration were closely associated with long-time residence. Those in-migrants who remained in Bottrop and formed the core of the new population did not share the dominant demographic traits of the total in-migration. The former wre likely to have been early arrivals, while the majority of in-migrants entered the city only after 1910. Three-quarters of all in-migrants were Catholic, but religion was not significantly related to persistence. The young and single came in large numbers but did not stay long. More mature in-migrants with families remained there is disproportionate numbers. There was an almost equal mix of veteran migrants and those who had left home for the first time, but this apparently had no effect on persistence. Polish in-migrants exhibited a high rate of group persistence. It must now be shown how those Poles were accommodated within the large society of the city and to what extent and to which ends ethnicity played a role in that process.

CHAPTER III

OCCUPATIONS AND MOBILITY

Until the last decades of the nineteenth century Bottrop's economy could not have supported large-scale in-migration. Until that time its economy was firmly based, as it had been for centuries, on agriculture. In 1800 the *Gemeinde* counted 317 farms of varying size, *Kötter* and *Bauernhöfe*. At the same time there were only 376 houses altogether in the central village and the surrounding *Bauernschaften*.[1] All but a small percentage of the population, then, was directly engaged in farming. Manufacturing existed on the artisan level, and was often carried on by the cottagers as a necessary supplement to income. Most prevalent among the cottage industries were the manufacture of wooden shoes and weaving. Both of these were undertaken by means of the putting-out system (*Verlagsystem*). Of 124 artisans listed in a census (*Personenstandsaufnahme*) of 1806/07, fifty-four were engaged in these two occupations. As late as 1837 weaving was the chief occupation of thirty-seven households.[2] The factory system first appeared in Bottrop in 1796 with the founding of a cotton spinning mill. The mill, the work of an outside entrepreneur, employed sixty to seventy workers, but the business was short-lived. The operation was abandoned scarcely a decade after its beginning.[3] For two generations thereafter manufacturing remained almost exclusively the province of the artisan. Disregarding tiny breweries and distilleries, the only exceptions were formed by a clay pipe factory (1840) and a brickyard (1841) that served local needs.[4]

41

Commerce was also served on a basic level. An early index of commercial establishments (*Verzeichnis der Winkelwarengeschäfte und der Wirtschaften zu Bottrop vom 30. Juni 1777*) shows that taverns were the most numerous of Bottrop's businesses. Eleven were located in the village, and an equal number were scattered throughout the *Bauernschaften*. Since the population of Bottrop lay under 2000 at that time, it meant that there was a tavern for every thirty or forty adult inhabitants. Clearly such an establishment could not support a family, and farming or the brewing of beer was commonly practiced by the proprietor. A number of small grocery stores also were to be found both in the village and the *Bauernschaften*. In the latter areas only the most common goods were handled—flour, coffee, sugar and the like—while the village store carried a wider variety of articles.[5] Commercial intercourse with the world outside the community was supplied by means of markets. As early as 1432 the Archbishop of Köln, overlord of Bottrop, had sanctioned the *Michaelismarkt* (September 29) during which local farmers sold the surplus from their harvests.[6] Finally, a worthwhile source of income for Bottropers was the Horse Market (*Pferdemarkt*). Wild horses roamed the lowlands north of the Emscher. In feudal times the horses were the exclusive property of the overlord. However, after the destruction of feudal law during the Napoleonic occupation they were freely hunted by the local population. After a spring roundup hundreds of these animals were offered for sale at the *Pferdemarkt*. The wild horses of the Emscher were avidly sought, especially in the southern Mark.[7]

For the greater part of the nineteenth century then, Bottrop stood aside from the rush of industrialization which was overtaking Germany. Quite probably the village at mid-century in size, economic structure and spirit more closely resembled its medieval self than the bustling industrial city of the twentieth century. Its isolation from the industrial age was physical as well. The means of communication and transportation were primitive. Through traffic was served by the Old Postroad (*Alter Postweg*) be-between Düsseldorf and Münster, but this lay four kilometers to the north of the village. The Vest Highway (*Vestische Landstrasse*)—paved only after 1868—linked Osterfeld with Recklinghausen and did pass through the village. The main avenues of communication, however, were the country roads—little better than paths—that stretched out to nearby villages. In wet weather these were often impassable. Essen, Bottrop's more advanced neighbor to the south, was linked to it by a footpath.[8] The railroad, in the form of the branch line Sterkrade-Bottrop-Wanne, did not reach Bottrop until 1873.[9] Bottrop was not unique in its isolation from modernization. The whole of *Kreis* Recklinghausen remained largely agricultural until the 1880s.[10] The comparative backwardness of this area well into the latter part of the nineteenth century is clearly shown in Table III-1.

According to the results of the Occupational Census (*Berufszählung*) of 1882 more than a third of the population of *Kreis* Recklinghausen, of which Bottrop was a part, was still dependent on agriculture for its subsistence.[11] No other contemporary political sub-division of the Ruhrgebiet counted even half that percentage of farming population. Recklinghausen was the only city of the Ruhrgebiet which at that date continued to be enumerated in census reports together with the rural areas of the *Kreis*. Had a *Landkreis* Recklinghausen—which would have included Bottrop—existed in 1882, its agricultural sector would probably have been larger than the reported figure. A comparison of the agricultural sector between other Ruhrgebiet *Stadt-* and *Landkreise* supports this supposition. The census category which included mining, industry and the construction trades was lower, considerably so, for *Kreis* Recklinghausen than any other area of the Ruhrgebiet. Even so, by 1882 just over half of the population gained its living from activities listed in that category. A portion of that number must have been traditional artisans, but the figure of 51 percent clearly indicates that as the new *Reich* entered its second decade even the economically most traditional section of the Ruhrgebiet was moving into the modern industrial age. Those service areas of an economy which mark the modernization process—commerce, communications, public administration and the professions—were particularly weak in *Kreis* Recklinghausen. Again, had a *Landkreis* existed its figures for those sectors—and those figures would have included Bottrop—would likely have been lower than those actually listed.

By the time of the next Occupational Census in 1895 the economic structure of the *Kreis* as a whole, and of Bottrop in particular had undergone considerable change. That portion of the population of *Kreis* Recklinghausen dependent on agriculture had decreased 45 percent in the thirteen years since the last Census. That figure, however, was still much the highest in the Ruhrgebiet. At the same time the mining, manufacturing and construction industries had increased their share of the economy by 33 percent. In these areas *Kreis* Recklinghausen's economic structure was now comparable to the rest of the Ruhrgebiet. In commerce, communications,

TABLE III-1

Comparison of the Economic Structure of Kreis Recklinghausen with the Other Kreise of the Ruhrgebiet in 1882 and 1895

	Agriculture/ Forestry		Mining/Industry/ Construction		Commerce/ Communications		Domestic Service		Public service/ Professions	
	1882	1895	1882	1895	1882	1895	1882	1895	1882	1895
Recklinghausen	37.0*	20.5	51.4	68.6	7.6	8.0	1.4	0.4	2.4	2.5
Dortmund Stadtkreis	1.6	0.7	70.1	69.6	20.8	21.1	2.3	3.2	4.9	5.1
Dortmund Landkreis	14.3	9.6	74.0	80.0	8.6	6.6	0.6	1.2	2.4	2.1
Horde	—	7.0	—	79.0	—	9.9	—	0.9	—	2.8
Bochum Stadtkreis	0.6	0.4	77.2	71.5	14.6	17.2	1.6	4.2	5.0	6.2
Bochum/Rest	7.8	3.4	81.4	83.2	8.2	9.5	0.6	1.2	1.9	2.4
Witten	1.8	—	72.8	—	15.4	—	5.9	—	4.0	—
Gelsenkirchen Stadtkreis	—	0.8	—	77.4	—	16.7	—	1.2	—	3.8
Gelsenkirchen Landkreis	—	2.1	—	86.0	—	9.2	—	0.5	—	1.9

TABLE III-1 (Continued)

	Agriculture/Forestry		Mining/Industry/Construction		Commerce/Communications		Domestic Service		Public service/Professions	
	1882	1895	1882	1895	1882	1895	1882	1895	1882	1895
Hattingen	—	7.8	—	77.9	—	9.8	—	1.6	—	2.7
Duisberg	3.1	1.6	66.0	69.5	19.0	22.4	7.1	1.6	4.6	4.4
Mulheim Stadtkreis	1.4	4.5	66.5	71.8	22.8	18.4	4.9	2.2	4.2	3.0
Mulheim/Rest	14.7	—	62.8	—	15.8	—	3.8	—	2.7	—
Ruhrort	—	13.2	—	65.8	—	15.6	—	0.7	—	4.4
Essen Stadtkreis	0.4	0.4	75.7	76.0	16.1	17.1	2.3	1.5	3.2	2.6
Essen-Altendorf	2.5	—	90.8	—	4.1	—	0.4	—	1.8	—
Essen-Borbeck	6.4	—	80.5	—	7.8	—	2.8	—	2.3	—

Sources: SDR (NF) Bd. Nr. 2 and Bd. Nr. 111.
* All figures are a percent of employed population.

public administration and the professions, however, the *Kreis* contined to lag well behind the most urbanized areas of the Ruhrgebiet, though it stood reasonably close to the *Landkreise*.

The beginnings of Bottrop's transformation from market village to industrial city can be dated a little earlier. In 1871 the Arenberg Bergbau (coal mine) GmbH began work to sink its second shaft, Prosper II. The company's initial venture, Prosper I in Ebel, had begun production eight years earlier. It was, however, contained within a different administrative jurisdiction, Essen, until 1929, and its location south of the Emscher, with inadequate lines of transportation to the north, assured that it was not the central influence of Bottrop's economic growth. Prosper II began producing coal in 1875. Its effect on Bottrop's economic life was immediate and profound. By 1895 it employed more than 3000 Bottropers.[12] That is, more than one-sixth of the total population of Bottrop was employed by the mine. If the ratio of working population to total population was about the same for Bottrop as it was for all of *Kreis* Recklinghausen, then about half of the people employed in Bottrop worked for Arenberg Bergbau. Other enterprises as well were affected by the opening of the mine. The quickening of building activity, both by the mine and private construction firms, led to the founding of two new brickyards. Old construction firms grew and new ones went into business. Grocery stores expanded to meet the needs of the swelling population. A brewery was converted from artisanal to industrial production techniques.[13] In short, during the last two decades of the nineteenth century Bottrop experienced an industrial revolution.

The occupational distribution ofthe sample group of Bottrop's in-migrants from 1891 to 1920 accurately reflects the most important source of its industrial boom. Of those in the sample group who listed an occupation at registration more than half (53.7 percent) were involved in coal mining. Prosper II had remained the city's only mine for twenty-five years, but during the first fifteen years of the twentieth century four new mines went into production. Together the five mines remained Bottrop's pre-eminent employers.[14] A little less than a third of the in-migrants gained their livelihoods either through manufacturing/processing or the construction industry. Only about one in-migrant in seven listed a non-industrial occupation.[15] There is some evidence of ethnic bias when the distribution is examined from the point of view of in-migrant origins (see Table III-2).

TABLE III-2

Occupational Distribution at Registration of the Sample Group
of In-Migrants According to Ethnic/National Group

Occupation at Registration	Poles Nr.	%	Germans Nr.	%	Foreign Nr.	%	Total Nr.	%
Mining	104	68.4	28	31.8	28	48.2	160	53.7
Industry/ Construction	34	22.4	36	40.9	27	46.6	97	32.6
Other	14	9.2	24	27.3	3	5.2	41	13.8
TOTAL	152	51.0	88	29.5	58	19.5	298	

Source: AEB.
x^2 = 41.77, df = 4, p ≤ .001.

Poles tended to be overrepresented among mine workers. Foreigners and German in-migrants were to be found in numbers above the average in the manufacturing/processing and construction areas. Germans placed almost as many in-migrants in the tertiary sector, i.e. commerce in goods and services, as they did in mining, the city's chief area of employment. The level of statistical significance (beneath the .001 level) shown by the table makes it probable that an ethnic imbalance with respect to occupational categories existed among the total in-migrant population.

Considered from a different perspective, it is clear that the particular distribution of the in-migrants among the economic sectors guaranteed a very high percentage of manual workers among them. In the mines, in factories and in construction work only a small percentage of while collar employees was necessary. At the end of 1905, for example, 98 percent of Arenberg Bergbau employees were manual workers.[16] In the tertiary sector a rather large number of nonmanual occupations were available. It must be remembered, however, that teamsters, servants and janitors are included in that sector as well as lawyers, merchants and clerks. It is not surprising then, to find that a breakdown of the sample group yields an overwhelming majority of manual workers (see Table III-3). Only about 4 percent of in-migrants were involved in non-manual occupations at all levels from clerk to professional. The percentage of Poles listed as skilled workers is, perhaps, surprising. It derives, for the most part, from the large number of Polish in-migrants who described themselves at registration as experienced miners.

TABLE III-3

Occupational Level of the Sample Group of In-Migrants According to Ethnic Group

Occupational Level	Poles Nr.	%	Germans Nr.	%	Foreign Nr.	%	Total Nr.	%
Un/semi-skilled	57	36.8	40	41.7	29	50.0	126	40.8
Skilled	96	61.9	46	47.7	28	48.3	170	55.0
Non-manual	2	1.3	10	10.4	——	1.7	13	4.2
TOTAL	155	50.2	96	31.1	58	18.7	309	

Source: AEB.

The occupational level of the in-migrants at registration was more strongly related to persistence (see Table III-4). Half of the un- and semi-skilled in-migrants in the sample group left Bottrop within a year of registration. The percentages of skilled workers and those who practiced non-manual occupations who left within the same period were significantly smaller—21.8 percent and 7.7 percent respectively. In the short term at least, those at the lowest levels of the socio-economic order were most likely to have been spatically mobile in Bottrop's highly fluid society.[17]

More important to the question of integration were the careers of those in-migrants who remained in Bottrop over a longer period of time. The problem of socio-economic mobility has long been of central interest to

TABLE III-4

Occupational Level of the Sample Group of In-Migrants at Registration and Persistence (one year or more)

Persistence	Un/semi skilled		Skilled and non-manual		Total	
	Nr.	%	Nr.	%	Nr.	%
to one year	65	51.6	38	20.8	103	33.3
one year +	61	48.4	145	79.2	206	66.7
TOTAL	126	40.8	184	59.4	310	

Source: AEB.
x^2 = 31.90, df = 1, p ≤ .001.

those investigating the formation of American society, and it has increasingly become a focus of attention for students of German society.[18] The movement of European immigrants into diverse sectors and strata of the American economic system has often been cited as a leading factor in the integration of those people into American society.[19] Conversely, the failure of American blacks to accomplish the same economic success is often adduced as prima facie evidence of the failure of racial integration in American society. The extent, nature and ethnic differential of mobility in Bottrop are the subjects of the following discussion.

Table III-5 gives an overview of the occupational ranking at registration of the sample group of in-migrants. They have been divided into cohorts according to date of registration. The occupational makeups of the three cohorts at the time of entry into the city were manifestly dissimilar, and there was a clear temporal ordering. The earliest arrivals were concentrated in the ranks of skilled workers; only one in eight was an un- or semi-skilled worker. The percentage of un- and semi-skilled workers was much greater —more than one third of the total—among in-migrants who registered during the following decade. Almost half of those who entered the city during the last ten year period were in the lowest occupational category. In each cohort the number that listed non-manual occupations was quite small,

TABLE III-5

Occupational Level of the Sample Group of In-Migrants
According to Date of Registration

Occupational Level	Cohort 1891-1900		Cohort 1901-1910		Cohort 1911-1920		Total	
	Nr.	%	Nr.	%	Nr.	%	Nr.	%
Un/semi-skilled	4	12.1	46	38.0	76	49.0	126	40.8
Skilled and Non-manual	29	87.8	75	62.0	79	51.0	183	59.2
TOTAL	33	10.6	121	39.2	155	50.2	309	

Source: AEB.
x^2 = 16.62, df = 2, p ⩽ .001, Cramer's V = .232.

and it was therefore included with the skilled category. The pattern was not random; it is significant beneath the .001 level, and some statistical significance exists between occupational level and date of registration. Possibly the relationship was due to difference in age. The median age of the in-migrants decreased in each succeeding decade, and the younger in-migrants would have had fewer years in which to acquire occupational skills.

Beyond the date of registration the cohorts displayed the same general tendencies. Table III-6 compares them at a time when all members of each cohort had been in Bottrop for at least ten years.[20] The percentage of the cohorts contained in the un- and semi-skilled category after at least a decade's residence in the city was significantly less than it had been at registration. In each case the percentage of skilled workers had risen—dramatically so for the 1901-1910 and 1911-1920 cohorts. There was also an increase of percentage for all three groups in non-manual occupations. It was smallest among the earliest of the in-migrants and largest among the most recent arrivals. This pattern suggests either a modification of the economic structure of Bottrop or a change of occupational expectation among the youngest in-migrants who were largely contained in the 1911-1920 cohorts.[21] Conversely, the difference in occupational makeup among

TABLE III-6

Occupational Level of the Cohorts Ten Years After Registration

Occupational Level	Cohort 1891-1900 in 1911		Cohort 1901-1910 in 1920		Cohort 1911-1920 in 1930		Total	
	Nr.	%	Nr.	%	Nr.	%	Nr.	%
Un/semi-skilled	1	3.2	5	12.5	6	15.4	12	10.9
Skilled and Non-manual	30	96.8	35	87.5	33	84.4	98	89.0
TOTAL	31	28.2	40	36.4	39	35.4	110	

Source: AbB.
$x^2 = 2.85$, df = $.2 < p < .3$.

the cohorts was much reduced. The 1901-1910 and 1911-1920 groups showed nearly identical patterns, and the oldest cohort did not deviate significantly from them. Thus, the tendency of the in-migrants, over time, to congregate in the ranks of the skilled workers was uniform, not confined to those entering Bottrop at specific dates.

That reduction of the proportion of in-migrants at the lowest level of socio-economic status over a period of time is, in itself, a fact of some interest. It is not, however, identical with a proof of upward mobility on the part of the in-migrants. The increased percentage of Bottrop's in-migrants in the middle and at the upper end of the socio-economic scale may simply have been the result of attrition. By 1930 more than 60 percent of the original sample group of in-migrants had migrated from Bottrop. Another 6 percent had died by that year. It is possible that these groups were made up largely of un- and semi-skilled manual workers. If this were true then the apparent upward movement of in-migrant occupational level which was demonstrated above would have been merely arithmetical rather than the result of real socio-economic mobility. To some extent that was, in fact, the case. In terms of occupational level, in-migrants of the sample group who remained in Bottrop for a period longer than a year had listed a higher status on their registration forms than the average of the total sample population.[22] The out-migration of persons of low occupational status, however, was not the whole story. The rising status of those who remained can be shown to have been the result of real upward mobility.

Just under forty-six percent of the sample group remained in Bottrop for more than five years. The mobility experienced by that group is summarized in Table III-7. In-migrants, it is clear, did not remain entirely motionless with Bottrop's socio-economic order. About one in five experienced some change in status by the end of a decade's residence. By far the most common movement was upward. The summary table, however, does not indicate the degree of movement. Most of those who moved up the socio-economic scale (87.0 percent) remained manual workers. That is, mobility consisted, for the most part, of entry by an un- or semi-skilled worker into a skilled trade. Only a few (8.6 percent) of the upwardly mobile were able to move from the status of manual worker to a

TABLE III-7

Economic Mobility of Bottrop's In-Migrants after a Residence of Five Years

	Nr.	Percent
↑	23	15.5
⇔	123	83.1
↓	2	1.4
TOTAL	148	

Sources: AbB; AEB.

non-manual occupation. An even smaller number (4.3 percent) rose within the ranks of the non-manual occupations. However, mobility into the non-manual occupations may not be an accurate measure of the socio-economic success (or lack of it) achieved by the in-migrants. Simply gaining a foot-hold in a skilled trade and remaining in Bottrop for an extended period of time could, in themselves, have been considered measures of success. If this were true, then upward mobility into the non-manual occupations, while not unwelcome, would have been subsidiary to the main goal of stability.

If the in-migrants, or some of them, achieved at least stability, it could have been the second generation which reaped further economic rewards. The American cultural tradition espouses this belief, and there is some evidence to support it.[23] Might not the same process have occurred in another

TABLE III-8

Occupational Mobility of the Children of In-Migrants by 1930

	Nr.	Percent
↑	15	9.0
⇔	124	74.6
↓	27	16.2
TOTAL	166	100.0

Sources: AbB; AEB.

rapidly expanding industrial society? In Table III-8 mobility is defined as the contrast between the occupational level of the children of in-migrants in 1930 and the last occupation practiced by the parent to 1930.[24] There is some difference between this pattern of mobility and that of the first generatin shown in Table III-7; in particular, the rate of downward mobility among the children is rather larger than that of the parents. However, this is probably due to the age of the children in 1930. At that time less than a third (30.9 percent) of them were over thirty. It is at least possible that with the passage of years the younger children reached or even passed the occupational level of the parents. It must also be borne in mind that the seemingly limited upward mobility of the second generation represents an advance beyond the highest level reached by the parents. The upward mobility of the children, as was the case with the parents, consisted largely of moving into skilled occupations. More than seven in ten (73.3 percent) of the second generation who advanced beyond the occupational level of the parent did so by adopting a skilled trade. The rest (26.6 percent) of the upwardly mobile second generation did manage to leap the barrier into the non-manual occupations. No child whose parent was of non-manual status had experienced upward mobility by 1930.

The gross statistics of the mobility of Bottrop's in-migrants do not, in themselves, appear overly impressive. All that one may reasonably infer from them is that the in-migrants, with regard to occupational level, were not wholly static. They furnish proof neither for nor against the economic integration of the in-migrants. It may be that their mobility can give some clues leading to a conclusion regarding that question. In order to discover such evidence, however, it is necessary to gain a different critical perspective. Viewed in isolation, it is not even possible to say whether a rate of fifteen percent upward mobility is a large or a small figure. That is, did Bottrop's in-migrants experience such a low rate of upward mobility that one may deduce that they became an urban proletariat, or was the rate of upward mobility sufficiently high to distribute the in-migrants and their children equitably throughout the city's economic structure? Even to begin to answer such questions there must be some point of reference. By comparing Bottrop's economic structure and the mobility of its inhabitants to that of other cities some basis may be formed for speculation about the importance of mobility among the city's in-migrants.

Table III-9 shows the mobility rates of manual workers for Bottrop and three other cities.[25] The figures given for Bottrop are for in-migrants only. The three other cities included in the table also had substantial numbers of in-migrants, but the figures given were calculated from samples of the total population. Slightly different categories of occupational classification were used for the various studies, and sampling techniques also varied. Thus, it is possible that the use of a standard classification for occupations and a standard sampling method would have produced a different ranking of the cities. If any confidence is placed in the technique of random sampling, however, such hypothetical standardization would not have substantially affected the pattern shown in the table. The similarity of the overall rates of upward mobility is striking. The lowest figure is that of Bochum, another industrial city of the Ruhrgebiet. The highest rate of upward mobility was to be found in Bottrop. The two American cities, however, have rates only fractionally under Bottrop. The rates of downward mobility are also comparable. Bochum had the highest rate of downward mobility, but it was only marginally higher than that of Boston. Bottrop had the lowest rate, but it was barely under Atlanta's. In gross terms, then, the

TABLE III-9

Comparative Mobility of Blue Collar Workers in Four Cities

	Bottrop 5 years +	Bochum 1880-1890	Boston 1880-1890	Atlanta 1870-1800
↑ to white collar	1.4%	7.6%	11.6%	11.0%
↑ within blue collar	14.2	4.0	3.2	4.4
↑ Total	15.6	11.6	14.8	15.4
⇔	82.8	83.6	80.8	83.0
→	1.4	4.8	4.2	1.6
Number in sample	140	377	334	182

Sources: Bottrop—AbB; AEB.

Bochum—David Crew, "Definitions of Modernity: Social Mobility in a German Town, 1880-1901," *Journal of Social History*, Vol. 7, Nr. 1 (Fall 1973).

Boston—Stephan Thernstrom, *The Other Bostonians: Poverty and Progress in the American Metropolis, 1880-1970*, (Cambridge: Harvard University Press, 1973).

Atlanta—Richard J. Hopkins, "Occupational and Geographic Mobility in Atlanta, 1870-1896," *Journal of Southern History*, XXXIV, Nr. 2 (May 1968).

mobility shown by Bottrop's in-migrants would not have seemed unusual elsewhere in the Ruhrgebiet, nor, indeed, in contemporary American cities.

Upon closer examination, however, an important difference between the four cities is observable. The percentage of manual workers in American cities who were upwardly mobile was weighted heavily in favor of those who moved into non-manual occupations. Bochum's upward mobile working class also followed that general pattern, although not to the same degree. Only in Bottrop did mobility not usually take the form of movement into the non-manual occupations. In Bottrop upward mobility almost always meant the acquisition of a skilled trade. From these figures it could be argued that Bottrop's in-migrants did not, in fact, become economically integrated. That is, they did not participate in the full range of the city's economic activities, but remained almost exclusively a working class.

This view, however, is contravened by a comparison of the economic structures of the four cities. Table III-10 presents such a comparison. Since Bottrop was not enumerated separately in the economic censuses until 1925, the figures for the earlier dates are for the whole *Kreis* Recklinghausen. However, there is no reason to believe that during the period under consideration Bottrop formed an exception to the rest of the *Kreis* in any way that is critical to this analysis. If any adjustments were to be made they would, in all probability, consist of decreasing the percentage taken up by agriculture and increasing the share held by manufacturing and mining. But even this is not for certain, for five of the six divisions of the *Gemeinde* Bottrop were *Bauernschaften.* If the secondary sector were ascribed a higher figure it would only strengthen the plausibility of the conclusion to be drawn from the table. That conclusion is, very simply, that the direction of upward mobility—toward skilled trades or non-manual occupations—was determined largely by the structure of the economy. That is, the larger the tertiary sector, the greater the chance of mobility into white collar jobs. As previously emphasized, it is in this sector that the non-manual occupations are concentrated. In order to avoid as far as possible distortion in the table the domestic services are listed separately since these jobs, though clearly not industrial working class, did not carry white collar status.

The highest rates of mobility into the non-manual occupations occurred precisely in those cities which had the largest tertiary sectors, Boston and

TABLE III-10

Comparative Economic Structures (in percent) of Four Industrial Cities

Sector	Bottrop*	Bochum	Boston	Atlanta
	1882		1880	
Agriculture	37.0	0.6	0.9	2.0
Industry, mining	51.4	77.2	35.8	24.4
Tertiary	10.0	20.2	51.7	55.8
Domestic service	1.4	1.7	11.4	17.8
	1895		1900	
Agriculture	20.5	0.4	0.7	0.8
Industry, mining	68.6	71.6	32.4	24.2
Tertiary	10.4	23.5	55.2	60.6
Domestic service	0.4	4.3	11.4	14.2
	1925		1920	
Agriculture	1.2	0.8	0.6	0.6
Industry, mining	84.4	72.0	37.0	27.8
Tertiary	12.4	23.4	56.4	63.6
Domestic service	2.0	3.7	6.0	7.9

Sources: Bochum and Bottrop—SDR (NF) Bd. 2, Bd. 111, Bd. 408.
Atlanta and Boston—U.S. Census Reports of 1880, 1900 and 1920.

Note; Since occupational categories were not always constant it was sometimes necessary to calculate the percentage.

* *Kreis* Recklinghausen for 1882 and 1895; Bottrop for 1925.

Atlanta. Bottrop, the city with the smallest (by far) rate of mobility into the non-manual occupations also had (again, by far) the smallest tertiary sector.[26] In the study of Boton it was calculated that in 1920 32 percent of the male work force was employed in non-manual occupations. The sheer size of this white collar sector, the vast number of jobs needed simply to maintain a constant percentage and the openings created by death, migration or retirement created opportunities for movement upward and out of the blue collar sector which could not have been conceived of in Bottrop. In 1925 in Bottrop it is certain that less than 10 percent of the work force was employed in white collar occupations.[27] Even in Bochum, from any perspective an industrial, working class city, the tertiary sector was double that in Bottrop, and the rate of nobility into non-manual occupations there was correspondingly higher.

Finally, this discussion must consider the possibility of an ethnic differential. It may be that the amount of upward mobility displayed by Bottrop's in-migrants was "normal" in comparison with other contemporary cities. Further, the direction of the mobility, i.e. into the skilled trades rather than non-manual occupations, was to be expected if one examined the particular structure of Bottrop's economy. If, however, the ethnically German in-migrants were disproportionately represented among the upwardly mobile, it might justifiably be argued that only that section of the in-migration became economically integrated. The Poles, who were a majority among the long time in-migrant residents, would have remained a species of helot. Confined to the lowest types of menial and unskilled labor, they would have served, on the whole, as a stepping stone to economic success for more fortunate Bottropers. The evidence, however, does not support such a conclusion.

Table III-11 shows that among in-migrants who remained in Bottrop for a period of at least five years Germans were only slightly more inclined than Poles to be upwardly mobile. Conversely, the Poles showed both a greater tendency to remain stable and a lesser degree of downward mobility. A calculation of statistical significance, however, reveals that the pattern shown in the table is very apt to be random. That is, the small difference in the percentages of upward mobility, stability and downward mobility which were found in this sample are likely to be meaningless. Another sample might turn the fractional differences in the other direction. Thus, it seems probable that there was little, if any ethnic difference in the rate of upward mobility among the first generation of in-migrants.

TABLE III-11

Comparison of the Economic Mobility of Polish and German In-Migrants after Residence of Five Years

	Poles		Germans		Total	
	Nr.	%	Nr.	%	Nr.	%
↑	15	15.6	6	16.2	21	15.8
	81	84.3	31	83.8	112	84.2
TOTAL	96	72.2	37	27.8	133	

Sources: AbB; AEB.
$x^2 = .011$, df = 1, $.90 < p < .95$.

Analysis of the mobility figures for the second generation is somewhat more complex. On the face of the matter it would appear that the second generation of German in-migrants displayed a signficantly greater amount

TABLE III-12

Comparison of the Economic Mobility of the Second Generation of In-Migrants in 1930

	Poles		Germans		Total	
	Nr.	%	Nr.	%	Nr.	%
↑	8	6.8	7	16.2	15	9.4
	109	93.2	36	83.7	145	90.6
TOTAL	117	73.1	43	26.8	160	

Sources: AbB; AEB.
$x^2 = 3.38$, df = 1, $.05 < p < .10$.

of upward mobility than their Polish counterparts. Table III-12 shows that the Germans moved upward at a rate more than twice that of the Poles. What the table shows, however, is not simple individual mobility, but rather inter-generational mobility. Thus, mobility, as measured here, is relative movement. The ability of the child to achieve upward mobility depend, in large measure, on the economic success of the parent. Since upward mobility in Bottrop, for the children as well as the first generation, most usually took the form of movement from an un- or semi-skilled job into a skilled trade, it follows that the children of un- or semi-skilled workers had the best chance to move beyond their parents. This was, in fact, exactly what happened. More than a sixth (18.6 percent) of the German in-migrant parents were on the lowest occupational status level at the latest date (to 1930) at which it was possible to trace them. Only 4 percent of the Polish in-migrant parents were in the same category (see Table III-13). For a number of the second generation Germans then, the attainment of a skilled trade represented definite upward mobility vis-à-vis their parents. At the same time, a like achievement for the Pole of the second generation quite probably meant only that he had reached the socio-economic status which his father already enjoyed.

The foregoing discussion has shown that, in their totality, the in-migrants were not relegated to the status of permanent economic step children. Had they not been able to move upward a case against their economic integration could have been made. The gross sum of mobility, however, was as great in Bottrop as in other contemporary cities, both German and American—the latter which, by tradition, guaranteed upward mobility to the willing.[28] The bulk of upward mobility in Bottrop, it is true, involved only movement from an un- or semi-skilled job into a skilled trade. Granted, most observers conclude that the leap from manual to non-manual occupation is the significant move upward. However, given the economic structure of Bottrop, the concentration of the in-migrants in mining and manufacturing and their movement into skilled occupations in those areas strongly suggest that they become integral members of Bottrop's economic system.

Nor was there any meaningful difference between ethnic groups. Regardless of ethnic group, those with little or no salable skill tended to move on after a brief residence in Bottrop. If, for whatever reason, the un- or semi-skilled in-migrant chose to remain in the city, he was likely to have

TABLE III-13

Crosstabulation of the Occupational Level of German and Polish In-Migrants at the Last Observation and the Occupational Levels of the Children in 1930

PARENTS	CHILDREN							
	Un/semi-skilled		Skilled		Non-manual		Total	
	P	G	P	G	P	G	P	G
Un/semi-skilled	—	2	5	6	—	—	5	8
Skilled	17	3	91	24	3	1	111	28
Non-manual	1	—	—	3	—	4	1	7
TOTAL	18	5	96	33	3	5	117	43

Source: AbB; AEB.

the opportunity to rise in economic status, at least to the skilled level. Again, this was the case for both German and Pole. Movement into the non-manual occupations was not a common experience for in-migrants. Only comparison with a separate sampling of old stock, native Bottropers would show if these positions were reserved for a native elite. Unfortunately, such a sample is not at hand. The very structure of the city's economy, however, would not have permitted large-scale movement from blue collar to white collar occupations. For most laborers, whether native or in-migrant, the acquisition of a job at the level of skilled workman must have been the limit of imaginable upward mobility.

CHAPTER IV

COAL MINES AND MINERS

Equitable participation in upward mobility, however it was defined and limited by German society of the late nineteenth and early twentieth century, was clearly important to the Polish in-migrants in Bottrop's new urban society, if only by preventing economic ghettoization. Equally as important was the nature of Polish in-migrant involvement in coal mining. Mining was the single most important industry in the Ruhrgebiet. In 1912 more than a third of all industrial workers in the Ruhrgebiet were employed by coal mines.[1] A decade before that almost two-thirds of the working men of the Ruhrgebiet were miners.[2] Even these figures, however, do not sufficiently emphasize the position of coal mining in Bottrop's economy. In 1910 93 percent of all industrial employees in Bottrop worked for the mines.[3] If job discrimination against Polish in-migrants was present in the mines, then for all intents and purposes, there was no possibility of their integration into Bottrop's economic system.

Openings outside the mines did, of course, exist, but they were few. In a government report of 1905 it was noted that only 294 non-coal mining industrial and construction jobs (*Zahl der in sonstigen Industriezweigen und in Bauhandwerk beschäftigtin Personen*) existed in Bottrop. Of these only seven (2.4 percent) were held by Poles. In the same year there were 697 tradesmen and self-employed artisans (*Zahl der Gewerbetenbenden und selbständigen Handwerker*) in the city. Forty-five (6.4 percent) of them were Poles. By 1910 some change had occurred. The number of

industrial and construction jobs had doubled (to 608), and about 19 percent (113) of them were held by Poles. Movement was less rapid among
the self-employed. Only a 5 percent increase (to 731) had occurred in this
sector, and a little over 9 percent (67) of those people were Poles.[4] A publication issued by the Bottrop Polish community in 1911 included a list of
twenty-two Polish firms in the city. Among them were three bookshops,
which were the objects of special attention by government agents.[5]

The variety of jobs to be found in a coal mine was, perhaps, rather greater than one might expect. The basic division was between those who actually worked in the pits (*Untertags*) and those who worked at the surface
installations (*Uebertags*). The latter division included about a fifth of the
total work force.[6] Part of that group was made up of coking plant workers.
Until after the first world war most of Bottrop's coal mines had such plants
attached to them. Only in 1928 was a single, central facility constructed
by the Rheinische Stahlwerke AG.[7] Other surface employees maintained
and ran machines which brought coal to the surface (*Fördermaschinist*),
lowered pit workers into the mine and returned them at the end of the
shift (*Seilbahnarbeiter*) and provided for a continuous flow of fresh air
and disposal of water (*Wettermaschinist*). A number of workers in the
skilled trades were also employed, such as carpenters, masons and electri-
cians, who constructed and maintained plant facilities. In addition, janitors, night watchmen and casual laborers were included in the work force
Uebertags.

The majority of mine employees worked in the pits where the variety
of jobs was not as great as among surface workers. A very few specialists
such as the explosives expert (*Schiessmeister*) worked *Untertags*, but, for
all practical purposes, the work force in the pits was divided among the
Schlepper, the *Lehrhauer* and the *Vollhauer*. All inexperienced workers
began as *Schlepper*. The job called for nothing in the way of skill; it simply
involved the moving about of coal wagons. After some time spent in this
work a man became an apprentice miner or *Lehrhauer*. In this position he
worked directly under the supervision of a *Vollhauer* learning the techniques of working the pit face. After acquiring the skills and experience
necessary for independent work he too became a *Vollhauer*. The appren-
ticeship was more than formal.[8] A *Vollhauer* required more than strength
and a freedom from claustrophobia. In the work of cutting tunnels through
the earth five hundred feet and more below the surface an intimate knowledge of mining techniques was more than merely desirable. During the

period under consideration this work was almost entirely skilled hand work rather than simple attendance on a coal cutting machine. Through 1925 more than half of the coal production of the Ruhrgebiet was the result of hand cutting with pick and mallet. Mechanization, in the form of the pneumatic pick (*Abbauhämmer*), was rapidly introduced after that date. Coal cutting remained, however, the work of a single individual working at the coal face. Even after World War II (1948) 85 percent of coal production was still won in this manner.[9]

How did the Polish in-migrant fit into this sytem? In theory, since the introduction of occupational freedom (*Gewerbefreiheit*) in 1869 he might legitimately aspire to any position from *Schlepper* to *Generaldirektor*. In practice, of course, the choice was rather more narrow. By a generous estimate the salaried employees of a mine included no more than 5 percent of the whole.[10] Skilled trades *Uebertags* might have been attractive, but again, few were available. By far the most open and remunerative position in Bottrop which a working class man might expect to gain was the job of *Vollhauer*. Of all non-salaried positions in the mine—*Uebertags* or *Untertags*—it was the second highest paid. In a wider comparison, the *Vollhauer* was among the most highly paid of all workers in an industrial setting.[11] If the Polish in-migrant was to participate in a full and important economic sense in Bottrop society, then the job of *Vollhauer* had to be open to him. In a purely arithmetical way it was. The doubling and re-doubling of the work force in the mines had forced mine owners to look outside the immediate environs for labor. Not only did the accept, but they actively recruited labor from the Polish areas of the *Reich*. Nor could the owners draw on self-renewing generations of miners. As early as 1893 only about a third (37.4 percent) of miners in the *Oberbergamt* Dortmund were following in their fathers' footsteps.[12] Ruhrgebiet coal miners had never formed the traditional, almost hereditary, guild-like body that had existed earlier in the coal fields of Saxony and the Siegerland. From its inception the Ruhrgebiet coal mining industry had demanded the labor of in-migrants.

Viewed in a different way the question might be, how well suited were the Poles for coal mining? Had they experienced in the mines? Had they any industrial experience at all? Both contemporary and modern accounts of Polish in-migrants make note of their rural origins.[13] This is not, however, identical with agricultural occupations. The majority of Bottrop's Polish in-migrants were natives of Upper Silesia, and in particular the two

Kreise Rybnik and Ratibor. In both of these *Kreise* agriculture was the primary occupation, but industry was not unknown in them. In fact, according to the Occupational Census of 1895 a third of Rybnik's total (both men and women) working population was employed in industry or mining. In Ratibor the figure was almost 40 percent.[14] Nor was it necessary to be a city dweller in order to pursue a non-agricultural occupation. In Upper Silesia many industries had moved into the countryside.[15] The location of coal mines in the countryside was even more common. Thus, the villagers, or even the countrymen, had the opportunity, in many cases, to gain some kind of industrial experience, or even to have worked in the mines.

Data gained from the sampling of in-migrants tend to support the conclusion that industrial or mining experiences was widely available to Polish in-migrants (at least the Upper Silesians) in their native areas. According to the registration forms two-thirds of the sample group of in-migrants were coal miners—*Schlepper, Bergtagelöhner, Hauer* or other. It may be, of course, that the figure is somewhat inflated. Some of the occupations listed at registration may have represented aspiration rather than reality. That is, the in-migrant may have listed the occupation he hoped to follow in Bottrop rather than the one he left behind in Czyprzanow. Leaving aside the question of veracity, it was unquestionably more useful for a job-seeking Polish in-migrant in Bottrop to describe himself to a prospective (probably coal mine) employer or a *Schlepper* rather than a milker or swineherd. On the other hand, it may be that the occupational registration entries are not significantly slanted. Contemporary opinion was that conditions in the Ruhrgebiet coal mines were much superior to those in the Upper Silesian fields.[16] Less subjectively, wages in the Ruhrgebiet mines were higher than in any other mining district. From 1886 to 1909 the yearly wage of an average coal miner ranged from 36.8 percent to 56.5 percent higher in the Ruhrgebiet than in the Upper Silesian fields.[17] Superior working conditions and higher wages may well have been as attractive to experienced miners as to agricultural workers.

Ultimately, however, the crucial question is whether or not the Polish in-migrants who went to work in the mines, regardless of occupation in their native villages, were eventually employed in responsible and well paid jobs, for all practical purposes as *Vollhauer*. Contemporary observers differed in their assessments of Polish occupational level in the mines.

A 1913 article in a popular magazine noted that Poles were usually employed as unskilled laborers in the mines.[18] A more serious analysis from the same period (1909) gives a much different picture. Aside from supervisory and management personnel, the highest class of workers in the mines were those operating specialized machinery (*Fördermaschinen, Wasserhaltungsmaschinen, Ventilatoren* and the like) and the experienced miners working at the coal face, the *Vollhauer*. The jobs involving the operation of the machinery were all occupied by native Germans (*ausschliesslich mit Einheimischen besetzt*). This may have been a matter of seniority, in which case, in-migrant Poles could have been expected to have acceded to these jobs in time. In any case, only 1 percent of mine employees were in this category. In the job most centrally important to coal production (*Kerntruppen im Heere der Bergarbeiter*), the *Vollhauer,* Poles were employed on equal terms with Germans.[19]

The author of the above account did not statistically document his conclusions, but he did quote foremen and officials of the mines who maintained that Poles and Germans were equally competent. This undocumented claim is supported by data gained from the sample group of Bottrop's in-migrants. Of the one hundred German-born in-migrants who remained in Bottrop for a period of at least ten years, seventy-nine were involved in coal mining. Almost without exception they were employed as *Vollhauer.* Sixteen of the seventeen Germans were in that category and sixty of the sixty-two Poles. One German and one Pole were listed as supervisory personnel (*Steiger*). Thus, on the basis of contemporary estimates and the information gleaned from a sampling of Bottrop's in-migrants there is no reason to believe that discrimination against the employment of Poles as *Vollhauer* existed in any important way.

Against the preceding argument must be set the Mine Inspection Decree (*Bergpolizeiverordnung*) of 1899. This decree forbade the employment of anyone in the mines who was not sufficiently fluent in German to understand the orders of his superiors and communicate with his co-workers. In addition, no one could attain supervisory rank unless he were able to read and write German.[20] The justification for the decree lay in the sharply rising numbers of accidents in the mines. Because of the rapid expansion in Ruhrgebiet coal mining, numbers of only partially qualified men had been put to work in the pits. Mining officials noted that whereas the rate of accidents among German workers tended to fall, among foreign workers the rate rose. Lack of communication was offered as a reason. That is, non-German-speaking workers, it was said, often carried out their work in a dangerous manner, or undertook tasks to which they were not equal simply because they did not sufficiently understand the instructions given them. The assertions of the mining authorities may have been entirely correct and completely without malice. However, the principal Polish-language newspaper in the Ruhrgebiet, *Wiarus Polski,* immediately attacked the decree as an anti-Polish act. Safety in the mines, it argued, would better be served by posting safety rules in translation. This was formally requested of the mining authorities, but after a long delay it was finally denied in 1903 for reasons of (German) national sentiment (*aus nationalen Gründen*).[21] The message seemed clear that *Wiarus Polski* had been correct. This impression could only have been strengthened by strident support for the decree and demands for its extension to all other industrial sectors by such anti-Polish organizations as the Pan-German League (*Alldeutscher Verband*).[22]

Given the advantage of some years perspective, it is possible to conclude that the mine authorities misread the problem. Regardless of language difficulties, experienced miners of any nationality would have avoided dangerous situations. What was needed in the Ruhrgebiet coal mines was a large body of experienced miners. Only time could provide that, as time would also tend to erase the language problem. It was probably true, as *Wiarus Polski* asserted, that a fundamental anti-Polish feeling was implicit in the decree. It was also correct, however, that the *Oberbergamt* Dortmunt was seriously attempting to prevent the recurrence of such tragic mine accidents as the one in Bochum which took 116 lives in 1898.[23] The results of the decree, however, were not detrimental to the Poles of the Ruhrgebiet. As has been shown above, Poles were not shunted into the lowest positions in the mines. They moved rapidly into well paid jobs. On the contrary, if a lasting effect was felt, it was the impetus given to the development of self-conscious Polish ethnic awareness among the in-migrant Poles of the Ruhrgebiet.

In addition to their purely economic aspect, the Ruhrgebiet coal mines offered opportunities for Polish in-migrants to participate in certain organizations which had crucial social and political impact. The most important of these was the Polish Trade Union, the ZZP (*Zjednoczenie Zawodowe Polskie*), which was founded in Bochum in November 1902. It was the last of the three great mine unions to be organized. The movement toward unionization among Ruhrgebiet coal miners in general had begun only in the last decade of the nineteenth century.[24] The Old Union (*Alter Verband*) came into being largely as a result of the strike of 1889. Justifiably or not, it was widely regarded as socialist in tendency, and thus was unacceptable to many miners. As a counterweight to it the Christian Miners Union (*Gewerkverein christliche Bergarbeiter*) was founded in 1894. It attempted to accommodate both Catholic and Protestant anti-socialist miners within its organization. It was unable, however, to allay the suspicions that it was an arm of the Center Party (*Zentrum*). Thus, it developed into an almost exclusively Catholic union.

Both the *Alter Verband* and the *Gewerkverein* early on made some efforts to attract the increasing numbers of Polish miners into their respective organizations. As early as 1890 as assembly of the *Alter Verband* resolved as soon as possible to begin publication of a Polish-language edition of their union journal.[25] The resolution was not implemented. In 1894 a reorganized *Alter Verband* again voiced support for a Polish-language journal. The journal should only begin publication, however, after 4,000 Polish-speaking members had been enrolled in the union. Should the number slip under 4,000 a grace period of four months would be permitted to reach that number again during which time publication would continue. If after that period the 4,000 barrier should not have been surpassed publication would cease. Again, no action was taken to realize the resolution. The following year a similar proposal was defeated at the assembly on financial grounds. Finally, in 1898, a Polish-language journal, *The Miner* (*Oświata*),appeared. An insufficient subscription forced cessation of publication two years later. In 1901 the *Alter Verband* authorized a bi-monthly publication of the General Association of Trade Unions, *Education* (*Sświata*), as their official Polish-language journal.

The *Gewerkverein* proceeded in a similar manner. It first voted its support of a Polish-language publication in 1897. Nothing came of it. In 1898 the resolution was again put forward. This time it was coupled with a provision to raise the dues in order to cover the cost of publication. The chairman raised several objections and the resolution failed. The *Gewerkverein* journal, *Der Bergknappe,* put forward another suggestion. The Polish newspaper, *Wiarus Polski,* it was pointed out, devoted a number of its pages to miners. Why not, suggested *Der Bergknappe,* funnel information that the *Gewerkverein* wished made known to the Poles through *Wiarus Polski*? That newspaper was, in any case, in fundamental agreement with the *Gerwerkverein*. The proposal was not greeted with any enthusiasm, and its memory rapidly faded. Unable to arrive at any population solution, the *Gewerkverein* assigned the question to a committee for further study.

The conclusion is unavoidable that either the *Alter Verband* and the *Gewerkverein* had no real desire to enroll Polish members, or they were simply not competent to recruit them successfully. The attempt of the *Alter Verband* may have been merely formal. Since most Poles were Catholic there would have been little reason to expect many recruits from among them. Rome, after all, was vocal in its opposition even to Liberalism. The *Alter Verband*'s resolution which required 4,000 Poles to be enrolled before beginning publication of a special journal for them might well be viewed as a sober recognition of the chances for large-scale enrollment. The *Gewerkverein,* on the other hand, had a real opportunity to attract Polish members into its ranks. Religion, for example, could have been the basis for an appeal in this undertaking. Its failure was, in large part, due to a lack of sensitivity concerning Polish ethnicity.

In Bottrop relations between the Poles and the *Gewerkverein* suffered considerable damage during the election of 1898 for *Knappschaftälteste*. The institution of the *Knappschaft* had developed out of traditional organizations of coal miners in the period when mining was very nearly a closed, hereditary occupation. Its object was to assist ill or injured miners or, if need be, their survivors. As the bureaucratic apparatus of the Prussian state evolved it recognized and legitimized the *Knappschaft* rather than abolishing it and assuming the responsibilities itself. The Prussian *Knappschaft* Law of 1854 organized the institution into a rational form and made membership in its mandatory for all miners. The result was the introduction into German coal mining—thirty years before Bismarck's social legislation—of a statutory social insurance system which provided for pensions to invalids, payments to widows and orphans and free medical treatment. The General Mine Law of 1865 granted the right of full self-administration to the *Knappschaft*.[26] The officers (*Knappschaftälteste*) of each local branch were chosen by indirect election. Their functions included the superintending of the treasury and the representation of individual grievances to the management of the mines. Half of the board of directors

(*Vorstand*) of the combined *Knappschaft* for the *Oberbergamt* Dortmund came from the ranks of the mine employees. They were chosen from among the local *Knappschaftälteste.*

By 1898 some Ruhrgebiet Poles were demanding representation among the *Knappschaftälteste.* In the summer of that year a deal was concluded (or seemed to have been) between August Brust, the chairman of the *Gewerkverein,* and the leader of the Ruhrgebiet Poles, Jan Brejski, the editor and publisher of *Wiarus Polski.* The Poles were to have one mandate each in Recklinghausen-Bruch and Bottrop. However, at a meeting of Polish miners in Bottrop in June, 1898 this offer was rejected. The leading speaker at the assembly, the miner Augustin Świenty, was insistent in his attack on anti-Polish tendencies within the *Gewerkverein.* He claimed that nine of the fifteen *Knappschaftälteste* who sat on the *Vorstand* were anti-Polish and he demanded the election of Polish representatives. His exhortations were successful; the assembly decided to choose two Polish candidates to stand for election in Bottrop.[27] This action led to a bitter exchange of letters in the *Bottroper Volkszeitung* between Świenty and Brust. Accusation of anti-Polish bias was hurled, and counter charge of outside agitator was returned.[28] Brust won the battle, as no Polish *Knappschaftälteste* were elected from that district. The victory, however, came at some cost. It left a residue of bitterness among the constantly increasing numbers of Poles, to which the *Gewerkverein*'s enthusiastic support of the language decree of 1899 incalculably added.

The founding of the ZZP, then, in November 1902 in Bochum was largely the result of the inability or unwillingness of the established unions to deal with the specific needs of the Polish mine workers. That it was solely the child of radical Polish nationalist aspirations was clearly incorrect, although there is no doubt that some, e.g. *Wiarus Polski,* hoped to use it as a vehicle for political education. It saw its task primarily as an economic one.[29] Its constitution provided for the disbursment of funds for unemployment compensation, sick pay and burial. Public meetings were to be held for discussion of conditions and rights of workers, informational pamphlets were to be distributed and a labor exchange set up. The Alliance of Poles in Germany (*Związek Polaków w Niemczech*), founded in 1894, had earlier made some effort to be recognized as the economic agent of the Ruhrgebiet Poles, but its frankly political character had put off most Polish workers.[30] The ZZP explicitly eschewed political activity, most especially of a socialist variety, but also including that of a Polish nationalist nature.[31] The specifically economic orientation proved successful. The two hundred founding members who gathered in Bochum in 1902 grew in a decade to more than fifty thousand, a membership which established it as a major power in the economic life of the Ruhrgebiet.[32]

The question remains of the effect that the ZZP had on the integration of the Ruhrgebiet's Polish population. There seems little reason to doubt that the fact of its existence, i.e. of a large, successful and specifically ethnically rooted union, inhibited the process of assimilation. Coal miners who belonged to the ZZP were clearly Poles and not Germans. The success of the ZZP and its acceptance as an equal by the other unions must have stimulated ethnic pride. But, paradoxically, the success of the ZZP was important to the integration of the Ruhrgebiet Poles. It must be remembered that the two terms, assimilation and integration, are not interchangeable. The former describes a process in which one identity is lost and another assumed. That is, an assimilated Poles would have become a German, without distinguishing language, customs or values. The Pole who was integrated into Ruhrgebiet society, however, could well have remained readily identifiable as ethnically different. But, he was also recognized as one who was competent to participate in the full range of economic, social and political activites that would have been available to a native of the same class and ability. It is unlikely that the first generation of Polish inmigrants would be assimilated, but it was necessary that they be integrated, not only for the sake of their own well-being, but also for that of their children. If the first generation created, or was forced into, a ghetto existence, the question of social acceptance would remain for each succeeding generation.

It is clear that at the turn of the century the Ruhrgebiet Poles were not assimilated. They were not, for example, indistinguishable from the general membership of the *Gewerkverein*. It was certainly no secret that certain of the membership were Poles. Yet, the leadership of the *Gewerkverein* did not realize that it was necessary to allow, or was not willing to permit, that Poles have access to positions which could prove crucial to their well-being. In 1898, although Poles made up two-thirds of the work force of Bottrop's mines,[33] they were denied a share of one-third of Bottrop's *Knappschaftälteste.* Early in the twentieth century other institutions were organized which were of importance to miners. By amendment to the General Mining Law in 1905 a renovated system of Workers' Committees (*Arbeiterausschüsse*) was established.[34] A Workers' Committee of at least three members was elected by secret ballot in each mine with more than a hundred workers. In brief, the task of the Workers' Committee was to protect the workers against arbitrary action of the employer and represent their grievances to him. That is, the Workers' Committees performed the functions in the mines which would have been the province of the still officially unrecognized unions. In 1909 the General Mining Law was again amended to provide for the election of security officers (*Sicherheitsmänner*) to regulate safety conditions in the mines. A *Sicherheitsmann* was chosen for each work crew (*Steigerabteilung*) by direct and secret ballot. In addition to maintaining safety standards, the Workers' Committees would be chosen from their midst.

If the Polish mine workers could be excluded from the ranks of the *Knappschaftälteste* and *Sicherheitsmänner,* then regardless of their relatively favorable employment position, they would have been denied significant control over their economic life which was available to others. With the founding and growth of the ZZP, however, it was no longer possible to deny a Polish voice in such areas. In 1898 the *Gewerkverein* had offered the Poles two *Knappschaftälteste* mandates for the entire *Oberbergamt* Dortmund. In 1912 throughout the *Oberbergamt* thirty-two Poles were elected *Knappschaftälteste.*[35] In 1910, overall, only 6.8 percent of the *Sicherheitsmänner* elected in the *Oberbergamt* were Poles, a figure far out of proportion to their representation (19.1 percent) among coal miners. However, in certain areas where Poles formed a significant part of the work force the figure was much higher. In the precinct (*Bergrevier*) Oberhausen 22 percent of the miners were Poles (excluding Masurians). In that *Bergrevier* fifteen out of the hundred *Sicherheitsmänner* elected were Poles. In the same year in *Bergrevier* Essen West, which included Bottrop, thirteen members of the ZZP were elected *Sicherheitsmänner* of a total of fifty-nine (22 percent). Twenty-seven percent of the miners of the *Bergrevier* were Poles (excluding Masurians).[36] In localities where the Poles, and thus the ZZP, were a force they were taken into account.

In the realm of their economic life the Polish in-migrants were probably most severely tested during strikes. It is in times of crisis that a society is most vulnerable to the centrifugal forces inherent in it. During these times the outsider is in a particularly sensitive position if he has maintained a separate identity, if he has not become a party to the whole series of social arrangements of which a part are now in dispute, if he is, in a word, not integrated into the society. If the crisis becomes severe enough, or if the outsider reacts to it in a manner seen as unsuitable, he may face constraints, sanctions, abuse or even expulsion. A strike is, at least potentially, a social crisis. Certainly it is for those directly involved in it. Thus, the German attitude toward the Poles during strikes was a valuable indicator of their integration. At the same time, the manner of Polish participation in strikes could effect German attitudes and behavior toward the Poles in the future.

Early on Poles had been suspected of being strike breakers and of depressing wages.[37] The Ruhrgebiet-wide strike of 1889 provided a test for these charges. Despite a background of increasing discontent the strike which broke out in May of that year came as a surprise to both miner owners and labor spokesmen.[38] Neither were the miners yet organized into unions. Thus, the strike was really a number of contemporaneous local strikes rather than a coordinated general strike with unified direction. In Bottrop a committee of four, two Germans and two Poles, was appointed by the general manager (*Betriebsführer*) of the mine to negotiate on behalf of the miners. Approval of agreements and instructions for further negotiations were gained by the committee at assemblies held every three or four days. The ethnic division of the Bottrop miners was clearly indicated by the separate meetings held by Polish and German miners. It soon became clear that the Polish miners contributed little direction to the strike movement. Individually, Polish miners participated wholeheartedly in the strike, but their lack of organization and competent leaders left them only a mass of individuals.[39] The strike waxed and waned in intensity for nearly a month before sputtering to an end by June. Bottrop's Poles, by their enthusiastic participation, had shown that the old accusations were false, but they had not been unified and had played only a subordinate role in events.

After the turn of the century, when Poles had become very numerous in the Ruhrgebiet, two major strikes occurred. The first was in 1905. In this strike the Poles took a more active part, for which the ZZP was largely responsible. It not only directed the activities of Polish miners, but it defined the nature of their participation in several critical ways. By its very existence it gave evidence of a continuing Polish ethnic identity in the Ruhr-gebiet. For better or worse during the course of the strike Poles would be identified as such. However, it also guaranteed that they could be relied on as a unified, disciplined force. In the ZZP they had an established, continu-ing organization rather than a temporary and inexperienced strike commit-tee. Thus, the Poles could coordinate their actions throughout the Ruhrge-biet and act in concert with the other unions. Finally, because the ZZP had survived and grown, the Poles had to be accepted in the highest councils of strike leadership as relative equals. Though not comparable in size to the *Alter Verband* or the *Gewerkverein,* the ZZP, after a slow start, had grown rapidly, and on the eve of the strike it had about twelve thousand members.[40] This growth is exemplified in the membership figures for Bottrop. By January 1904—a little more than a year after is founding—fewer than two hundred members of the ZZP were to be found in Bot-trop. By mid-year there were just over four hundred, and at the beginning of January 1905, 559.[41]

The strike broke out on the sixth of January at the Bruchstrasse mine in Bochum-Langendreer.[42] Its immediate cause was not a demand for high-er wages—indeed, wages had been rising during the immediately preceding years—but rather a dispute over working conditions. The owner of the mine, Hugo Stinnes, took the strike as an occasion to reaffirm his distain for unions, and he refused to negotiate. The unions attempted to localize the strike at Bruchstrasse, but a series of wildcat strikes followed through-out the Ruhrgebiet. On January 12 representatives of the *Alter Verband,* the *Gewerkverein,* the ZZP and the Hirsch-Duncker Union met in Essen to decide on a unified strategy. Executive authority over the four-union alliance and responsibility for negotiations with the Association of Mine Owners (*Bergbaulicher Verein*) was placed in the hands of a seven-member commission (*Siebener Kommission*) which included two representatives of the ZZP. On January 15 the *Bergbaulicher Verein* refused all negotia-tions with the *Siebener Kommission.* The following day the unions called for a Ruhrgebiet-wide strike.[43] On January 17 almost three-fourths of the Ruhrgebiet miners (*Untertags*) went on strike. The next day that figure rose to 85 percent. For twenty-one days at least 75 percent (most days over 85 percent) of Ruhrgebiet miners were out. In absolute num-bers this meant more than 200,000 men.[44] Without question this was the most extensive labor action ever seen in the Ruhrgebiet.

The course of the strike in Bottrop proved the militancy of the Polish miners. In a report by the *Kreis* authorities at the end of the strike to the provincial-appointed-governor (*Regierungspräsident*) in Münster, Bottrop's Poles received special mention.[45] The Poles, the report stated, were among the earliest supporters of the strike. Almost without exception, and with evident enthusiasm, they joined the ranks of the strikers. They were active participants in the numerous assemblies of miners, where their representatives made addresses in Polish. There was, however, no attempt to stir nationalist passions. The speakers concerned themselves wholly with labor issues, and even called on the Poles to maintain an orderly conduct (*Mässigkeit, Ruhe und Ordnung*). Early on in the course of the strike the assemblies were divided along ethnic lines. Notices of the meetings appeared in the *Bottroper Volkszeitung* and were signed jointly by the four unions, but they announced separate assemblies. The Polish and German miners of Prosper II met separately. The Rheinbaben employees were overwhelmingly German, and the Poles there voluntarily ceded their claim to delegates to the Germans.[46] The only exception to the generally peaceful conduct of the strike occurred on the evening of the eleventh of February when a confrontation between miners and police at Prosper II became violent. Thirteen Poles were arrested and warrants were issued for six others.[47]

The *Siebener Kommission* finally called for a resumption of work on the tenth of February, and the strike rapidly wound down. From the point of view of Ruhrgebiet Poles the strike had been a success. As a result of it the General Mining Law underwent the revision that resulted in the creation of the Workers' Committees. Poles soon gained significant representation on these important bodies. Then too, they and their union had proved their mettle in a major industrial confrontation. There remained no shadow of a suspicion that Poles were unreliable allies in such a crisis. As an example, when the directive to resume work went out on the tenth of February, the majoirty of miners complied with it. However, on the thirteenth of February most of the miners in Bottrop remained out. The Poles were, according to the above mentioned report, the last to pick up their tools. Just such solid adherence to the strikers' cause had won the Poles the respect of the other unions.[48] The ZZP itself derived great benefit from the strike. Beyond its now recognized claim to be a major force in the Ruhrgebiet, its conduct during the strike had won it thousands of new members. By the end of the year it had more than doubled its membership. In Bottrop, by October 1905, almost 2100 men had enrolled.[49]

The second major strike took place in March 1912.[50] It underscored significant changes in attitude both of and toward the Poles. Several of the motives behind the strike differentiated it clearly from the earlier great strikes.[51] Above all, the strike had specifically economic goals. The question on which the miners went out was one of higher wages. Previously wages had played only a secondary, or at best co-equal, role while demands for the creation of Workers' Committees, *Knappschaft* reform and more stringent safety measures were put first on the strikers' lists. Further, the demand for higher wages was made at a time when wages were already rising after a setback from 1908 to 1910. Profits, however, were rising even more rapidly. Thus, the demand was, in essence, for a more equitable distrubution of the wealth. The strike was also seen as a gesture of solidarity with Belgian and English miners who were striking at the same time. A desire to test the increasing strength of organized labor—almost a third of Ruhrgebiet miners belonged to unions in 1912[52] — against the recently reorganized owners (*Zechenverband*) also played a part. These motives meant that the striking unions—the Triple Alliance (*Dreibund*)—could not expect the public support that had been theirs during the previous great strikes. For the *Alter Verband,* accustomed to being execrated as socialists, this was perhaps inconsequential. For the Poles, as recent additions to Ruhrgebiet society, it meant new risk. Finally, the strike, particularly on the part of the *Alter Verband,* was used in an attempt to paint the *Gewerkverein* as a "yellow dog" union because it had declined to join the strike.

On the part of the Poles, participation in the strike marked a complete break with the *Gewerkverein.* Earlier most Poles who had been organized had belonged to it. The *Gewerkverein*'s unwillingness to recognize Polish aspirations had been the impetus which led to the founding of the ZZP. Even in the strike of 1905 there had been a great deal of cooperation between the two; witness the matter of delegates at Rheinbaben. Now the Poles not only showed their independence from the *Gewerkverein,* they actually stood in opposition to it. In Bottrop this was a particularly bold move. Organized miners in Bottrop were divided almost wholly between the ZZP and the *Gewerkverein.* The general alliance with the *Alter Verband* had no real benefit for Bottrop's Poles. That they had entered into

it at all, given the historical dislike of the Ruhrgebiet Poles for the Socialists, surely indicated a confidence on the part of the ZZP that it was too
strong to be devoured by the *Alter Verband.* This confidence was justified
in Bottrop. The *Bottroper Volkszeitung* was a *Zentrum* journal, and, of
course, supported the anti-strike position of the *Gewerkverein.* Throughout the strike it railed against the strikers, often characterizing them as
"terrorists" and "anarchists."[53] Yet, the importance of the Poles in Bottrop's society was such by 1912 that even as the newspaper condemned
the strike, which was almost unanimously supported by the Poles, it was
careful to put the blame on the *Alter Verband* (*Anarcho-Sozialisten*) and
a few selected "radical" Poles. The strike came to an end at the end of
March with little or no economic advantage to the *Dreibund.* Probably
more important for the Poles, however, it had resulted in no discernible
setback.

The economic opportunity offered by the coal mines of the Ruhrgebiet, then, was a real one. The Ruhrgebiet did not attract Poles from Upper Silesia, Posen and East Prussia in order to use them as a base of unskilled labor upon which others could rise. The chance for advancement
into non-manual fields for Poles, as for Germans, was limited. The jobs
which offered the best chance for a decent living in Bottrop—the *Vollhauer*—were open to Poles, and they filled them to the satisfaction of their
employers. Nor were the Poles absorbed into an amorphous Ruhrgebiet
working class. On the contrary, they organized themselves their own union,
by means of which they were able to force acceptance, not as assimilated
in-migrants, but as a distinct ethnic group which formed a valuable part of
the economic system of the city and the Ruhrgebiet as a whole.

CHAPTER V

RELIGION AND EDUCATION

Many of the various expressions of culture which mark human society are the direct concern of only a minority of its members. Nondomestic labor, particularly in modern, urban societies,, has tended to be alloted to adult males. The creation of art is, of necessity, the work of a gifted few. Political life has, until recently, been the province of an hereditary—if not uniquely gifted—ruling class. Religion and education, however, directly affect almost all members of society. In their institutional forms, church and school, the two are powerful inculcators and guardians of social values. A migrant group which settles in a new area may be accepted into the institutions of the host society and remade by the values which they define and teach, or the foreigners may be rejected and confirmed in their status of outsiders. Conversely, the foreigners may either welcome or spurn the acceptance, or acquiesce in or fight against the rejection. Thus, there are several possible combinations of attitudes and actions with regard to church and school which can help an observer judge whether or not migrants have been integrated into a host society.

The importance of organized religion as an instrument of social integration depends on the part which it plays in the host society. What, for example, is the extent of church membership in the community? Is church membership merely formal or does it represent deeply held beliefs? Is there religious homogeneity or are there are variety of confessional allegiances? If organized religion can claim only a small percentage of the members of a society as adherents, the nonadherence of an in-migrant population may be inconsequential. In the same way, if a society is divided into several confessional groupings the acceptance of still a different form by in-migrants could well be of little or no import.[1] The sincerity of religious belief held by Bottropers is impossible to ascertain. Formal adherence, however, can be measured.

TABLE V-1

Bottrop's Church Affiliated Population, 1890-1930

Year	Catholic or Evangelical		Non-affiliated*	
	Nr.	%	Nr.	%
1890	13,586	99.9	9	0.1
1900	24,789	99.8	58	0.2
1910	46,985	99.6	177	0.4
1930	84,556	98.6	1,139	1.3

Sources: JSB, Nrs. 3, 4 and 6.
*Includes a very small number of Jews together with persons of no known affiliation.

The percentage of Bottrop's population which admitted to church membership was uniformly high over a forty year period. Indeed, membership was all but universal. Even if that membership were only formal it must be assumed that the figures in the table above were not obtained by chance. That is, even if religious belief were tepid or absent altogether social conformity in Bottrop demanded at least formal church membership.

If it is accepted that affiliation with a church was regarded as desirable social behavior, the degree of confessional division must still be determined. That is, were the inhabitants of the city divided relatively equally between Catholicism and Lutheranism, or did one of the two dominate in the community? That question is also susceptible to measurement.

During the period under consideration in this study Bottrop was clearly a Catholic city. The ratio of Catholics to Lutherans, it is true, declined over the years, but with three quarters of the population still professing

Catholicism in 1930 it seems not misleading to maintain that designation for the entire period.

TABLE V-2

Confessional Division of Bottrop's Christian Population, 1890-1930

Year	Catholic		Evangelical	
	Nr.	%	Nr.	%
1890	12,695	93.4	891	6.6
1900	22,550	91.0	2,239	9.0
1910	40,954	87.2	6,031	12.8
1930	63,675	75.3	20,881	24.6

Sources: JSB, Nrs. 3, 4 and 6.

The confessional structure of the city would appear not unfavorable to the Polish in-migrants. They were, it will be remembered, overwhelmingly Catholic (81.0 percent). The Polish in-migration was also greatest during the period when Bottrop was most Catholic. Over 60 percent of the Polish in-migrants entered the city by 1910. At that time seven of every eight Bottropers were Catholic. At variance with the supposition that religious commonality was of value in attaining integration is the finding concerning the relationship of religion to persistence (see pp. 36-37). Although the Catholic in-migrants found in this sample showed a greater inclination than the Protestants to remain in Bottrop for a year or longer, that difference was not statistically significant. This could be evidence that church membership was largely formal, involved little personal interaction and resulted in small degree of mutual social acceptance among co-religionists. On the other hand, having religious observance in common with other inhabitants may have enabled Polish in-migrants to overcome, at least in part, ethnic disadvantage and attain the rate of persistence that they, in fact, did.[2]

The earliest Polish in-migrants in Bottrop were without religious apparatus of their own. There was only one church, St. Cyriakus, in the city, and it was there that they were required to go it they wished to fulfill religious obligations at all. No Polish-speaking priest was resident in Bottrop. Services were entirely in German, which many of the Poles had not yet mastered.[3] In August of 1872 a priest from Posen, Johann Kontecki, took up residence in the *Oberbergamt* Dortmund and moved among the various Polish communities there. However, political considerations intervened and his ministry was short-lived. It was in 1872 that Bismarck opened his campaign, the *Kulturkampf,* against the Catholic Center Party. By 1873 he was able to secure passage of legislation, the May Laws (*Maigesetze*), which gave him extensive control over the Catholic Church and its activities in Prussia. Kontecki was required to leave the Ruhrgebiet, and during the height of the *Kulturkampf* other Polish priests were forbidden to work in Westphalia or even enter the province.[4] Despite the May Laws a certain Pastor Brylski from Kloster St. Annaberg in Upper Silesia, who was in exile in Holland when the *Kulturkampf* began, was active in the Ruhrgebiet during the middle and late 1870s. The local German ecclesiastical leader, Pastor Englert, was responsible for obtaining his services. Brylski was able to attend to the spiritual needs of the Poles in private homes. He visited Bottrop regularly for several months every year, and was highly regarded by the local Poles. Ultimately he fell afoul of the authorities and emigrated to America.[5] The years of the most active persecution of the *Kulturkampf* in the 1870s were later remembered by Bottrop's Polish community as dark, immoral and irreligious.[6]

When the *Kulturkampf* slackened in the early 1880s (although the May Laws were not repealed until 1885) things took a better turn for the Poles. In 1881 enforcement of the laws was relaxed and Polish-language services were allowed in the church so long as German remained the language of sermons delivered from the pulpit, and in addition, confessions could be heard in Polish. Pastor Englert wholeheartedly supported the relaxation.[7] His repeated invitations resulted in visitations to Bottrop by Polish-speaking priests two or three times a year. In 1885 an attempt was made to introduce vernacular services for the Poles on a regular basis. The diocese of Kulm, in West Prussia, was given formal obligation for the Poles of Bottrop, and it sent the priest Raschke to Bottrop.[8] His arrival was the occasion for great celebration in the Polish community. The Germans seem not to have been disconcerted by the presence of a Polish priest. The *Bottroper Volkszeitung* reported favorably on Raschke's arrival and the consequent jubilation. Many of Bottrop's Germans joined in the welcome; a number of them decorated their homes with banners in honor of the Polish priest.[9]

Raschke departed within a year, but by October of 1886 another Polish priest, Pastor Szczotowski, began to make regular visits to the city, although he did nto take up residence there. Szczotowski's visits continued for three years. Thereafter a series of Polish-speaking priests visited Bottrop on a more or less regular basis, but none of them actually lived in the city.[10]

By the end of the nineteenth century the lack of a regular ministry in Polish, the growth of the Polish in-migrant community and the emergence of Polish spokesmen combined to create the conditions for the first serious dissension between Poles and Germans in Bottrop. The lack of regular religious services in Polish had, by that time, come to vex many Poles, and some of the more forceful members of the Polish community determined upon action. On March 20, 1898, a meeting of Polish miners was held at a tavern in Bottrop. Among the speakers was Franz Swoboda of that city. He called in strong and unequivocal terms for the permanent installation of a Polish priest in Bottrop.[11] Pursuing this demand, Swoboda called a meeting of local Poles at the end of April, 1989 to discuss possible action. Only forty-six people attended the meeting, but they were activists. It was suggested that a petition be sent to the bishop of Münster concerning the position of the local Poles, and thirty people volunteered to collect signatures.[12] Within two weeks enough interest had been aroused in the Polish community to attract more than 350 people to another meeting which was dominated by Franz Swoboda and his brother Aloys. In a rousing speech Franz Swoboda described the terrible consequences of the *Kulturkampf* for Catholics in general and Poles in particular. He noted that Bottrop was inhabited by more than 7,000 Poles, and he demanded that they receive proper religous care, which was only possible under the direction of a Polish-speaking priest. Aloys Swoboda polled the assembly on the question of whether or not everyone wholly understood the sermons delivered in German and received a unanimously negative answer. He then read a petition which he had drawn up to the bishop of Münster asking that a Polish-speaking priest be sent to Bottrop. The suggestion was made and accepted to ask that the local church administration pay the costs of a resident Polish priest.[13]

The German reaction to the meeting and the petition seemed out of proportion to the actions of the Poles. A Polish priest had been in residence, earlier, and the Germans had welcomed him. Following that, Polish priests had visited Bottrop at the invitation of the German pastor and there had been no visible opposition. However, the report of the April meeting in the *Bottroper Volkszeitung* leaves no doubt that in 1898 there existed in the city vociferous opposition to the Polish demand. Was it possible, the newspaper asked, that Poles were so little educable that eight years of German school had not given them command of the language? How, in that case, did Polish men ever get along in the army? The newspaper had certainly thought that the Poles were smarter than that. It still thought so. The demand must have been the work of a radical minority of young upstarts. Clearly the responsible members of the Polish community were not behind it. They had no desire for a Polish priest. The whole thing was simply a ploy on the part of the radicals to establish a completely Polish parish in Bottrop, and that attempt would never succeed. In closing, after complimenting the Polish establishment on their opposition to the Young Turks, the editorial suggested that if the brothers Swoboda did not like it in Bottrop they were free to leave.[14]

The charges of the *Bottroper Volkszeitung* were answered by *Wiarus Polski*. Bottrop's Poles, it said, had never laid claim to their own parish. The question was one of adequate spiritual care. This German reaction was simply another example of their insensitivity to Polish needs. The overflowing hall at the meeting disproved the assertion that a tiny group of radicals alone were interested in the question. Finally, in answer to the suggestion that dissatisfied Poles leave, it must be remembered that because of the policy of Germanization in the East it was almost impossible for Poles to return there.[15] *Wiarus Polski*'s claim of wide support for a permanent Polish priest was justified. Within two months 3,425 signatures had been gathered for the petition. The Polish leaders strictly followed canonical procedures and presented the petition to the highest local ecclesiastical authority, the German pastor, Müller. As in the past, the German cleric gave support to the Poles. He not only gave his permission for the presentation of the petition to the bishop, but he also indicated his agreement with it. The bishop received the petition with some scepticism. They wanted, he assumed, a Polish nationalist installed in Bottrop. The Bottrop Poles denied this. All they desired was a resident priest who could speak Polish. Finally the bishop's misgivings were overcome and he promised to send a Polish-speaking priest to the city, but he added that fulfillment of the promise would take two years.[16]

The storm seemed to have dissipated, but very shortly the question of a Polish controlled parish was revived. Near the end of the nineteenth century Bottrop's population had grown to a point where a single church could not adequately serve all the city's Catholics. In 1895 it was decided to build a second church, St. Johannes, which was dedicated in 1898. However, it was located in the northeastern part of the city, a relatively lightly settled area.[17] Many Poles, already dissatisfied with the irregular visitations by Polish-speaking priests, were further disgruntled by the building of a new church in the *Bauernschaft* of Boy where so few of them lived. Even while St. Johannes was under construction it became apparent that Bottrop's growing population would soon outstrip the facilities of the two churches. Therefore, local ecclesiastical authorities determined, in July 1898, to petition the bishop of Münster for permission to put up a third church. A building site had already been donated on the southern edge of the old central village.[18] The bishop did not grant his permission until March 1899. He expressed disappointment with the proposed location. The new church, he felt, should be built in Lehmkuhle. That area had lately become heavily settled, primarily by Poles, and the bishop specifically mentioned the need to provide for them.[19] In the end, the donation of the land fixed the location of the new church, but it was clear that its parishioners would be drawn largely from Lehmkuhle. Thus, the German inhabitants of the city would be faced with what, for all practical purposes, would be a Polish parish.

Work on the new church, Herz Jesu, was begun without interethnic strife. The land on which it was built was donated by a German woman. Eighty-five citizens of Bottrop donated RM 50,000 towards its construction, and Arenberg Bergbau, GmbH, which had an interest in maintaining some degree of satisfaction among its Polish employees, contributed an additional RM 20,000. In October 1902 the church was dedicated.[20] The completion of Herz Jesu provided the opportunity for the fulfillment of Polish aspirations regarding the practice of their religion. At the same time it seemed to quicken the fears of at least some Germans. From the beginning permission had been given by the bishop of Münster to conduct services in Polish. In addition, Polish hymns were allowed to be sung at low mass after the consecration. Pastor Müller of St. Cyriakus had petitioned the bishop for these favors.[21] Most important, just before Easter of 1903 a Polish-speaking priest took up residence at Herz Jesu, five years after the bishop of Münster had made his promise. The new priest, chaplain Vennekamp, represented a compromise. He was a German who had become fluent in the Polish language. His presence in Bottrop assured the bishop that Polish nationalism would not find any aid in the Church. On the other hand, Vennekamp's language facility stood him in good stead with the Poles since he was able to perform his ministries of comfort, hear confessions and, above all, give sermons in Polish.[22]

Although Herz Jesu had, from the beginning, a distinctly Polish cast, German fears of a Polish takeover were not immediately realized. The local church council (*Kirchengemeindevertretung*) and its executive committee (*Kirchenvorstand*) which had authority over the three churches were, at first, dominated by Germans. In 1902 only three out of thirty members of the former body and one of ten members of the latter were Polish, percentages far under Polish representation among the whole congregation. Two years later the make up of the bodies was the same.[23] However, late in 1904 Bottrop's single parish was divided among the three churches. To Herz Jesu was alloted the southeastern part of the city which included part of the *Bauernschaft* Batenbrock and almost all of *Bauernschaft* Lehmkuhle, both areas heavily populated by Poles. The congregation of Herz Jesu parish rivaled that of the historic St. Cyriakus in size—11,252 and 13,996 respectively—while St. Johannes took the care of 3,387 souls.[24] More important than size, the division meant the creation of three separate *Kirchengemeindevertretungen* and *Kirchenvorstände*.

The church elections of 1902 had been severely criticized by *Wiarus Polski*. The Germans were accused of preventing Poles from voting, and a complaint was filed with the bishop of Münster.[25] Following the division of Bottrop into three parishes, the Poles were confident of electing their condidates, in whatever numbers they wished, to the governing bodies of Herz Jesu in 1905. Similar situations existed in other parts of the Ruhrgebiet. In those parishes some voices called for an exclusively Polish composition of the *Kirchenvorstände*. Moderates urged a division of the seats with Germans. A compromise was reached which was intended to guide Polish electors in all church elections throughout the Ruhrgebiet. It was announced in *Wiarus Polski*. In those cases where Poles had been accepted in the German-dominated *Kirchenvorstände*. Germans would be allowed seats in the new Polish parishes. In areas where Poles had been excluded no German should be elected.[26] Despite the publication of this plan the results of the election in Herz Jesu came as a surprise to many Germans. The Polish slate for *Kirchenvorstand* was easily elected. A few days later the parish chose a *Kirchengemeindevertretung* composed largely of Poles. In all, Poles gained nine of the ten seats in the former body and twenty-two out of thirty in the latter.[27]

Germans reacted with astonishment and outrage. The *Bottroper Volks-zeitung* characterized the successful Polish candidates as radicals and the election itself as a provocation (*hetzerische Treiben*). Its opinion, it said, was faithfully conveyed in an editorial from the *Essener Volkszeitung,* which it reprinted. Radical Poles, according to that editorial, had been successful in carrying through their plan to elect exclusively Polish church authorities in Herz Jesu. The outrage among Germans over this brutal exercise of power (*brutalen Gewaltakt*) was certainly understandable, especially when one realized that it was Germans who had contributed such large sums for the building of the church. So much had been done for Polish parishioners in Herz Jesu that it was impossible to grasp what it was that the agitators wanted. Things were at a sorry pass when it was possible for strangers, immigrants, to displace old German inhabitants of the city. The action of the Poles was certainly in stark contrast to the elections in the other parishes of the city where the Germans had been so generous as to elect some Poles to the church council (". . .so nobel waren, einige Polen in die Gemeindevertretung zu wählen.")[28] Neither the *Essener Volkszeitung* nor the *Bottroper Volkszeitung* mentioned that not a single Pole was elected to the *Kirchenvorstand* of either St. Cyriakus or St. Johannes, or that Polish representation on the *Kirchengemeinde-vertretungen* of the two churches was limited to two members each.[29] It was high time, the editorial concluded, that the government take steps to keep a closer surveillance on the radical element among the Poles.[30]

Thus, the relationship between German and Polish Catholics in Bottrop had, by 1905, come to be one marked by mutual distrust and even open animosity. An aspect of culture which the two held in common, and which might have been expected to foster a greater understanding and acceptance between them, was threatening, through its institutional manifestations, to further alienate the two. Yet, that did not happen even though the Poles did not retreat in religious matters. They did not surrender the concessions already won regarding pastoral care in Polish, rather they continued to push for the extension of it. Reports of the *Kreis* authorities to the provincial governor repeatedly referred to the use of Polish in connection with the Mass, Sunday afternoon devotions and sermons.[31] By 1913 three churches in Brottop offered spiritual care in that language. At Herz Jesu, with the Polish-speaking Kaplan Vennekamp in residence, Polish-language services were held every Sunday. At St. Johannes in Boy and the new Liebfrauenkirche in Eigen there were no resident Polish-speaking priests, but a Franciscan who lived in Düsseldorf visited both of the churches at regular intervals.[32]

These activities did not draw the condemnation of the *Bottroper Volkszeitung*. Nor did the government intervene to prohibit religious observance in Polish, as the *Essener Volkszeitung* had once urged. Some restrictions were imposed. Instruction in Polish for children was allowed for first communion and confession, but general religion classes had to be conducted in German.[33] It was not permitted to perform baptisms, marriages or burial services in Polish. Requests for concessions in these areas were not successful, and as late as 1917 and 1918 conferences of pastors serving Polish congregations were still petitioning the bishop of Münster for them.[34] Overall, however, pastoral care in the Polish language continued to expand throughout the Ruhrgebiet. By 1911 more than fifty Polish-speaking priests were active in the region.[35] The attitude of the ecclesiastical authorities went beyond simple tolerance. They actively sought to provide clerics competent to conduct ministries in Polish. In 1916 Polish was made an obligatory subject in the Catholic seminary in Paderborn.[36] Ultimately, the Catholic church had seventy-five Polish-speaking priests at work in the Ruhrgebiet providing services in about a hundred churches.[37]

Neither did the Poles give up control of the governing bodies of Herz Jesu. If, however, the newly elected Polish members had ever had radical notions of whatever kind, they rapidly disposed of them. At the first meeting of the new *Kirchenvorstand* in December 1905 the pastor carefully defined the limits of its authority and cautioned members against anti-German behavior. The lecture seems to have been effective. A short time later, when one of the Polish members resigned from the *Kirchenvorstand,* a German was chosen to replace him.[38] Throughout the city the pattern of representation in church governing bodies which had resulted from the elections of 1905 was maintained with little change in the elections of 1910.

Table V-3 gives a comparison of the ethnic composition of the bodies after each election. Germans gained some additional representation in

TABLE V-3

Membership of Catholic Church Governing Bodies in Bottrop, 1905 and 1910

Church	Kirchenvorstand					Kirchengemeindevertretung				
	1905		1910		Total	1905		1910		Total
					1910					1910
	G	P	G	P		G	P	G	P	
St. Cyriakus	10	–	10	–	10	28	2	28	2	30
St. Johannes	8	–	8	–	8	22	2	22	2	4
Hezu Jesu	2	8	3	7	10	8	22	12	18	30
Liebfrauenkirche	–	–	9	1	10	–	–	27	3	30
TOTAL	20	8	30	8	38	58	26	89	25	114

Sources: "Nachweisung uber die in der Gemeinde Bottrop vorhandenen Polen and Masuren, 14. Februar 1911" (RM VII–Nr. 37, Bd. 1).
"Beteiligung der Polen an den kirchlichen Vorstanden und Gemeindever-tretungen, 1911" (RM VII–Nr. 35a, Bd. 1).

Herz Jesu parish, but Polish control there was not seriously threatened. The *Bottroper Volkszeitung* did not decry the results of the 1910 elections in the alarmist fashion that it had in 1905. In the parishes of St. Cyriakus and St. Johannes Poles continued to receive token representation on the *Kirchengemeindevertretungen* while being excluded from the *Kirchenvorstände*. A new church, Liebfrauenkirche, had been built in the years between the elections to serve Eigen where much settlement had taken place around the Rheinbaben mine. In that parish Poles gained representation on both bodies.

How important, then, were the issues of Polish priests and Polish parishes in Bottrop? Without question they had created dissention between the ethnic groups. For years Poles had demanded pastoral care by Polish-speaking priests and condemned Germans for their seeming denial of it. *Wiarus Polski* regularly carried reports out of Bottrop which voiced these sentiments.[39] Many Germans interpreted these demands as thinly disguised attempts to extend the cause of Polish nationalism. Polish leaders, according to a contemporary German critic, stirred up support for Polish-langauge services even though they themselves never attend church. Thus, it was mere nationalist provocation.[40] The charge may have been true. It was not impossible that some viewed the question purely as a matter of political tactics. However, there is no doubt that many, perhaps most, of Bottrop's Polish inhabitants desired Polish-language church services and took advantage of them whenever they were available. The *Bottroper Volkszeitung* reported overflowing churches after Polish-language services were introduced on a regular basis.[41] Polish domination of the Herz Jesu governing bodies does not, in perspective, seem unreasonable. Poles heavily outnumbered Germans in the parish. As had been the case in the *Knappschaft* election of 1898, the Poles were simply seeking equitable representation.

That Polish penetration of church administration was not unique to Bottrop. The same thing occurred throughout the Ruhrgebiet wherever Poles formed a significant part of the population. In 1912 Poles were only 6.1 percent of the population of the Ruhrgebiet. At the same time, 6.1 percent of the memberships on the Catholic *Kirchenvorstände* and 6.0 percent on the *Kirchengemeindevertretungen* were Polish.[42] The Polish members, however, were not distributed uniformly throughout the Ruhrgebiet, but concentrated in certain areas. More than two-thirds of the Polish members of the administrations held their seats in only thirty-three *Kirchengemeinden* of the Ruhrgebiet which had 10.6 percent of the seats of the whole region. In those parishes Poles made up almost 40 percent of each body. Thus the situation in Herz Jesu was not unique, but rather a part of the general pattern in the Ruhrgebiet.

The confrontation between German and Polish Catholics then, while tense and, at times, even bitter, was relatively brief. The Poles had never been without some sympathy and support from Germans. Early on Bottrop's pastors had made efforts to secure religious care for them in their own language. Even during the difficult years of the *Kulturkampf* the city's German pastor had aided the Poles in circumventing government sanctions. The reaction of local Germans as reported in the *Bottroper Volkszeitung* has already been mentioned. It was only when Poles began demanding what Germans had already been assisting them in gaining, i.e. pastoral care in the Polish language, that animosity arose. It seems probable that for the Germans the question was one of Polish nationalism, or

TABLE V-4

Polish Participation in Catholic Church Administrative Bodies in the Ruhrgebiet in 1912

	Kirchenvorstand	Kirchengemeindever-tretung
Total seats in the Ruhrgebiet	2934	8642
Seats in 33 districts	311	916
%	10.6	10.6
Polish seats in the Ruhrgebiet	179	521
% of total seats	6.1	6.0
Polish seat in the 33 districts	123	353
% Polish seats in the 33 districts	39.5	38.5
Polish seats in the 33 districts as a % of total Polish seats	68.7	67.8

Source: "Zahlmässige Angaben uber das Polentum im rheinischwest-falischen Industriebezirke, 1912" (RM VII—Nr. 37, Bd. I).

their apprehension of it. No doubt the issue was made vital by the well known struggle between Germans and Poles in Posen. Just what form Polish nationalism was to take in Bottrop and what its objectives would be there were unclear. Even in its most strident editorials the *Bottroper Volkszeitung* never suggested that the local Poles were aiming at an autonomous enclave within the city, or that a march eastward could be expected at any time by a Polish army of liberation raised in the Ruhrgebiet. It can only be concluded that what manifested itself was a fear of change and its possible consequences rather than unalterable antipathy to Poles. Support for this position is inherent in the resolution of the conflict, or rather, in the lack of a resolution. There was, in fact, no dramatic climax. As it became clear to the Germans that the Poles regarded Herz Jesu as a center of religious practice rather than politics the issues of Polish priests and Polish parishes simply faded away.

The controversy which surrounded the education of Polish children differed markedly from the origins and development of the religious question in Bottrop. The latter was largely local in scope. Since its most critical point was control of a single parish, resolution of the problem was always within the capability of the city's inhabitants. Polish vexation concerning the education of their children was engendered by legislation which was valid in all of Prussia. Moreover, the problem (as the government saw it) which the legislation was intended to remedy was located in the East, particularly Posen, and it was there that the main battles were fought. The religious problem, though intense, was short-lived. The most critical point was the church election of 1905, and temperatures abated rapidly thereafter. The educational question began quite as early as the religious one, but it survived the demise of the Wilhelmian *Reich*. Throughout that period it simmered constantly without erupting into open conflict. Resolution was only reached after World War I under circumstances completely altered from those which gave rise to the problem, and which, in fact, obviated it. The struggle, such as it was, for Herz Jesu was born and died while the Kaiser still reigned. Finally, the point of dispute between Germans and Poles which created the greatest emnity in the religious context was over institutional power, control of the administrative bodies of the local parish. To a considerable degree the educational question involved only Polish in-migrants and their children, but, in any case, it never involved a German-Polish struggle for the control of local schools. The Poles never attempted—nor could they have—to seize the schools, the institutional apparatus of education. At most, the effort was to introduce a Polish element into them.

By the beginning of the twentieth century education had been a public concern in Prussia for almost a century and a half. In 1763 Frederick the Great issued his General Regulations for Village Schools (*General Landschulreglement*) which mandated universal and compulsory education in Prussia. This goal, needless to say, was not immediately attained. For example, school inspectors in Cleve, a relatively advanced part of Prussia, found during an inspection of 1802 and 1803 that conditions there fell far short of those aimed at in the Regulations. All children between the ages of six and thirteen were required to attend school for six hours a day. No fees were charged the poor. Nonetheless, attendance was found to be extremely irregular. The quality of instruction and its circumstances scarcely encouraged it. Often classes were held in a single room of a private house which was rented for the purpose. Where school buildings did exist they were most often in poor repair. Forty-three percent of the sixty-seven teachers in the province were incompetent. Few of them had even set foot inside the teachers' training school set up in Cleve in 1784. The starvling wages made it necessary for them to carry on another trade to support themselves. Beyond that, the curriculum was very limited. Religion, reading, writing and arithmetic were the only subjects taught.[43] Nevertheless, the direction had been set, and education in Prussia steadily improved. In 1816 forty-three pecent of children of school age were attending classes. By 1846 the figure had risen to 68 percent, and in the 1860s ninety-seven percent were in school. The quality and scope of instruction similarly improved.[44] Without question, in 1900 Prussia boasted one of the best, if not the best, and most comprehensive school systems in Europe.

The basis for the Polish question in Prussian education was also created by Frederick the Great. The dismemberment of Poland, which began during his reign, brought millions of Poles under Prussian rule. For a hundred years the ethnic question lay dormant in the schools. Aside from the compulsory study of German, children were allowed to study subjects in their native tongue. In the East this caused little difficulty since, in practice, most Poles attended Catholic schools and most Germans Evangelical. However, during the years 1872-1874 the curriculum was reformed and unified. Henceforth, German was specified as the language of instruction in all subjects save one. Since Polish could no longer be used as a language of instruction, it followed that it was not necessary to teach it as a subject. Thus, at a stroke, Polish was almost eliminated from Prussian schools in the East. This was clearly an attempt by the Prussian government to solve the ethnic problem in the East. The Polish language would fall into disuse and ultimately be forgotten. Prussia's Polish subjects would, in the end, become German. The one exception to the general exclusion of the Polish language in the schools occurred at the point where education touched religion. Polish children were allowed to receive religious instruction in their own language. Gradually, however, that privilege too was withdrawn.[45] The Poles, who had meekly accepted the expunging of their language from the academic curriculum, found this to be the sticking point. In Wreschen, in Posen, in 1901 it led to a strike in the schools. Polish children turned in their German catechisms and refused to recite in German in religion classes. They were physcially disciplined by teachers, and parents entered the schools to stop the beatings. The arrest and trial of several of the parents followed, and they received prison terms for their actions.[46] In September 1906 in the city of Posen resistance flared anew. By mid-winter the new strike had spread to West Prussia and even into Upper Silesia. It was estimated that a hundred thousand Polish school children took part in the strike at its height. The government retaliated with fines, prison sentences, the expulsion of students from gymnasia who had younger brothers or sisters who were striking and the firing of parents of striking children from government posts. By May 1907 the strike was over with the state victorious in all areas.[47]

With the migration of hundreds of thousands of Poles into the Western coal fields the question of Polish language education became an issue in the Ruhrgebiet. There the presumptuous goal set by German nationalists—the Germanizing of the Polish nation, or at least that part of it under Prussian rule—seemed, almost accidentally, attainable. In the East the Germans were a distinct minority, usually clustered in cities and towns and surrounded by a sea of Poles. That the exclusion of the Polish language from the schools in the East would have, sooner or later, resulted in a transformation of nationality by millions of Poles is, at least, arguable. In many cases German must have been merely an academic language, heard only in schools, while Polish remained the usual mode of social intercourse. The relative ease with which peasant dialects were elevated to literary languages among the Slavs of the Habsburg Empire during the nineteenth century might have been taken by German nationalists as a cautionary sign of how shallow was the imprint of an official language. In the Ruhrgebiet, however, the situation was reversed. There Poles were in the minority. While Polish was certainly their domestic language and was often used among co-workers in the mines, German was obviously the language of the Ruhrgebiet. Thus, if Polish was to be preserved among the second generation of in-migrants, there would have to be an active effort to teach it.

Some Poles recognized this early on. Shortly after they began arriving in the Ruhrgebiet in large numbers, after 1890, appeals began to be made to parents to preserve their language and pass it on to their children. In 1894 a report from the Recklinghausen *Kreis* authorities to the provincial governor in Münster described a Polish assembly in Bottrop which was attended by some two hundred people. The speakers were almost exclusively concerned with the maintenance of the Polish language, and, one after the other, they called for a continuing effort to inculcate it in the children.[48]

Thereafter, the authorities constantly sought evidence of instruction in the Polish language on a formal basis. Although desired and urged by many Poles, this, in fact, did not occur. Over the years the *Kreis* authorities consistently reported that no such classes existed.[49] Just as consistently the necessity for language instruction was preached by the Polish leaders. *Wiarus Polski,* the leading organ of Polish opinion in the Ruhrgebiet, took the lead. As early as 1898 it claimed, extravagantly, that Polish children, without exception had been assimilated by the Germans.[50]

In every issue of the paper editorials argued against the use of German, even rising (or sinking) to verse.

"To Polish Women Concerning the Protection of the Mother Tongue"

> Shame, shame to you daughter of Poland
> who betrays the national virtue,
> whose innocent, rosebud mouth
> is defiled by foreign tongue.[51]

Despite the urgings of *Wiarus Polski,* and, quite probably, the genuine concern of many Polish parents the struggle to maintain the language in the second generation was a difficult one. The children, even when residential patterns had created a largely Polish district in Bottrop, for example, still went to German schools. The school reform which had been designed to deal with the Poles of Posen was in force throughout Prussia. Thus, even religious classes in Polish were not available to the children of the eastern in-migrants. The Poles recognized the futility of formally opposing government policy in the West. It might have been argued that mass protest had some chance of success in the East. However, in the Ruhrgebiet, where Poles were a minority, it was clearly without hope. During the great school strike of 1906 only one case was reported in the entire Ruhrgebiet.[52] The problem of dialect was also present. In Bottrop a majority of the Polish in-migrants were from Upper Silesia. There the language spoken was not the Polish of Posen, but the so-called water Polish (*Wasserpolnisch*). Quite probably then, the teaching of literary Polish to the children of Upper Silesian in-migrants could only occur outside the home, that is, in a classroom. There, of course, the Poles were confronted by the structures of the law.

Partial relief was found in the relaxation of the enforcement of the law. In 1911 instruction for confession and first communion were allowed in the Polish language, although the general religion classes contined to be held in German (see page 88). Nevertheless, the language battle was being lost by the Poles. In some cases Polish young people were joining German clubs.[53] That issue of the preservation of Polish culture in the West was the focal point of a Polish congress held in Winterswijk, Holland, on November 1 and 2, 1913.[54] The question of education for the children was one of the main topics of consideration. The debate concerning this issue was, in the eyes of many, the most important of the congress. Parents, particularly mothers, the final resolution read, should more than ever see to it not only that the children could read and write Polish, but also that only Polish was spoken and sung in the home, prayers offered only in Polish and only Polish religious services attended. Further, on days of historical commemoration (*Gedenkfeier*) the parents should lecture their children on the particular meaning of the event to Poles. In every area where Poles were to be found a man of good reputation should be chosen as guardian of the children. His task would be to visit Polish homes to see that the children were receiving Polish language-instruction. On holidays he should assemble the children of the town for lectures and songs in Polish. Because of the exclusion of the language from the schools, the resolution called for the writing of Polish primers and the formation of children's libraries. Finally, the proposal was made to found holiday resorts (*Ferienkolonien*) in Holland, directed by Polish women from the Rhineland and Westphalia, where Polish lessons and classes could he held outside the reach of Prussian law.

The time expended on the question of education at the congress and the detail in which remedies were proposed illustrate the great concern of Poles. Had no problem existed or if it were only marginal, such great pains would not have been taken. Yet, in practice, there was little to be done. If Poles were to live in the Ruhrgebiet German had to be learned. Children, of course, had to use Polish at home. But what of their children? Probably the only hope of preserving the language among the Ruhrgebiet Poles lay in the creation of formal and regular Polish schools, or at least language classes. These, however, were proscribed by law, and to World War I that law was not altered. When, in April 1914, a Polish teacher from Cracow visited Bottrop to encourage Polish parents in their efforts to maintain the Polish culture in the second generation, she was harassed by the authorities. At a meeting of over three hundred Polish women she gave a speech dealing with the education of Polish children and the maintenance of the Polish language. However, notice of the meeting had not been published in the newspaper, as required by law. Therefore, both organizers of the meeting, two Bottrop women, and the speaker were subject to penalty. Because the authorities believed that the purpose of the meeting was the organization of formal Polish classes, they decided to prosecute. The three were convicted and received both fines and jail sentences ranging from three to ten days.[55] In its final report on the matter, the Church and School Department (*Abteilung für Kirchen-und Schulwesen*) of the Prussian government reiterated its absolute opposition to Polish-language classes.[56]

Only at the end of the First World War were the Poles able to gain the legal right to educate their children in their own language. As things came apart at the end of the war the language laws were annulled.[57] A new Prussian ordinance of December 31, 1918, gave Poles the right to have their own schools. This right, however, was only valid in East Prussia and in border territories.[58] Polish-language classes, on the other hand, could be organized in any part of Germany. Bottrop's Poles moved swiftly to take advantage of the new circumstances. They petitioned the city council (*Gemeinderat*)—Poles had elected seventeen members to that body in March of 1919—for access to school buildings. The council approved the request and placed a number of school rooms at the disposal of the Polish community for use in reading and writing instruction in Polish. A further request for a money grant to underwrite the instructions was, however, refused.[59] In their annual account to the provincial head at the end of 1919 the *Kreis* authorities reported that in Bottrop Polish children were hearing lectures in the Polish language in Polish history and literature, political economy, natural science and hygiene. Enthusiasm for the courses had, at first, been high, but attendance had gradually fallen off. At the time of the report about one hundred children were still attending the lectures.[60]

In 1928 a new ordinance was passed which further encouraged minority education. No restrictions were to be placed on children of minority groups who wished to transfer from a German school to one of their own. However, some demonstration of minority status was necessary. In general, the rule in Weimar Germany was that anyone who declared himself part of a minority was. (*Minderheit ist, wer will.*) However, when it was a matter of transferring to a minority school, proof had to be given that the child was, indeed, of Polish nationality, i.e. *Nationalität* rather than *Staats-angehörigkeit.*[61] The reason for this, quite simply, was money. According to the new law private schools opened for children of a minority group could be eligible for state financial aid. Opening such a school required no minimum number of pupils. However, a lower limit was set for eligibility for state aid. In school districts of twenty thousand people at least forty students had to attend classes; in districts of between twenty thousand and fifty thousand—eighty pupils; in districts of between fifty thousand and 100,000—120 pupils; and in districts over 100,000—240 pupils. If these numbers could be met, then 30 percent of the costs would be borne by the government. Further, it was required that at least one hundred German citizens (*Staatsangehörigkeit* though not necessarily *Nationalität*) be members of the school's founding board.[62] A school association was founded in Bottrop in September of 1928 with a Polish member of the city council at its head. The city administration made spare classrooms available to it, and some 130 children were enrolled. The new Polish school thus qualified for state aid. The school begun earlier was still in existence, but by 1929 it counted only thirty-three children in attendance.[63]

In Weimar Germany Poles achieved what would have been a major, if not unbelievable, victory under the old imperial regime. Not only did the republic permit the opening of Polish-language schools, in some cases it even subsidized them. Yet, in the 1920s its scarcely mattered. The point of such schools—or in Wilhelmian Germany, the desire for them—had been to protect and pass on the language and thus the Polish culture. The careful tending of the Polish cultural heritage had been made necessary by the partitioning of Poland in the eighteenth century. As a consequence of the First World War it was no longer necessary to preserve the nation as a people. The nation was again a political fact. For those in Bottrop or the other cities of the Ruhrgebiet whose first consideration was the manifestation of Polish nationality the way was now open to the final achievement of that goal. It merely required a railway ticket. Many did choose that way. Many, however did not. For the latter the benefits to be found in Bottrop, or the Ruhrgebiet generally, outweighed the desire to live in a purely Polish environment. Few of them were even willing to take advantage of the opportunity offered them to foster Polish culture in the second generation.

According to a government report of 1910 there were 3,489 Polish children of school age in Bottrop.[64] Even if one assumes a migration of extensive proportions after the war, there must have remained in the city considerably more than the one hundred-odd children who were enrolled in the Polish schools. Perhaps parents were simply unable to convince their children of the desirability or worth of such an education. Whatever the reason—migration, indifference of parents or disinclination of children— a decade after the end of World War I there remained in Bottrop little more than a handful of Poles who actively sought the preservation of their language and culture.

From the discussion of Polish education in Bottrop the conclusion emerges that the issue was not one which divided German and Pole. The prohibition of education in the Polish language, and of Polish-language classes themselves, was an act of the Prussian government on which the influence of Bottrop was microscopic, if it existed at all. Even had Germans in Bottrop supported the idea of specifically Polish education they could not have implemented it. If the membership of the Bottrop school board (*Schulvorstand*) had been exclusively Polish it could not have revised the school curriculum. Thus, there existed in the area of education no prize to be contended for by German and Pole as there had been in the cases of the Herz Jesu governing bodies and the Workers' Committees. After the war, when the possibility was created for the Poles to found specifically Polish educational institutions, little happened. Poles did not move *en masse* out of the public school system. The language-education question had always been one of acculturation rather than integration. School children were not segregated along ethnic lines. Polish children were obliged to go to German schools, and there is no indication that Polish parents expected otherwise. In so far as Polish language and culture were taught in the home and the children valued and preserved it, assimilation was avoided. Integration into the educational system, however, was mandated from the beginning of the in-migration and few recoiled from it when it became possible to do so.

CHAPTER VI

MARRIAGE

Throughout his life a person performs a variety of functions in a society. He will act as part of an economic system, a religious community and a political body. For analytical purposes the various functional areas are often treated in isolation although, in fact, there is a good deal of interplay among them. For example, the economic aspects of a person's life may be treated in terms of income level, employment in a specific economic sector or job mobility. However, these economic factors affect, and are affected by, other aspects of the person's life. The type of employment—manual labor, white collar or professional—may depend on the extent of the person's education. The reward gained from that economic activity will, in turn, greatly influence the choice of residential area. In the same way, friendships and casual associations can be determined or limited by economic status. A Ruhrgebiet miner might well have belonged to the *Alter Verband* or *Gewerkverein,* and he probably drew his friends from among his co-workers and fellow unionists. He would not have belonged to a tradesmen's association, nor would he have associated with university professors. In so far as economic factors influence the choice of residential area they can also, for example, indirectly dictate membership in a particular religious congregation and the social or service organizations based on it. That confessional membership may, in turn, be the object of discrimination which causes exclusion from some economic areas, e.g. exercise of professions, upper level management in business or service in government positions.

A minimum of reflection thus calls to mind the interaction of the wide range of human activities and relationships. In one area, however, the interconnection is always obvious. Marriage always admits to impediments. The choice of a spouse is ever constrained by bounds of social and economic status, racial, religious and ethnic difference and even political complexion. Marriages across these lines are, rightly, viewed as aberrations. Such a union may, in fact, be made not despite but rather because of its eccentric nature, as a conscious gesture of defiance or rebellion. If economic status, social class and the like play a considerable role in determining the composition of secondary groups such as trade unions and social organizations—and thus personal relationships resulting from them—they must certainly be crucial to the formation of primary groups, particularly the most fundamental of them, the family. Relationships established in a secondary group are likely to be more or less impersonal and formal, involving only part of the personality. In the primary group, above all the family, contact is personal and intimate, involving the entire personality.[1] A close examination of the various factors which make up the marriage patterns of Bottrop's in-migrants then, may well reveal much regarding their status in the city.

The following analysis of marriage patterns in Bottrop is based on information gained from the sampling of in-migrants who entered the city between 1891 and 1920. Additional data which deal specifically with their marriages were obtained from the city's marriage license bureau (*Standesamt*). Both the marriages of the in-migrants and of their children will be considered in the following discussion. By the end of 1933 all members of the second generation who were included in the sample were twenty-three years of age or older. Almost half of them (44.6 percent) were at least thirty years old, while more than a third (38.5 percent) were between twenty-five and thirty. Thus most of them had reached an age by which marriage was likely to have taken place.

The analytical units differ in size for the various characteristics under consideration. This is due in part to the changing methods of record keeping in the *Standesamt* over time. In addition, not all in-migrant and second generation marriages occurred in Bottrop. Those which took place outside the city were not recorded in the *Standesamt*. Some authors have cited the propensity of the Polish in-migrants to make such marriages. Many Poles, it is maintained, demanded vacations in order to return home and marry.[2]

The assertions, however, are not accompanied by statistical proof. In this study it was found that 9 percent of all the marriages contracted by the sample group during their residence in Bottrop took place outside the city. In the absence of comparative data it cannot be asserted that this figure is a high, low or average one. In any case, the practice declined over the years. One in-migrant marriage in six was celebrated outside Bottrop while fourteen out of fifteen of the second generation married in the city. Thus, material suitable for analysis was available for more than 90 percent of the marriages. Finally, a few of the sample group married a second time. However, these were so few that they were not included in the analysis.

The percentage of in-migrants and their children who were of marriageable status was large (see Table VI-1). Of the 322 in-migrants who were selected in the sample almost two-thirds were single at the time of registration. A few of that number were elderly widows or widowers, but by far the greatest portion of the single in-migrants was youthful. More than three-quarters were under twenty-five. Among the ethnic groups foreigners (66.1 percent) and Germans (68.0 percent) had the largest percentages of unmarried people in their ranks, but the Poles (60.1 percent) were only marginally behind. Men outnumbered women among the single in-migrants by a ratio of three to one. The same ratio existed between Catholics and Protestants. Many of the children of the in-migrants also reached marriageable age during the period under study. Altogether 441 children were born through 1910 to parents who had entered Bottrop during the sample period. Of that number 70 percent remained in the city long enough—to the age of fourteen—to be individually recorded by the Registration Office. Seventy-two percent and 70 percent respectively of Polish and German members of the second generation passed their fourteenth birthday in Bottrop; just over half of the foreign children did so. Since the incidence of marriage at that age is low, and some of the children may have left the city shortly thereafter, the figure of 70 percent shown in the table is undoubtedly an overestimation of the proportion of the second generation which was eligible for marriage while still resident in Bottrop. In that second generation the sexes were more evenly divided among the in-migrants. Males made up just over half (50.4 percent) of it. As was the case with the in-migrants, the second generation was largely Catholic—80 percent.

TABLE VI-1

In-Migrants and Their Children Eligible for Marriage

	In-migrants	Children	Total
Total	322	441	763
Eligible for Marriage	205	311	516
Percentage	63.8	70.5	67.6

Source: AEB.

Many of the in-migrants and their children in that marriage pool did get married. Twenty-seven percent of the in-migrants and over 54 percent of their children contracted marriage during their period of residence in Bottrop. Taken together, 43 percent of those eligible took that step. This figure includes only first marriages celebrated in the city of Bottrop. Marraige was clearly in the normal course of things. In 1910 less than 28 percent of the men over twenty-one years of age and 25 percent of the women over fifteen in *Kreis* Recklinghausen had never been married.[3] The bachelor or spinster of middle years must have been an uncommon figure. He or she may well have found difficulty in fitting into the accepted social pattern. A comparison of the rates of persistence for married and single people of the same group in Bottrop shows that marital status was more closely associated with long term residence than hitherto suggested. Note one of the sample group of in-migrants who remained unmarried still resided in the city at the end of 1933. Over half of them who were married at the time of registration or who married at a later date were still there at that date. The period of residence for the latter ranged from thirteen to forty-three years. The pattern shown in the table is a statistically significant one, and the association between marital status and long-term persistence is strong. While being married did not prevent a goodly number of in-migrants from leaving Bottrop, bachelorhood or spinsterhood virtually guaranteed departure.

When in-migrants who were single at registration are considered alone the results are still more striking. The rate of persistence—defined as residence through 1933—for in-migrants single at registration was eight points

TABLE VI-2

Persistence and Marital Status in Bottrop

	Single		Married		Total	
	Nr.	%	Nr.	%	Nr.	%
Resident in Bottrop at at the end of 1933	—	—	80	52.3	80	26.9
Migranted out of Bottrop by the end of 1933	144	100.6	73	47.7	217	73.1
TOTAL	144	48.5	153	51.5	297*	

Source: AEB, ASB.   * Excludes those deceased by 1933
x^2 = 100.41 , df = 1, p ≤ .011, Phi = .589.

lower than the rate for all in-migrants. However, in-migrants who married while resident in Bottrop had a rate of persistence (72.5 percent) higher even than those who had been married at registration (52.3 percent).

The same pattern is visible is visible among members of the second generation. By the end of 1933 nearly half of that group who remained unmarried was still to be found in the city. Of those who had married, however, over 85 percent still resided in Bottrop. In both cases the figures are considerably higher than the comparable percentages for the in-migrants as a whole or those who had married while living in Bottrop. It is probable that the pattern of the second generation would have been different if the study had ended at a date five or ten years later. A certain number of them would have migrated out of Bottrop by that time. If the pattern of the first generation is followed, however, the loss would have been greater among the unmarried. Even with this limitation the crosstabulation yields a statistically significant result. The relationship between persistence and marital status among the second generation, even in the short run, is of considerable strength although it falls short of those shown in the previous two tables. The strength of the associations yielded by all three tables make it imperative to examine closely who among the in-migrants and

TABLE VI-3

Persistence and Marital Status in Bottrop
In-migrants Single at Registration

	Single		Married		Total	
	Nr.	%	Nr.	%	Nr.	%
Resident in Bottrop at the end of 1933	–	–	37	72.5	37	19.0
Migranted out of Bottrop by the end of 1933	144	100.0	14	27.5	158	81.0
TOTAL	144	73.8	51	26.2	195*	

Source: AEB, ASB.   * Excludes those decreased by 1933.
x^2 = 124.26, df = 1, p ⩽ .001, Phi = .813

TABLE VI-4

Persistence and Marital Status in Bottrop—The Second Generation

	Single		Married		Total	
	Nr.	%	Nr.	%	Nr.	%
Resident in Bottrop at the end of 1933	63	47.7	150	85.2	213	69.2
Migrated out of Bottrop by the end of 1933	69	52.2	26	14.7	95	30.8
TOTAL	132	42.8	176	57.1	308*	

Source: AEB, ASB.   *Excludes those deceased by 1933.
x^2 = 49.78, df = 1, p ⩽ .001, Phi = .402.

their children married and with whom the marriages were contracted. More specifically, it must be determined what the characteristics of the in-migrants and their children were and to what extent they were matched by the characteristics of the spouses.

One of the most striking features of the in-migration was its heavily male composition. That men outnumbered women so greatly among the single in-migrants was, perhaps, not at all surprising. That predominance of men, however, had important implications for in-migrant marriage. If male in-migrants were restricted in their choice of spouse to female in-migrants alone, then two-thirds of them would have had to remain single. If the circle of potential spouses were widened to include the natives of the city the single male in-migrants would have had little better chance to marry since old-stock Bottropers made up only a fraction of the city's population. All in all, the prospects were not bright for the single male in Bottrop. In contrast to Prussia as a whole Bottrop, and indeed the entire Ruhrgebiet, contained fewer women than men. Table VI-5 shows that discrepancy clearly. At the beginning of the era of the great in-migration Bottrop contained 20 percent more men than women. Their numbers gradually drew closer, but even at the end of World War I, in which so many men were killed, women were still less than half the city's population. The marital prospects of single, in-migrant males were even less favorable if the numbers of men and women of marriageable age are compared. In 1900 in the *Landkreis* Recklinghausen there were 747.8 women to every 1000 men among persons over the age of eighteen. By 1910 the preponderance of males in that age group had decreased slightly. However, at that date the ratio of women to men still stood at 797.6 to 1000.[4]

For many of the male in-migrants then, the choice was clear. If they wished both to marry and remain in Bottrop, a spouse had to be brought to the city. That could be accomplished in two ways. A number of the male in-migrants married outside the city sometime after the date of registration. Of all marriages (including second marriages) contracted by male in-migrants through 1933, 20 percent took place outside the city. The second generation of males—to whom the second generation of females stood in a ratio of 980.8 to 1000—contracted less than 7 percent of their marriages outside Bottrop. In addition, some in-migrant males relied on the good offices of friends and relatives at home who undertook to

TABLE VI-5

Ratio of Women* to Men in Bottrop, The Ruhrgebiet and Prussia from 1895 to 1919

	Bottrop	Ruhrgebiet	Prussia
1895	818.7	911.4	1,036.6
1900	843.7	876.5	1,031.0
1905	860.4	901.2	1,023.6
1910	868.6	909.1	1,023.6
1919	924.3	977.5	1,090.4

* Per 1000 men.
Source: Muller, *Die Bevolkerungsentwicklung, Zahlentafel* 9.

find a suitable bride and send her to the Ruhrgebiet where the ceremony would take place.[5] Unfortunately, it is impossible to determine just how common that practice was. If no spouse could be found either in or outside Bottrop, the chances of out-migration were great. Although single males made up almost half the total of the sample group of in-migrants, not one remained in the city at the end of 1933. It is all but certain that this was not true for the whole in-migrant population, but the sample finding does indicate the rarity of single men taking up permanent residence in the city.

For in-migrant women the male to female ratio was clearly more favorable with regard to marriage. If numbers were any guide women should have been able to find spouses more easily than men. Published statistics reinforce the findings of the sample. In *Kreis* Recklinghausen in 1910 the percentage of unmarried women over the age of fifteen was smaller (24.7 percent) than the percentage of single men over twenty (27.9 percent).[6] The figures shown below in Table VI-6 were taken from the sample group. Among in-migrants and their children women married at a rate almost twelve percentage points above men. Calculations reveal that the difference in percentage between marriage rates of men and women is significant. The sex ratio in Bottrop and the figures for *Kreis* Recklinghausen lend credence to the sample finding.

Published statistics also show that there were almost inflexible age limits for marriage. In *Kreis* Recklinghausen in 1910, 98.7 percent of men who married did so between the ages of twenty-one and fifty. In the same year 96.9 percent of women who married were between sixteen and

TABLE VI-6

First Marriages in Bottrop—In-migrants and the Second Generation

	Men	Women	Total
Nr. eligible for marriage	312	204	516
Nr. married in Bottrop	121	103	224
Percent married in Bottrop	38.8	50.4	43.4

Source: ASB.
$H_0 : P_1 - P_2 = 0; Z = 2.60.$

forty years old.[7] Bottrop's pattern was in general accord with that of *Kreis* Recklinghausen. Figure VI-1 displays that pattern. It includes all the marriage partners who were available as a result of the sample selection—in-migrants and their children and the spouses of both. Only those whose marriages were contracted in Bottrop were included. The prime years for marriage were even fewer in Bottrop than in the *Kreis* as a whole. Most women did not marry before the age of nineteen. Just under 11 percent were wed before that age. Twenty-one was the effective lower age limit for marriage for men. Only 3.1 percent of them married before that age. For both men and women considerably fewer marriages were contracted after the age of thirty. Over 95 percent of the women in Bottrop did so by the age of thirty. The corresponding figure for men was also over 95 percent. For the whole of *Kreis* Recklinghausen the percentages were 88.6 percent and 79.4 percent respectively.[8]

The generally early marriages which occurred in Bottrop were likely related to the city's economic structure. Because the coal mines were the city's chief employers, and they experienced an almost constant shortage of labor, securing and holding a job must have been relatively easy. Further, in a relatively short period of time a miner could move from *Schlepper*

FIGURE VI-I

The Age-Sex Structure of the Marriage Partners of the Sample Group
of In-migrants and Their Children

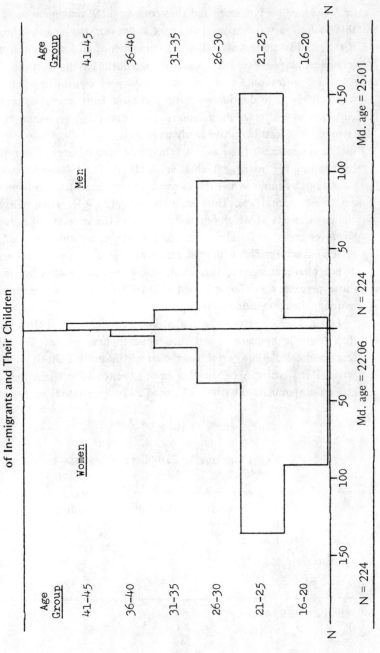

Source: ASB.

to *Lehrhauer* to *Vollhauer* and thus command the maximum wage available to him, a wage higher than most other working men in other jobs. If the city had contained a rather larger number of professional people and service employees the average marital age might have been higher. Years spent in professional training and at low paid clerical apprenticeships would likely have discouraged early marriage. Thus, insofar as economic considerations affected the decision to marry, Bottrop's economic structure favored, or at least permitted, early marriages.

The limitations of age are, one may say, natural ones. There may be laws barring the marriage of children. Aside from that, however, such considerations as earnings and the exigencies of sexual maturity will probably determine marital age. Thus, with the exception of child marriage, the choice of an age at which one will marry and the selection of a spouse of whatever years are largely matters of preference, without threat of social or legal sanction. This is not the case with regard to other characteristics of potential marriage partners. Public abuse or ostracism may be the lot of those persons who choose to ignore certain of society's rules regarding marriage. Religion is one such sensitive area.

In all, a lesser percentage of Protestant in-migrants and their children than Catholic in-migrants and their children married (see Table VI-7). Statistical calculations reveal that the sample finding is unlikely to be aberrational. It is virtually certain that among the total in-migrant and second generation population Catholics married at a higher rate than Protestants,

TABLE VI-7

First Marriages of Catholics and Protestants

	Catholic	Protestant	Total
Nr. eligible for marriage	404	112	516
Nr. married	188	36	224
% married	46.5	32.1	43.4

Sources: AEB, ASB.
$H_0 : P_1 - P_2 = 0; Z = 2.72$

although the difference between the rates was probably not the same in the sample. To some extent this must have been due to the age structure of the Protestant residents in Bottrop. A larger percentage of Protestants (24.8 percent) than of Catholics (13.9 percent) either entered the city after the prime age for marriage or left before reaching those years.[9] In addition, the absoute number of Protestants in Bottrop was smaller than that of Catholics, so the pool of potential marriage partners was smaller. Thus, it is possible that single Protestants had greater difficulty than Catholics in making a suitable match. This hypothesis is supported by the higher percentage of Protestants who married outside the city. More than 14 percent of Protestants who married did so outside the city, while the comparable rate for Catholics was less than 6 percent.[10]

Exogamous marriages—in a religious sense—were, of course, possible. Table VI-8 shows the extent of inter-faith marriage among the members of the sample group and their children. Overall, just above 15 percent of the marriages contracted by in-migrants and their children in Bottrop were across confessional lines.[11] Women of the sample group were slightly more likely than men to have entered into an inter-faith marriage. However, there is a good chance that the small difference between the two shown in the sample group was the result of chance. Protestants were more likely than Catholics to have married outside their faith. That propensity would have increased the marital prospects for the numerically smaller group.

The three remaining divisions are more interesting. The second generation was more willing than their parents to take a spouse of another faith. To a great extent that generational division was also a chronological one. More than 80 percent of in-migrant marriages were contracted by the end of 1918, while seven out of eight marriages of the second generation took place between 1919 and 1933. A study of another Ruhrgebiet city, also predominantly Catholic, found that inter-faith marriagess rarely took place until after the First World War.[12] The findings from the sample of Bottrop's in-migrant generated population clearly support that study. Until the end of World War I inter-faith marriage was almost unknown in Bottrop. After the war it became common, if not usual. From 1919 one marriage in five was made across confessional lines. The greatest difference in rate of inter-fatih marriage was found when the sample group was divided along ethnic lines. Germans married outside the faith at a rate three and a half times greater than Poles. This fact reinforces the argument made in Chapter V concerning the strong adherence of Poles to Catholicism.

TABLE VI-8

Inter-Faith Marriage in Bottrop—In-migrants and Second Generation

	Intra-faith		Inter-faith		$H_0 : P_1 - P_2 = 0$ (Inter-marriage) Z score
	Nr.	%	Nr.	%	
Men	107	88.4	14	11.6	
Women	83	80.6	20	19.4	
Total	190	84.8	34	15.2	1.62
1st generation	52	92.8	4	7.1	
2nd generation	138	82.1	30	17.8	
Total	190	84.8	34	15.2	1.94
Catholic	164	87.2	24	12.8	
Protestant	26	72.2	10	27.8	
Total	190	84.8	34	15.2	2.30
1891-1918	68	97.1	2	2.8	
1919-1933	122	79.2	32	20.8	
Total	190	84.8	34	15.2	3.46
Poles*	141	91.0	14	9.0	
Germans	40	67.8	19	32.2	
Total	181	84.6	33	15.4	4.22

Source: ASB.
N = 224.
*German-born only. N = 214.

Socio-economic barriers also limited marriage in Bottrop. In contrast to inter-faith marriage, which may have been regarded as unwise and perhaps deserving of opprobrium, marriage across socio-economic lines could, in a tangible sense, work to the benefit or detriment of either of the partners. In a society in which economic considerations played an important part in marriage, to marry beneath one's class could not be a decision lightly taken. Table VI-9 summarizes the marriages of the in-migrants and their children in socio-economic terms.

TABLE VI-9

Inter-Class and Intra-Class Marriage by In-migrants
and the Second Generation

	Nr.	Percent
↑	33	15.0
↔	142	64.8
↓	44	20.0
Total	219	

Source: ASB.

The table is based on a division of the sample population into three groups: un- and semi-skilled workers, skilled workers and while collar. The last is undifferentiated. That is, no attempt is made to distinguish between clerk and professional. Bottrop was, overwhelmingly, a working class city. There were simply not enough white collar cases in the sample to allow a meaningful internal analysis of the white collar group. Only 8.6 percent of the marriages involved a white collar spouse. In most instances the status of women has been determined by the occupation of their fathers. Many women, of course, did work, but the occupations involved were usually unskilled manual jobs such as domestic service or factory labor. For example, if a woman who worked as a maid, and whose father was a skilled workman, subsequently married a skilled worker it is unreasonable to conclude that she was marrying into a higher socio-economic class. Exceptions to this rule of classification are formed by women, usually in their late twenties, whose marriage records listed their own occupations while omitting those of their fathers. In such cases it has been assumed that the women lived independently of their families and had, in fact, established their own socio-economic stati.

Marriages most usually took place between partners of the same class. Slightly less than two-thirds of all marriages were of this kind. One person in five married below his class. About a fifth of such marriages (20.4 percent) were unions between skilled workers and the daughters of tenant farmers (*Häusler*). Since all of these marriages involved Polish in-migrants the finding seems to verify the contention of contemporary observers that many of the Polish in-migrants married "mail order" brides. Just over 11 percent of the marriages downward across socio-economic lines involved white collar in-migrants or their children and working class spouses. Half of these were between clerks (*Büro-und Handlungsgehilfe*) or small shop-keepers (*Händler*) and the daughters of skilled workers. The remainder of the marriages downward were between partners of the skilled and un- or semi-skilled working class.

In-migrants and their children made marriages upwards across socio-economic lines about as frequently as they did downwards. Fifteen per-cent accomplished the former. Of these marriages just over 36 percent saw a working class in-migrant or member of the second generation marry into the white collar class. To an even greater degree (66.6 percent) than mar-riages in the opposite direction these were between skilled workers and members of the petty bourgeoisie. The other 60-odd percent of the mar-riages upwards were between persons of the skilled and un- or semi-skilled working class. If the line between working class and white collar is to be considered the crucial social distinction and that between un- or semi-skilled and skilled working class of lesser importance, than the following fact may be noted. Less than 8 percent of in-migrants and their children who married did so across class lines either into or out of the white collar class. In contrast, just over 15 percent contracted inter-faith marriages. It appears that, with respect to marriage in Bottrop, the material con-siderations were more weighty than the metaphysical.

Some interesting patterns appear when the marriages are divided in certain ways (see Table VI-10). The smallest difference is seen when the division is a chronological one. There the rate of inter-class marriage is five points higher than 1919 than after. As has been shown, the chrono-logical divisin is largely congruent with the generational. Thus, it is some-what surprising to note a twenty-five point difference in favor of the first generation. Men and Germans were also more likely to have contracted inter-class marriages than women and Poles respectively. The largest dif-ference in percentage was that between Protestants and Catholics (26.2 percent). However, further thought must be given to the differences shown in the table. It will be remembered that a number of the inter-class mar-riages (11.6 percent) consisted of unions between skilled workmen and farmers' daughters. In the sample group these were all contracted by Polish,

TABLE VI-10

Inter-class Marriage in Bottrop—In-migrants and Second Generation

	Intra-class		Inter-class		$H_0 : P_1 - P_2 = 0$ (Intermarriage)
	Nr.	%	Nr.	%	Z score
1891-1918	41	61.2	26	38.8	
1919-1933	101	66.4	51	33.6	
Total	142	64.8	77	35.2	0.75
Poles*	104	68.0	49	32.0	
Germans	32	57.1	24	42.8	
Total	136	65.0	73	34.9	1.47
Men	69	58.4	49	41.5	
Women	73	72.2	28	27.7	
Total	142	64.8	77	35.2	2.12
Catholic	127	69.0	57	31.0	
Protestant	15	42.8	20	57.1	
Total	142	64.8	77	35.2	2.98
1st generation	24	46.1	28	53.8	
2nd generation	118	70.6	49	29.3	
Total	142	64.8	77	35.2	3.22

Source: ASB.
N = 219.
*German-born only. N = 209.

Catholic, male in-migrants before 1910. That is, they were unique to a certain class of people at a particular time and, as such, had a skewing effect on the figures. When they are removed from the computations a somewhat different picture emerges.

More inter-class marriages (4.2 percent) were contracted after 1919 than before. That difference, however, is still very likely the product of chance results obtained in this sample (Z = 0.60). The generational difference is reduced to 14.8 percent, though the larger figure remains with the first generation. It may simply be that the in-migrants had less of a choice in the matter of marriage and took what was available. However, it should be noted that the results obtained from the sample are open to some doubt ($Z = 1.85$). The difference between men and women also fell—to 9.0 percent—and even that figure should be suspect ($Z = 1.40$). In two of the divisions the difference of percentage rose. Germans were more likely—by 15.1 percent)—than Poles to have married across class lines. There are only four chances in a hundred that the ethnic difference was not real. Protestants entered into inter-class marriages almost 30 percent more frequently than Catholics. That difference was almost certainly an accurate reflection of a difference in the whole population ($Z = 3.45$).

The most striking results shown in the table then, are those yielded by divisions along ethnic, religious and chronological lines. The religious and ethnic differences are very largely due to Protestant and German marriage into and out of the white collar class. Germans contracted such marriages at a rate nearly three times that of the Poles. The small number of Poles of bourgeois status (see Chapter IV) must certainly provide part of the explanation. The same pattern exists with regard to religion. The Protestant rate of marriage into and out of the white collar class was two and three-quarters greater than that of Catholics. Any explanation of that here would be surmise, but one might note that the Polish community was almost wholly Catholic. Finally, the lack of any real difference based on the chronological division is instructive. That over a forty-three-year period, marked by transition from Imperial Germany to the Weimar Republic to the eve of the Third Reich, so little had changed, is testimony to the endurance of social convention.

In addition to mixed marriage in religious and socio-economic terms, marriage between ethnic groups occurred in Bottrop. The question of inter-ethnic marriage has been of at least passing interest to a number of writers concerned with the social history of the Ruhrgebiet. It has commonly been framed in terms of inter-marriage between old-stock natives and in-migrants. There is general agreement that such marriages represented only a small portion of the marriages which took place, and that they occurred for the most part, after World War I.[13] Findings from the sample of Bottrop's in-migrant generated population give no cause to dispute this contention. Of all marriages contracted in Bottrop by the sample group through

TABLE VI-11

Inter-Ethnic Marriage in Bottrop: In-migrants and Second Generation

	Intra-ethnic		Inter-ethnic		$H_0 : P_1 - P_2 = 0$ (Intermarriage)
	Nr.	%	Nr.	%	Z score
Catholic	110	72.4	42	27.6	
Protestant	17	65.4	9	34.6	
Total	127	71.3	51	28.6	0.73
Men	70	68.6	32	31.4	
Women	57	75.0	19	25.0	
Total	127	71.3	51	28.6	0.94
1st generation	43	82.6	9	17.3	
2nd generation	84	66.6	42	33.3	
Total	127	71.3	51	28.6	2.14
Poles	98	76.0	31	24.0	
Germans	29	59.2	20	40.8	
Total	127	71.3	51	28.6	2.21
1891-1918	56	84.8	10	15.2	
1919-1933	71	63.4	41	36.6	
Total	127	71.3	51	28.6	3.06

Sources: AEB, ASB.
N = 178.

1933 only 6.2 percent were unions of in-migrants or their children and persons of old native stock.[14] Although that figure is low, it must be remembered that natives formed only about a quarter of the city's population in 1920. Thus, it appears that a substantial number of them, perhaps 20 percent, who married during the period under study were espoused to an in-migrant or the child of an in-migrant.

Such marriages were, of course, not all inter-ethnic marriages since a considerable part of the in-migrant populations was itself ethnically

German. More commonly, inter-ethnic marriages were marriages between in-migrants or children of in-migrants. Table VI-11 shows the patterns of inter-ethnic marriage among Bottrop's in-migrants and their children. The table excludes two groups: foreigners and German subjects who married foreigners. Thus, it displays only inter-ethnic marriage between *Reich* subjects of German and Polish ethnicity. Within the second generation, the marriages of children who were themselves products of inter-ethnic marriages were all considered to have been inter-ethnic no matter the cultural background of the spouse.

The differences in rates of inter-ethnic marriages between Catholics and Protestants and men and women in the sample population were not statistically significant. The probability is very great (46.5 percent and 34.7 percent respectively) that there was no real difference for those groupings in the whole population. The remaining three categories show differences in rates of inter-ethnic marriage that are very likely to reflect real differences that existed in the whole population. Less than a quarter of Poles contracted inter-ethnic marriages, and even that relatively small figure is largely the result of second generation inter-marriage. About 30 percent of the children of in-migrant Poles married Germans. That generational differences holds good for the entire sample. Inter-ethnic marriages occurred twice as frequently in the second generation as in the first. An even greater difference, however, is shown in the chronological division. Most commentators have contended, rightly, that inter-marriage between native and in-migrants was rare until after World War I. It can now be seen that inter-ethnic marriage was also relatively rare until that time. From the end of the war until the final days of the republic however, inter-ethnic marriages constituted more than a third of all marriages.

Of the three types of inter-marriage examined that between partners of the working class and the white collar class was the least common. This is no surprise and is clearly the result of Bottrop's particular economic structure. Inter-faith marriage was also uncommon. Again, this should have been expected given the confessional make-up of the city. Inter-ethnic marriage took place rather more frequently, especially after World War I. However, it is important not to overvalue its consequence for the Polish community. More than seven in ten of the second generation, of whom one might have expected a lessened sense of ethnicity, still contracted marriage within the ethnic group.

CHAPTER VII

HOUSING AND RESIDENTIAL PATTERNS

In direct, physical terms housing was the most difficult problem which faced the Ruhrgebiet during the period of industrial expansion. When the boom began around 1870 its population, largely rural, numbered considerably fewer than a million—perhaps 600,000 or 700,000. By 1910, when the area had taken on its urban, industrial aspect, about three million people inhabited the land between the Ruhr and the Lippe. The need for new housing was thus enormous. It directly concerned, of course, those who had to find lodgings, the in-migrants. No less concerned, however, were the owners of the mines and foundaries. The expansion of industrial plants and the production of an ever increasing tonnage of coal were directly tied to the availability of labor. Whatever the technical advances of the machine age mechanization, particularly in the mines, had not yet reached the stage of automation. The problem in the early part of the twentieth century remained one of assuring an adequate supply of labor rather than one of technological unemployment.

Industrial growth, then, was immediately dependent on the expansion of housing facilities. Beyond its economic implications the housing problem posed difficult, and potentially explosive, social questions. Could entrepreneurial capitalism meet the demand and do so at the cost bearable by a largely working class population? Certainly an exploitative housing policy would only exacerbate social tension. What kind of housing was

119

desirable or practical? At one extreme the construction of tens of thousands of privately owned homes might have produced distinct social benefits. However, time, cost and the availability of had rendered such a solution impractical. At the other extreme multitudes of tightly clustered tenements might have been erected rapidly and cheaply, but a rise in disease and crime rates and the increased alienation of the working class might well have followed. These and other ramifications of the housing problem were part of the history of industrial expansion in the Ruhrgebiet.

Until the mid-nineteenth century coal mining occasioned little or no housing problem in the Ruhrgebiet. In 1800 each mine of the Ruhrgebiet employed, on the average, only ten miners. By 1850 mining had moved north of the Ruhr and deep-shaft operations had begun, but the average number of workers per mine had only increased to sixty-four. Thereafter the size of the mines and the numbers of employees increased rapidly. Between 1860 and 1870 the average number of workers in each mine rose more than 100 percent (from 104 to 234). Between 1880 and 1890 the increase was 82 percent (from 397 to 722). In 1897, for the first time, the mines of the Ruhrgebiet employed an average of over one thousand workers in each operation.[1] Mining was no longer a part-time job engaged in by local people to supplement income. The in-migrantion which was to transform Ruhrgebiet society had begun, and the task of housing an urban, industrial population had to be faced.

Early on mine operators chose not to involve themselves with the problem. Sound liberal economic policy would have dictated a market solution to the housing shortage, and, after all, only very recently (1859 and 1865) had they been able to effect legislation which had withdrawn the paternal authority of the Prussian government from the day to day operation of the mines. A few companies experimented with company housing, but these were only local and tentative efforts. In 1857 the mining company Concordia, in Oberhausen, finished construction of several housing units which contained forty-four apartments (*Wohnungen*). The following year Gutehoffnungshütte, also in Oberhausen, established a workers' settlement (*Arbeiterkolonie*) of ten units with forty apartments.[2] In 1873, however, only 1,521 company-owned housing units with a total of 5,772 apartments were to be found in the whole of the Ruhrgebiet.[3] In 1875 the same mines employed over 83,000 workers.[4] Most owners seemed to prefer to rely on the results of entrepreneurship to house their workers even though it was becoming increasingly obvious that those results were sadly lacking. In 1872 a strike broke out among the miners of the Essen district. Among their grievances, miserable housing conditions were prominently mentioned. Certainly, the mine owners replied, the rapid population increase in Essen and vicinity had given rise to certain regrettable circumstances (*Uebelstände*), but that, of course, was not the fault of the mine operators.[5] If the mine owners' basic tendency was toward a policy of laissez-faire in the area of housing, it was reinforced in Westphalia by the Settlement Law (*Ansiedlungsgesetz*) of 1870. According to the provisions of that act—at least in the interpretation of many local authorities—the mining companies were obligated to assume the entire tax bill for administrative, church and school costs for any new workers' settlements which they built.[6]

Whatever the theoretical benefits of reliance on private initiative for a solution to the housing shortage, in practice, satisfactory results were not forthcoming. Throughout the 1870s and 1880s the problem continued to grow. When housing was available the rents were often at scandalous rates.[7] Worse, the housing was often in slum condition. A housing inspection in Hörde (Dortmund) in 1895 documented the deplorable state of private housing. Seventy percent of the inspected housing was in a state of disrepair (*vernachlässigt*), 60 percent was damp and 55 percent dirty. Fully 40 percent of the housing would not pass building codes (*vom baupolizeilichen Standpunkt aus unzulässig*). The apartments housed an average of 5.5 people each, and 62 percent of them had only one or two rooms.[8] The existence of such conditions had long been know to both local and provincial authorities. There was general agreement that a solution of the housing problem was vital to the working class, and, further, that such a solution was necessary to combat increasing social and political dissatisfaction among workers. Unfortunately, it was also agreed that direct intervention by the government was not feasible. Rather the political authorities advocated support of private construction activity. A few cities, above all Dortmund, attempted to remedy the situation. The city of Dortmund not only subsidized private building, but even founded public interest building societies (*gemeinnützige Baugesellschaften*). Most of the Ruhrgebiet cities, however, declared that they were not in a position to undertake such financial support, and, in any case, the propertied middle class (*besitzende Bürgertum*) had no interest in such schemes. A few even denied that there was any necessity to undertake anything at all in the way of construction of housing for workers.[9] Thus, it was clear that the housing problem would not be solved by either private initiative or public policy.

However great or little interest mining companies had in their employees as human beings or in the conditions of their lodgings, they had considerable interest in them as workers, and more particularly as reliable and stable workers. While the steady expansion of both mining and industry in the Ruhrgebiet had attracted hundreds of thousands into the area, it consistently outran the supply of labor. There was an almost constant labor shortage. Since the skills necessary for mining were the same regardless of mine, changing employers in the Ruhrgebiet was not difficult. For whatever good or inconsequential reasons more and more miners took advantage of that opportunity. The rate of labor turnover, as recorded in the annual report of the *Allgemeiner Knappschaftverein* in Bochum, was calculated by dividing the number of workers entering and leaving the employ of Ruhrgebiet mines during a year's time by the average number of workers for that year. From 1896 through 1913 the total turnover fell below 100 pecent in only four years, one of which was the year of the great strike, 1905. Six times the figure rose over 120 percent.[10] The magnitude of the turnover had undesirable consequences for the mining companies. Had it been merely a question of experienced miners moving from job to job it would have been a lesser problem. However, only about half of the turnover was accounted for by these men. Many experienced miners simply left the area or found other employment. The other 50 percent consisted of new, unskilled workers. This meant that until the new workers acquired the necessary skill the level of production fell and the accident rate rose.[11] Therefore it was greatly in the interest of the mine operators to reduce personnel turnover as much as possible.

Despite protestations of loyalty to liberal economic theory—at least vis-à-vis the government—the mine owners showed little inclination for a free market solution to the problem of labor turnover. That is, they did not attempt to attract and hold a stable work force by the expedient of paying higher wages and offering better conditions than their competitors. One method of retaining a stable body of employees that was favored by mine operators was the limited lock-out (*Aussperrung*). This technique was refined after the strike of 1905. In case of a local strike the miners involved might attempt to find work at another mine in order to support themselves for the duration of the strike. The neighboring mines, or even all those in the district, would then pledge themselves not to hire any man who had been in the employ of the struck mine. This method had a serious drawback. It might very well have been illegal. The Freedom of Movement Law of 1860 had specifically outlawed conspiracy to enforce lock-outs as a method of labor management. Naturally the owners attempted to maintain the secrecy of these machinations. However, when the unions protested to the authorities in November of 1905 the owners abandoned the lock-out rather than submit it to a legal test. In any case, the chronic labor shortage had tempted some mine owners to ignore the lock-out, thus greatly limiting its effectiveness.[12]

Another system was used by the so-called "family mines." These were the large mining companies which operated several mines each in the Ruhrgebiet. They created the transfer (*Ueberweisung*) system. Anyone working in one of the "family mines" who gave notice and then attempted to gain employment in another of the "family mines" was obligated to produce a certificate. This document was bestowed by the last employer, and it stated that he had no objection to the employment of the bearer. ("Gegen die Einstellugn des Hauers_____ist nichts einzuweden.") In part this was an attempt to exclude so-called trouble makers, but its most important object was to reduce the labor turnover. It was employed for a number of years, but to only limited effect. Most of the mines of the Ruhrgebiet were not "family mines" and thus not part of the system.[13]

A comprehensive attempt at the regulation of the movement of labor was begun in 1908. In January of that year a Ruhrgebiet-wide organization of mine operators was founded, the *Zechenverband*. It was intended to be a more closely organized association than the old *Bergbaulicher Verein*, and so be much more effective in controlling the labor market. The method of control was again to be the limited lock-out, but this time it would be made legally irreproachable. Under the law of contract a worker was obligated to give fourteen-days notice when leaving his job. In the new system of the *Zechenverband* the name of any worker who violated this provision would be placed on a black list. The list was made current every two weeks and forwarded to the member mines. Anyone whose name appeared on the list would be denied work at any member mine for a period

of six months. The blacklisted worker could return to his previous place
of employment and reume work there. While the system lasted, however,
only about 10 percent of the blacklisted workers made use of that provision. The black list was, to some extent, effective in dealing with the
problem, but it did not solve it. Each new blacklist contained 4,000 to
5,000 names. The unions vigorously protested the use of black listing and
were widely supported by public opinion. The *Reichstag* felt compelled
to take up the question, but it did not condemn the practice.[14] Within
two years the *Zechenverband* inaugurated a new system; it formed a central labor exchange (*Arbeitsnachweis*). Labor exchanges had previously
been used both by local governments and unions. The central exchange,
however, was to be controlled entirely by the employers. All Ruhrgebiet
mines were obligated to fill their labor requirements through the central
exchange. Anyone simply appearing at a mine asking for work would be
turned away. A worker had to procure from the central exchange a reference (*Nachweisschein*) which was valid for only one mine. If he did not
report to that mine within two working days of receipt of the reference,
he could not receive another for two weeks. Upon protest of the unions,
it was agreed by the *Zechenverband* that the reference would be directed
to the mine favored by the applicant if a job were available there.[15]

None of the sanctions tried by employers to control the turnover were
fully effective. Neither, however, were they the only methods tried. Early
on some mining companies began to experiment with the provision of
housing as a means of promoting employee stablility. A number of barracks (*Menage*) were constructed to house men, but these were only marginally useful. They were only for the use of single men, many of whom,
in any case, preferred to board with families. By 1907 only fifty-four of
them with fewer than 3,500 inhabitants remained.[16] Attempts were also
made to provide financial support for mine employees to build their own
homes. The company would give building subsidies (*Bauprämie*), make
available low cost loans or sell lots and building materials cheaply.[17] Little
success accured to these efforts, however. To 1900 the mines of the Ruhrgebiet had subsidized, in one way or another, the building of houses by
their employees in the amount of nearly RM 3,000,000, but only 775
houses had been built.[18] Not only was the number of houses disappoint-
ingly small, but often the miners had difficulty meeting mortgage payments, or even built houses solely as speculative ventures.[19] Encouraging

the building of private, single-family homes by miners clearly was not an effective way of producing general labor stability, however well it may have worked in a small number of instances.

The only course which held hope of significantly reducing the housing problem to manageable proportions was the construction of housing by the mines themselves. Beyond the amelioration of a social problem—and more important to the mine companies—the construction of mine-owned housing might possibly be of advantage in attacking the problem of the labor shortage. The existence of guaranteed housing could, in itself, be an attraction to in-migrants. Additionally, once installed in company housing, workers might be less prone to further migration. (A rather more coercive element was also involved which will be dealt with later.) From the 1890s company housing began to be built at in increasingly rapid rate.

The construction of company housing reached a peak in the immediate pre-World War I years. By the end of 1914 almost ninety-five thousand apartments had been built.[20] Through the first two years of the war building continued although it was hindered by the shortage of labor and the rising cost of building materials. From 1916 construction practically ceased. All building activity not directly connected with the war effort was prohibited. Only in exceptional cases was permission for private construction granted.[21] In the first year after the war's end, just over 1,100 new apartments were built. Through 1923 the number rose steadily, but it only reached 3,364 in that year. From 1924 through 1930 only 4,146 new apartments were added to the total.[22] In large part this was due to the horrendous inflation and its aftereffects. To some extent, however, a new government housing policy discouraged the construction of company housing. By government decree (*Verordnung vom 22. Juli 1919*) the mines were unable to evict workers who had left their employ and install new employees in their places. By May of 1930 almost a quarter of company-owned apartments were occupied by persons not employed by the owners.[23]

Until the post-war years, however, the construction undertaken by the mines companies made it possible to house an increasingly larger percentage of Ruhrgebiet miners in company-owned apartments. Table VII-1 shows that trend. By 1914 almost two of every five coal miners in the Ruhrgebiet lived in company housing. Although that figure was almost 95 percent higher than in 1901, the total number of company-owned apartments had only risen by about 60 percent in the same period. The disparity between

TABLE VII-1

Ruhrgebiet Miners and Company Housing, 1893-1914

	1893	1901	1907	1914
Nr. of miners	146,440	243,926	303,089	388,385
Company-owned apartments	10,525	26,250	52,900	94,027
Ratio of apts. to miners	1:13.9	1:9.2	1:5.7	1:4.1
Nr. of miners in company-owned apts.	10,607*	47,980	83,280	148,583
% of miners in company housing	12.5*	19.6	27.4	38.2

Sources: Adelman, *Die soziale Betriebsverfassung*, pp. 162-164; Hundt, *Bergarbeiter-Wohnungen*, pp. 8-9; Koch, *Die Bergarbeiterbewegung*, p. 139.
* For 1893—only heads of household.

those figures can be accounted for by two things. In many cases sons in the family were also miners, and many families took in boarders (*Kostgänger*). For example, in 1900 Neu-Essen disposed of 509 apartments in which 730 miners lived. Of these, 509 were heads of household, 121 were sons of those men and 100 were boarders.[24]

The typical form taken by company housing was the development of colonies in the neighborhood of the mine. Since the colonies were erected on land which was already owned by the mining companies, the difficulty and expense of acquiring building sites was avoided. In addition, the construction of apartment complexes reduced the municipal obligations of the mining companies for such things as the laying of new streets. After early, unsuccessful experiments with barracks, the most commonly constructed types were units containing only a few apartments. Most of them housed four or fewer families. The individual apartments were also more commodious than had previously been the case. In contrast to the conditions in privately rented apartments (see p. 121) company-owned units typically contained four or more rooms.

There were several advantages for miners who were able to obtain company housing. Rents tended to be considerably lower than those for privately owne apartments. On the average, company-owned housing was available at about half the cost of private housing.[25] Those rates were made possible by the policy of charging rents which only just covered the construction costs and mortgage interest, the so-called "welfare rents" (*Wohlfahrtsmieten*).[26] The colonies were usually in the neighborhood of the mines. This meant that transportation costs or time consuming journeys on foot could be avoided. Most of the apartments (in 1901, 86.2 percent) had yards (*Garten*).[27] There it was possible to put in vegetable gardens. Additional land for that purpose was often available from the mining companies at very low rates. In addition to the garden, facilities for keeping a few head of livestock were almost always offered. These features enabled the miners, if they so chose, to make considerable savings on food costs. In a number of the colonies various other facilities such as buyer cooperatives (*Konsumanstalten*), child care and public baths were to be found. In all, company housing was clearly intended to serve as an inducement to miners to remain on the job.

How successful was this policy is impossible to determine. No records exist which specify the length of service of workers at individual mines and discriminate between those living in company housing and elsewhere. There are, however, some indicators.

The figures given in Table VII-2 are for only a handful of mines and are valid for only one year, thus, they cannot be accepted as conclusive. They are, however, suggestive. Most of the mines shown in the table counted a larger percentage of their workers in company housing than the average for the Ruhrgebiet in that year (19.6 percent). All of them offered the housing at a lower rate than private housing—some considerably lower. Each of the mines had a labor turnover lower than the average for the Ruhrgebiet in that year (120 percent). The most striking figures in the table, however, are the percentages of turnover among inhabitants of company housing. In those areas the turnover ranged from only 2 percent to 20 percent of that of the total work force. The relationship among rents, number of workers in company housing and turnover is not consistent for even the mines listed in the table, no doubt a result of variation in local conditions. Also, the figures show only that the colonies retained miners for the period of one year. They say nothing concerning changes over a

TABLE VII-2

Company Housing and Labor Turnover in Selected Mines, 1900

Mine Company	% of Workers in company Housing	% of Total Labor Turnover	% of Turnover in company Housing
Kolner Bergwerke-Verein	27.5	58.2	12.0
Neu-Essen	43.9	49.9	3.0
Prosper	22.4	101.9	10.5
Gutehoffnungshütte	11.4	78.2	1.6
Concordia	10.4	72.3	5.0
Deutscher Kaiser	79.9	77.9	5.0

Source: Adelman, *Die soziale Betriebsverfassung*, p. 173.

long period. The continued construction of company housing in the Ruhr-gebiet, however, indicates that the companies themselves considered the policy an advantageous one.

Along with the advantages for the miners attendant upon company housing there were two important disadvantages. One concerned the term of the lease. The miner was able to rent company housing only as long as he remained in the employ of that mine. If he went to work for another company the lease was terminated. Workers who transferred to another mine owned by the same company and pensioners were not affected by this condition. This practice had been usual since the earliest days of company housing. It was from the beginning unpopular with the miners, and the labor unions struggled against it from the time of their foundings. During the strikes of 1905 and 1912 the abolition of this type of lease was demanded by the unions, but neither time were they successful even in extending the notice of eviction to one month.[28] Not until after World War I was a change made.

It is impossible to determine to what extent this practice actually in-fringed on the freedom of movement of the miners. In all fairness, there was something to be said for the position of the mining companies. Low rent housing and its various ancillary services obviously constituted a species of fringe benefit for the miners. Clearly those miners who ntended to migrate out of the Ruhrgebiet would not have been coerced by the terms of the lease. However, even those who found work outside the immediate vicintiy of the mine might well have found it more inconvenient to assume travel costs or to spend hours moving between home and job than to secure housing near the new place of employment. A further objection to the policy was that the mine owners used the threat of eviction in order to discourage union membership and to circumscibe the freedom of the colony dwellers in other ways. Although this may have been the intention of the companies, there is some evidence to suggest that it met with only limited success. During the strike of 1912, for example, miners who occupied company housing were no less willing to walk out than other miners, even though many mines made use of their contractual rights and ordered the immediate eviction of the strikers.[29]

The second disadvantage of the colonies was their location. Particularly in the mining cities north of the Emscher, which had grown overnight from villages, the colonies were separated from the city centers and from each other. Beyond practical difficulties such as shopping, the physical separation of miners, usually in-migrants, from the native population of the city and from each other made more problematic the development of integrated, stable urban societies. Examples drawn from contemporary expressions of opinion indicated the potential danger. An essay of 1913 claimed that Polish houses were uncomfortable and dirty. Further, Poles were unable or unwilling to busy themselves with the growing of gardens, a healthy practice common among the other residents of the colonies. The latter charge is, of course, at odds with the frequently heard complaint that Poles were unfit for work in the mines because they were too firmly wed to their rural, agricultural backgrounds.[30] The word *"Kolonist"* itself ranked with *"Polak"* (actually the Polish word for a male Pole) as a term of abuse. In one town as late as 1914 an old inhabitant was astounded by the assertion of a miner that the inhabitants of the colonies, were, after all, human too.[31]

The housing problem developed relatively late in Bottrop. The city's first mine, Prosper II, was begun only in 1871, and it did not begin production until 1875. The labor necessary for the enterprise was, in the beginning, drawn largely from Bottrop itself and the surrounding country-side. The new housing that was erected was not concentrated in the vicinity of the mine but scattered throughout the *Gemeinde*. Younger sons of farmers who would not inherit the estate were more and more often drawn into the mine. If a plot from the farm fell to such a person as an inheritance, he was likely to build his home there regardless of the distance to the mine. In-migrants who possessed the capital necessary to build their own homes found that land located at some remove from the mine was considerably cheaper. Local entrepreneuers also invested in housing, often with capital gained from the sale of land to the mine. A number of three and four story apartment buildings were erected in various parts of the city.[32] Even the first company-built housing was not located immediately adjacent to the mine. Arenberg Bergbau's purchase of land was piecemeal. In 1874 the company owned only the land on which its above-ground facilities stood, about 60 hectares.[33] It built its first housing north and west of the mine in the direction of the old central village. Thus, during the early days of mine development in Bottrop there existed no miners' quarters. The mine workers took lodgings wherever they were available. The only common denominator of miners' housing during that period was that it was located neither in the old central village nor clustered around the new mine shaft.

In the 1890s mining, and thus population, began to expand greatly in Bottrop. It was no longer possible to leave the question of housing to the vagaries of individual enterprise. In order to attract and retain a labor force for the ever growing mines the company itself had to develop a housing policy. As did other mining companies, Arenberg Bergbau made attempts to encourage its employees to purchase or build their own homes, but it met with as little success as had other companies. By 1905 the company formally recognized the failure and discontinued the granting of home loans.[34]

The failure of the policy of encouraging homeownership, apparent long before its formal dissolution, and the inability of private initiative to provide suitable or sufficient housing inevitably led the company to an ever increasing reliance on its own resources to solve the housing problem. The years from the turn of the century to the beginning of the First World War saw the greatest activity. It was during this period that most of Bottrop's company housing was put up and the various miners' quarters developed.[35]

For the most part these were oriented toward specific mines, and they can be distinguished with a great degree of exactitude. The company housing of Prosper II and Prosper III lay closest both to each other and the old central village. Since the two mines were part of the Arenberg Bergbau operation, and movement between the two had no effect on the lease of an employee, they can be treated as a single unit. The Prosper housing was located in an arc curving east of the city center from north to south-west which roughly approximated the old *Bauernschaften* of Batenbrock and Lehmkuhle. Further north in Eigen lay the settlement of the mine Rheinbaben. Vereinigte Welheim sunk its shaft and errected its housing in Boy, near Bottrop's eastern border with Gladbeck. The area occupied by Jacobi, in the southwestern part of the city, was split by the line dividing Bottrop from Oberhausen. Some of the miners' housing there, however, was located in Fuhlenbrock.

The first steps toward the development of large-scale company housing were taken by the Arenberg Bergbau shortly after Prosper II went into production. In the early 1880s the Engelbert Kolonie was built, clustered along the Prosperstrasse west of the mine. It was a relatively small settlement, consisting of only forty two-family houses. The tentative nature of the project was shown not only by its limited size, but also by the type of housing erected. The units were small, one-story affairs without cellars or yards. Each apartment, however, was assigned a stable.[36] When the great stream of in-migration from the East began to flow into Bottrop, especially after 1900, the need for additional housing became more pressing. From 1906 to 1908 a large number of new units were erected in an arc west of the mine. Some were built along already established highways (*Landstrassen*), but the number of buildings erected necessitated the laying out of new streets. The new units were considerably larger than those put up in the previous century. Each one-and-half story building contained four apartments. They boasted not only the requisite stables, but also a large back yard for each apartment.[37] By the time the second Arenberg Bergbau shaft, Prosper III, went into production in 1908 already existing housing prohibited the construction of a single, closed miners' colony. At first construction took place to the north of the mine, but its extension was limited by the southern reach of Rheinbaben. Thereafter housing for Prosper III was spotted all around the mine property (*Zechengelände*) wherever space became available.[38]

The location of Rheinbaben on the northern edge of the city allowed that mine a relatively free hand in the construction of a miners' colony. Its housing stretched away from the mine to the west and south. The oldest buildings, built around 1902, were erected along the Gladbeckerstrasse, close to the northern boundary of the city. As was the case with earliest Prosper housing, these units were built close together with no space for yards. They were intended to put miners under roof as quickly as possible, and the amenities which were to be found in housing constructed at a later date were largely absent. Between 1912 and 1914 more numerous and attractive buildings were erected. The mine had been able to purchase a large estate, the Nesselhof, which allowed it sufficient space to carry through plans for an extensive housing project. Care was taken to make the new buildings as attractive as possible. They were spaced more widely apart than the older units, thus allowing for the allotment of both front and back yards to each apartment. The front yard was planted with shrubs and trees, while the back yards were of sufficient size to allow for a considerable vegetable garden along with the ubiquitous stable.[39]

The two remaining areas are of only minor interest during this period. Vereinigte Welheim went into production in 1914, and its housing complex was not yet completed by that date. The Welheim colony was built to the south of the mine and was clearly separated from the rest of the city by the fields and meadows surrounding it. Few of the in-migrants who entered the city before 1920 were to be found in that section of Bottrop. Jacobi, although located in part in Bottrop, was considered part of the Oberhausen-Osterfeld mining district. Its first company housing was located in that city. As the housing shortage manifested itself there, the company attempted to purchase land in Bottrop. This proceeded slowly, however, since that area of the city was divided among numerous small landowners who proved loath to give up their land. Only in the 1930s was Jacobi able to go forward with the building of company housing in Bottrop.[40]

This historical sketch of the growth of company housing in Bottrop, while not a complete picture of the development, does point to an important spatial characteristic. As Bottrop expanded rapidly from a meagerly populated, agricultural *Gemeinde* to an important urban center of the mining industry the old structure of central village and surrounding *Bauernschaften* remained largely intact. Each of the mines, located in one of the

Bauernschaften, became a magnetic pole for that area. Housing was most rapidly developed in the vicinity of each mine. The new streets were laid out to facilitate access to the mines. Small businesses—corner groceries, newsstands and bakeries—sprang up in the midst of the settlements. Even railroad construction was designed to service the mines. This kind of development meant that those aspects of urban life which favored the creation of an integrated, centralized city, e.g. central administration, provision of utilities and municipal elections, were balanced by centrifugal forces. If the various areas of the city were drawn economically in different directions and the neighborhoods were, at the same time, ethnically homogeneous, closed communities—and remained that way—then the city would have remained an entity in legal terms only.

Through examination of the Bottrop *Adressbücher* it has been possible to trace the spatial movement of the individuals selected in the sample of in-migrants who settled in the city between 1891 and 1920.[41] To avoid tedious repetition of such phrases as "the section of the city adjoining the mine Rheinbaben," the names of the old *Bauernschaften* had been used: Lehmkuhle—Prosper II; Batenbrock—Prosper III; Eigen—Rheinbaben; Boy —Vereinigte Welheim; Fuhlenbrock—Jacobi. The city center is referred to as the *Altstadt.* As used here these terms do not denote exactly the same areas as the historic terms. However, they do follow closely the respective "spheres of influence" of the mines (with the exception of the *Altstadt*) since the division was made largely on the basis of landownership by the mines.[42] Not every house in each *Bauernschaft* was, of course, owned by the mines. However, since the *Adressbücher* give, in addition to name and occupation, the ownership of the residence, it has been possible to make the decision between company and private housing.

Table VII-3 shows the concentration of the in-migrants in various parts of the city at the end of each of the first three decades of the twentieth century. For purposes of analysis the city is divided into three parts. The Altstadt and Fuhlenbrock, the western section of the city, comparises one part. They held no company housing during this period. The second part, Eigen and Boy in the north and northeast, was separated from the central city by the Arenberg Bergbau holdings. The third, the eastern arc of Batenbrock and Lehmkuhle, was the domain of Arenberg Bergbau.

At each of the three times shown in the table Bottrop's in-migrant-generated population (in-migrants together with the mature second generation and spouses) was to be found in heaviest concentration in the area

TABLE VII-3

Residential Districts of the In-Migrant-Generated Population
in Bottrop, 1910-1930

District	1910		1920		1930	
	Nr.	%	Nr.	%	Nr.	%
Altstadt/ Fuhlenbrock	37	21.8	63	20.8	84	16.4
Eigen/Boy	33	19.4	73	24.2	137	26.8
Batenbrock/ Lehmkuhle	100	58.8	166	55.0	290	56.8
TOTAL	170		302		511	

Source: Sample; AbB 1911, 1920 and 1930.

dominated by Arenberg Bergbau, Batenbrock/Lehmkuhle. That company
was the city's largest employer and disposed of the most extensive system
of company housing. In 1910 Altstadt/Fuhlenbrock and Eigen/Boy held
almost equal percentages of the in-migrant population. The Altstadt was
favored by tradesmen and artisans, while Fuhlenbrock held the land most
readily available for private building. Although Jacobi had gone into production in 1912 most of its employees lived in Oberhausen where all of its
housing units were located. The percentage of the in-migrant population
resident in Altstadt/Fuhlenbrock declined marginally in 1920 and showed
a further decrease in 1930. Vereinigte Welheim in Boy did not go into production until 1914 and its own housing units were not completed until
after that date. By 1920 Eigen/Boy held about a quarter of the in-migrants
and at the end of the following decade the percentage had increased slightly.
When the districts were examined for the year 1910 with reference to
ethnicity a somewhat different pattern is revealed. (See Table VII-4).
    Calculations show that the pattern of ethnic residence is statistically
significant. There is less than one chance in a thousand that such a pattern would be observed in a sample taken from a population in which
there were no relationship between ethnicity and residential district. It

TABLE VII-4

Ethnicity and Residential Districts, 1910

District	Poles Nr.	%	Germans Nr.	%	Total Nr.	%
Altstadt/ Fuhlenbrock	17	13.4	20	46.5	37	21.8
Eigen/Boy	25	19.6	8	18.6	33	19.4
Batenbrock/ Lehmkuhle	85	66.9	15	34.8	100	58.8
TOTAL	127	74.7	43	25.2	170	

Sources: Sample; AbB 1911.
$x^2 = 21.6$, df = 2, p $<$ .001.

should be remembered, however, that the table does not present an accurate picture of the total ethnic residential pattern in the city since the
sample did not include old-stock, native Bottropers. Thus, it is likely that
Germans more heavily outnumbered Poles in Altstadt/Fuhlenbrock,
which was the only district that had not passed very largely into mining
company possession. Much of the old, native population must also have
lived in Eigen since the majority of Rheinbaben employees were German.[43] The figures shown in the table for Batenbrock/Lehmkuhle are
very likely much closer to reality, for Arenberg Bergbau relied heavily on
labor recruited from the East.

The table demonstrates the existence of a Polish quarter in the city,
although it is important to note that it did not hold all of Bottrop's Poles.
Two-thirds of the Polish population were resident in Batenbrock/Lehm-
kuhle thus giving that district a distinctively Polish cast. That is, in 1910
Bottrop contained a Polish enclave which, if not a ghetto, must at least
have seemed manifestly non-Westphalian to the German residents of the
city. The historic basis for the ethnic residential pattern shown at the end
of 1910 was good and sufficient. Arenberg Bergbau had actively recruited
Poles in the East, particularly in Upper Silesia, and had guaranteed them

that they would be able to live together. That desire on the part of in-migrants moving into an alien city and culture was not surprising. How-ever, if the Polish in-migrants eventually decided on permanent settle-ment in Bottrop, and continued to dwell exclusively in a purely Polish enclave within the city, they certainly risked being seen by the other in-habitants as perpetual outsiders.

The passage of a decade produced very little change in the pattern of ethnic residence in Bottrop. (See Table VII-5.) The percentage of the

TABLE VII-5

Ethnicity and Residential Districts, 1920

District	Poles		Germans		Total	
	Nr.	%	Nr.	%	Nr.	%
Altstadt/ Fuhlenbrock	24	10.7	39	50.0	63	20.8
Eigen/Boy	56	25.0	17	21.8	73	24.2
Batenbrock/ Lehmkuhle	144	64.2	22	28.2	166	55.0
Total	224	74.2	78	25.8	302	

Sources: Sample; AbB 1920.
$x^2 = 56.5$; df = 2, p $<$ .001.

Polish population living in Altstadt/Fuhlenbrock and Batenbrock/Lehm-kuhle declined slightly. There was a corresponding increase in Eigen/Boy where a quarter of the Poles now resided. The German in-migrant popula-tion had shifted marginally toward a higher concentration in Altstadt/ Fuhlenbrock and Eigen/Boy. In the latter district German and Polish in-migrants were represented in relative equilibrium. Again, the pattern is statistically significant, and the Batenbrock/Lehmkuhle district remained the center of Bottrop's Polish community.

Although the overall ethnic distribution of Bottrop's in-migrant-genera-ted population had changed little in ten years there had been considerable

TABLE VII-6

Ethnicity and Movement, 1910-1920

| | Poles | | Germans | | Total | |
	Nr.	%	Nr.	%	Nr.	%
Population in 1910	127		43		170	
Out-migration	23	18.1	2	4.6	25	14.7
Inter-district movement	23	18.1	6	14.0	29	17.0
Intra-district movement	43	33.8	17	39.5	60	35.2
Stable	23	18.1	14	32.6	37	21.8

Sources: Sample; AbB 1911 and 1920.

movement on an individual level. Barley a fifth of the 1910 population had remained completely stable during the decade. More than two-thirds had been involved in movement of some kind. About one in seven left Bottrop between 1910 and 1920. (An additional 11 percent died during that period.) The most common type of movement was intra-city, either between or within districts. The ethnic comparisons are obvious. Poles were much more likely than Germans to have migrated out of the city.[44] In view of the resuscitation of the Polish national state after World War I that finding is scarcely surprising. Its complement is to be found in the differences of percentage for stability. Intra-city movement, however, had no ethnic bias. Poles and Germans were almost equally as likely to have moved to a different part of the city or changed residence within a district. The small differences shown in the table are not statistically significant; they might well be reversed if another sample were to be taken.

The high rate of spatial mobility displayed in the table, however, did not vitiate the Polish enclave in Batenbrock/Lehmkuhle. In 1920 as in 1910 it held about two-thirds of Bottrop's Poles. Table VII-7 shows how that was accomplished.

TABLE VII-7

Sources of In-Migrant-Generated Population, 1920

| | Batenbrock/Lehmkuhle | | | | All Others | | | | Total | |
| | Poles | | Germans | | Poles | | Germans | | | |
	Nr.	%	Nr.	%	Nr.	%	Nr.	%	Nr.	%
Population in 1920	144		22		80		56		302	
Holdover from 1910	50	34.7	9	40.9	16	20.0	22	39.2	97	32.1
In-migrants	28	19.4	9	40.9	21	26.2	16	28.6	74	24.5
Intra-city movement	15	10.4	3	13.6	14	17.5	5	8.9	37	12.2
Second generation	51	35.4	1	4.5	29	36.2	13	23.2	94	31.1

Sources: Sample; AbB 1911 and 1920.

Overall the in-migrant-generated population of Bottrop's districts in 1920 was divided farily equally among three groups: the holdovers from 1910, people who moved in (intra-city and in-migrants) and the children of in-migrants who came of age. When the figures are broken down by district and ethnicity, however, some interesting contrasts are revealed. Holdovers made up a considerable part of the in-migrant-generated population for both Germans and Poles in all parts of the city. For Germans there was almost no difference in percentage between Batenbrock/Lehmkuhle and the other districts. However, the Polish population of Batenbrock/Lehmkuhle in 1920 was composed of holdovers from 1910 to a degree significantly higher than the corresponding figure for the rest of Bottrop.[45] In-migration between 1910 and 1920 contributed relatively more to the German population than the Polish in Batenbrock/Lehmkuhle. Elsewhere there was no real difference. Intra-city movement was a discernable factor for both groups throughout the city, but it was a comparatively important one only for the Poles outside of Batenbrock/Lehmkuhle. The largest component of the Polish population in all parts of Bottrop in 1920 consisted of children who had come of age, a fact attributable to the generally earlier arrival of Polish in-migrants. The second generation was a negligible part of the German population in Batenbrock/Lehmkuhle, but elsewhere it make up almost a quarter of the whole. In sum, the Polish enclave in Batenbrock/Lehmkuhle maintained itself with a group of long-term residents at its core. A maturing second generation added to its numbers, and it continued to attract some new residents both from within and outside the city. As in 1910 a not inconsiderable number of Bottrop's Poles lived elsewhere in the city.

An ethnic-residential pattern was still highly visible in Bottrop in 1930. (See Table VII-8.) The most important change as compared with 1920 was the greater proportion of the German in-migrant population resident in Batenbrock/Lehmkuhle. That figure is an indication of the limitations of the table. It must be borne in mind that that figures no longer reflect the true ethnic mixture in any of Bottrop's districts. The sample from which the figures were drawn included only in-migrants who arrived in Bottrop by the end of 1920. After that date migration into the city continued. For the decade 1920-1930 over 100,000 people migrated into Bottrop, a number about 20 percent greater than its population in 1930. The out-migration durikng that decade was even greater. Almost 115,000 people left the city between 1920 and 1930.[46] Too great an act of faith

would be required to believe that all of the first number were included in
the second. Further, it is highly unlikely that many of the post-1920

TABLE VII-8

Ethnicity and Residential Districts, 1930

District	Poles		Germans		Total	
	Nr.	%	Nr.	%	Nr.	%
Altstadt/ Fuhlenbrock	32	9.0	52	33.3	84	16.4
Eigen/Boy	94	26.4	43	27.6	137	26.8
Batenbrock/ Lehmkuhle	229	64.5	61	39.1	290	56.8
TOTAL	355	69.4	156	30.5	511	

Sources: Sample; AbB 1930.
$x^2 = 51.6$; df = 2, p < .001.

in-migrants were Poles. Thus, Polish domination in Batenbrock/Lehm-
kuhle would have been greatly reduced, although a large majority of
the city's Polish population continued to live there.

Again, the similarity between the figures for 1920 and 1930 with respect to ethnicity and district masks a very considerable movement of the
in-migrant population (see Table VII-9.) The total percentages of those
who migrated out of Bottrop or moved to another district in the city are
almost unchanged from the comparable figures for 1910-1920. Change of
residence within the districts had been somewhat reduced. The most striking figure, however, is that for stability; it is almost twice as great as it had
been for the preceding decade. When an ethnic comparison is made the
most notable result is the absence of difference. Calculations indicate the
unlikelihood of ethnic bias with respect to the movement of the in-migrant
population. Only in the case of stability does there appear to be any reasonable change that a real ethnic difference existed.[47]

A division between older and newer residents of the city does yield
some interesting—and statistically significant—contrasts.[48] In-migrants who

TABLE VII-9

Movement of the 1920 In-Migrant-Generated Population, 1920-1930

	Poles		Germans		Resident in 1910		In-mig. 1911-1920/ 2nd generation		Total	
	Nr.	%	Nr.	%	Nr.	%	Nr.	%	Nr.	%
Population in 1920	224		78		134		168		302	
Out-migration	37	16.5	14	17.9	16	11.9	35	20.8	51	16.8
Inter-district movement	34	15.2	9	11.5	8	6.0	35	20.8	43	14.2
Intra-district movement	56	25.0	15	19.2	16	11.9	55	32.7	71	23.5
Stable	89	39.7	38	48.7	86	64.2	41	24.4	127	42.0

Sources: Sample; AbB 1911, 1920 and 1930.

had been present in Bottrop at least from 1910 comprise the older population. Those who entered the city between 1911 and 1920 together with the members of the second generation who had reached maturity during that decade make up the newer population. The smallest difference between the two groups is in the percentage of those who migrated out of the city. That is attributable to the attraction of the revived Polish national state for a number of the older in-migrants. Even so, the respective percentages may be termed close only in comparison with those for the other categories. The newer population was considerably more disposed than the older inhabitants to all types of movement. Conversely, the latter group had very clearly become a settled population. Almost two-thirds of them moved not at all during the decade, while less than a quarter of the newer population exhibited the same stability.

Table VII-10 analyzes the composition of the Polish population in the city's districts in 1930. Since the table is based on a sample of the pre-1921 in-migration it could not reflect additions to the German population which resulted from the influx of the 1920s. Few Poles would have entered Bottrop during that period, however, so the analysis of the Polish population may be presumed to be reasonably accurate.

TABLE VII-10

Sources of the Polish In-Migrant-Generated Population, 1930

	Batenbrock/ Lehmkuhle		All Others		Total	
	Nr.	%	Nr.	%	Nr.	%
Population in 1930	229		126		355	
Holdover from 1910	52	22.7	22	17.4	74	20.8
Holdover from 1911-1920	51	22.2	20	15.8	71	20.0
Intra-city movement	26	11.4	28	22.2	54	15.2
Second generation	100	43.8	56	44.4	156	43.9

Sources: Sample; AbB 1911, 1920 and 1930.

The patterns for Batenbrock/Lehmkuhle and the rest of Bottrop in 1930 stook in every much the same relationship to each other as they had in 1920. The holdover population was slightly more important in Batenbrock/Lehmkuhle than elsewhere. This was true both for the older segment of the population and that part which was added between 1911 and 1920. As in 1920 intra-city movement played a less important role in the formation of the Polish population in Batenbrock/Lehmkuhle than in other parts of the city. The maturing second generation wa again of equal importance in all areas of Bottrop.

The table also points up the ability of the Polish community in Batenbrock/Lehmkuhle to sustain itself. By 1930 the holdovers from 1910 made up less than a quarter of the total. Persons who were added to the district's adult population between 1910 and 1920 contributed a like number to the whole. During the 1920s it was able to attract some who had lived in other parts of the city. However, the young formed by far the greatest single part of the population, a circumstance which pointed to the maintenance of the Polish community even after the passing of the original in-migrant settlers.

What role then did ethnicity play in the shaping of Bottrop's residential structure? From the foregoing discussion it may be seen that the Polish enclave, which was formed in the pre-World War I era and continued to exist into the final years of the Weimar Republic, was only one of the conspicuous features of the city's urban aspect. The fragmentation of the city was another. Its social and economic focus was split among the central city and business district and the several areas dominated by the mines. A third was that domination of Bottrop's economy by the coal mines and their central importance in the housing market. The interrelationships of those three factors show that ethnicity—however prominent in Bottrop—played only a subsidiary role.

It is clear that the Polish enclave in Batenbrock/Lehmkuhle was not the cause of the city's fragmentation. That is, Bottrop was not split along ethnic lines into Poland and German districts. Rather the fractionation of the city may be traced to the development of the mines. Their need to attract and hold a large labor force resulted in the large-scale building of company housing as near as possible to the pits. Each of the city's mines then became the focus for a part of its population. The old central village and the western part of the city, where much of the land long continued to be privately held, formed yet another subdivision, one which was free from sole influence by any single mine. The Polish enclave in

Batenbrock/Lehmkuhle was simply a part of that larger system.

It is equally obvious that the Polish enclave was not a ghetto. Poles were not required to live there, nor did only Poles reside in the district. At all times a substantial part of the Polish population was to be found in other parts of Bottrop. Poles moved freely among the city's districts and did so at a rate scarcely distinguishable from that of the German in-migrants. The choice of Batenbrock/Lehmkuhle as district of residence by a large majority of the city's Poles was voluntary. It originated in Arenberg Bergbau's recruiting activity which had attracted them to Bottrop and specifically to the Prosper mines. The expansion of company housing—arguably the most desirable type of working-class housing in the city—provided economic and domestic incentive for the Poles to remain in the district. Thus, it was not anti-Polish discrimination but historical and economic factors—reeinforced by the intangible force of ethnic kinship—that produced and sustained Bottrop's Polish enclave.

CHAPTER VIII

NATIONALISM

Polish nationalism is, intrinsically, a subject of some interest. Its roots are not to be found in the mid-nineteenth century, as are those of other east-central European countries, but extend back to the medieval and renaissance periods. It was not necessary to revive the language (or construct one out of a peasant dialect) nor manufacture a literature and cultural tradition. A Polish state of varying degrees of sovereignty had, in fact, existed in modern times. Its partition among the tree powerful Polish neighbors resulted in some friction among those powers. However, it had the more important effect of precluding any Polish attempt to enlist aid in a struggle for independence from any government that could provide immediate, material help. The two unsuccessful attempts at rebellion, in the 1830s and 1860s, discredited the narrowly conceived Polish nationalism based in the hereditary aristocracy (*szlachta*), impelled the broadening of nationalist thought to include the middle and lower classes and led to the generation of nationalist fervor among those groups. This democratization of Polish nationalism was clearly successful in the German East, and its effects were perceptible among the working class Polish in-migrants in the Ruhrgebiet.

In broadest interpretation, any action on the part of a Polish in-migrant in the Ruhrgebiet which served to distinguish him from his German co-inhabitants and accentuate his specifically Polish cultural heritage could be seen as a manifestation of nationalism. Isolated actions, however, would likely have been viewed merely as a kind of eccentricity and the numbers of instances diminished in time. In order for a minority group to preserve its sense of ethnic identity, and thus make possible a continued expression of nationalism, organization is necessary. Among the Poles of the Ruhrgebiet nationalism found institutional form in the variety of associations and societies (in German—*Vereine*) which were founded in increasing numbers as the Polish population of the region grew. It was these *Vereine* which directed and reinforced the nationalistic tendencies of the Polish in-migrants. The goals of the numerous *Vereine* varied as their individual nationalist emphases dictated. *Vereine* were founded which were intended to lend a particularly Polish cast to virtually every aspect of the in-migrant's life. Within the context of this institutional activity the nationalism of the Ruhrgebiet's Polish in-migrants may fruitfully be examined.

The first Polish *Verein,* Unity (*Jedność*), in the Ruhrgebiet was founded in Dortmund in 1877. It was a church-related organization, and its stated goals were the maintenance of religious practice and domestic morals and customs (*die Pflege religiöser und heimischer Sitten und Bräuche*). In the same year a *Verein* devoted to the procurement of Polish language publications, the People's Library (*Czytelnia Ludowa*), was founded in Bochum.[1] By the early 1880s the Catholic press, both German and Polish, was incessantly discussing the situation of Poles in the Ruhrgebiet, and the founding of Polish *Vereine* shared first attention with the question of Polish-language religious services. The government first took official notice of the spreading movement in 1883 when it requested information from local authorities in the Ruhrgebiet concerning the numbers of *Vereine* in each jurisdiction. Several *Vereine,* it found, existed in the Westphalian Ruhrgebiet, i.e. *Regierungsbezirke* Arnsberg and Münster, but none, as yet, in *Regierungsbezirk* Düsseldorf. No particular importance was ascribed to the *Vereine.* They were regarded simply as implements of the Center Party, designed to attract Polish voters to its banner.[2]

The real beginning of Polish organization in the Ruhrgebiet can be dated in 1890 with the arrival in the region of Dr. Liss, a Polish clergyman from the diocese of Kulm in West Prussia. He was charged with the religious organization of the Poles in the Ruhrgebiet, and his organizational talents were up to the task. Within three years more than a hundred religiously affiliated *Vereine* had been founded. Liss, however, went beyond the narrow limits of his charge. He recognized that the Church could maintain its influence among the Polish in-migrants in the Ruhrgebiet only if it paid some heed to Polish nationalism. Thus, *Wiarus Polski,* founded by him in Bochum in 1890, served not only as a link among the numerous religious *Vereine,* but it also became the voice of Polish nationalism in the West. Liss also introduced the use of *Verein* badges and banners that were paraded in Church processions and displayed during religious feasts.[3] The *St. Josefat-Kollekte,* a fund to support Polish students studying for the priesthood, was another Liss project that was founded in 1892. Three years later it was supporting a dozen students.[4]

Liss' success discomforted political authorities. Pressure was brought to bear on his ecclesiastical superiors, and in 1894 he was recalled. By that time, however, the base of Polish organization that he had established in the Ruhrgebiet was too firm to be shaken even by the loss of its leader. In the same year that Liss was recalled the Brejski brothers, his successors at *Wiarus Polski,* established the Alliance of Poles in Germany (*Zeiązek Polakżw w Niemczech*) which was intended to be an organization of all Poles in the Ruhrgebiet. It never achieved that goal, but rather developed into a leadership association to which belonged the chairman of most of the Polish *Vereine* in the Ruhrgebiet.[5] By 1896 seventy-five Polish *Vereine* were in existence in the West,[6] and in 1900 it was estimated that eight thousand Poles counted themselves members of a *Verein.*[7] As the *Verein* movement grew problems appeared within it. From the beginning, the *Vereine* had been closely associated with the Church. It was the custom for each *Verein* to have as president (*Präses*) a cleric. Since there was virtually no Polish priests in the region the positions had to be filled by Germans. By 1900 many Poles were demanding that the German *Präsidenten* be replaced by Poles, if necessary by laymen. Ecclesiastical authorities could not comply with the first demand and would not hear of the second. The argument was more than a squabble over the ethnic credentials of the clergy. It also bespoke of an increasing trend toward secular concerns within many *Vereine.* Within a short time some of them had broken with the Church and oriented themselves toward specifically nationalist goals. Thereafter, many newly founded *Vereine* began life as secular organizations.[8] In 1904 over 150 religious *Vereine* with more than 15,000 members moved to counteract the secular trend. They founded the Mutual Aid Society of Polish-Catholic Associations in Rhineland-Westphalia and the Neighboring Provinces (*Verband gegenseitiger Hilfe polnisch-katholischer*

Vereine in Rheinland-Westfalen und in benachbarten Provinzen), which pledged itself to detect and eradicate all political activity in the religious *Vereine.*[9]

Despite the split the growth of Polish organization in the Ruhrgebiet continued. In 1910 the government reported that there were 660 Polish *Vereine* with over 60,000 members in the Ruhrgebiet.[10] Overall Polish organization, however, was weak although the number of individual *Vereine* was large. A permanent governing body with independent funding was lacking.[11] The Association of Poles in Germany, though it included most of the *Verein* leaders of the Ruhrgebiet, was too unwieldy (about a thousand members) to exercise executive authority. It gradually lost influence and finally amalgamated with the Guard (Straż) association of Posen.[12] In an attempt to find a means to provide direction for Ruhrgebiet Poles a Polish Congress was held in Winterswijk, the Netherlands, on the first and second of November, 1913. It was called by Jan Brejski, now sole editor of *Wiarus Polski.* The goal of the Congress was to unify the Ruhrgebiet Poles in order to strive more effectively to preserve faith and language, and to advance the Polish community in both a moral and material sense.[13] In fact, the Congress moved decisively toward these ends. An Executive Committee (*Komitet Wykonowczy*) was established that was expected to provide central direction for all organizations of Poles in the German West. In addition, the various types of *Vereine* were instructed to confine their activities to specific goals and not encroach upon others ("...die verschiedenen Arten von Polenvereinen ihre Tätigkeit hinfort auf ganz bestimmte Ziele beschränken und die gegenseitizgen Grenzverhältnisse achten.")[14]

The outbreak of war in 1914 prevented the effective implementation of the plans of the Congress, and the *Verein* movement as a whole suffered during that period. By 1916 the situation, from the Polish perspective, had deteriorated to the point that *Wiarus Polski* felt it necessary to mount a campaign to revive it.[15] Still, the *Vereine* were active enough during the war to claim the attention of three conferences of the Ruhrgebiet dioceses which were held between November 1917 and October, 1918. The religious *Vereine,* it was agreed, must devote themselves strictly to church affairs and not be drawn into politics. They might, however, be permitted the expression of national characteristics so long as these were not political. (Förderung nationaler Eigenart im Rahmen der Staatsgesetze gilt aber nicht als Politik.")[16] Further, it was felt that the Church should attempt to exercise some control over the secular *Vereine*.[17] This might perhaps be accomplished by exploiting a split which had arisen between the leadership in Bochum and that in Posen. While both were agreed that no German might become chairman, or even member, of a Polish *Verein,* the Bochum position favored allowing German clerics honorary positions in Polish *Vereine*. The conference also leaned in that direction.[18]

The immediate post-war period saw the peak of Polish *Verein* activity in the Ruhrgebiet. The Executive Committee, established by the Polish Congress of 1913, met in March of 1919 and developed a comprehensive detailed organization for the Polish *Vereine* in the region. Eight committees were formed, each with a specific jurisdiction in such areas as political affairs, finance, eduation and social welfare. It was the task of one of the eight to act as arbiter in inter-Verein disputes.[19] The new system of organization met with a great deal of success. Within a year virtually all Polish *Vereine* and other organizations were affiliated with the Executive Committee. The flurry of *Verein* activity was due, in part, to the relaxation of wartime restraints. Another influence must have been an intensification of Polish pride consequent upon the revival of the Polish national state a century and a quarter after it had vanished from the map of Europe. Polish nationalist feeling could now be based not merely on an idea, but, more firmly, on political and geographical fact.

If the post-war Polish national state was, initially, a stimulus to Polish nationalism and its institutional manifestations in the Ruhrgebiet, it was, in the long run, a prime cause of its decline there. While *Verein* membership may have assuaged the nationalist impulse in the pre-war period and provided an immediate outlet for it directly after the war, the existence of a Polish offered the chance to sate it. That is, the Ruhrgebiet Pole who held nationalism to be the supreme value could realize it most genuinely by the simple expedient of a day's rail journey. There is no doubt that many acted on this opportunity. For them nationalism was more important than any material advantage to be gained in the Ruhrgebiet. In this way numbers of people were lost to the Polish *Verein* movement in the Ruhrgebiet after the war. A subsidiary effect must also have been felt. Those who remained showed, by the very fact of their continued residence in the Ruhrgebiet, that nationalism was, at best, of secondary importance in their lives. Thus, it could not be expected that the Polish

Verein movement could be sustained with both the same fervor as in the immediate post-war period. The figures support this supposition. In May 1920, over 1,450 Polish *Vereine* were officially registered.[20] By 1926 there remained only about seven hundred in the Ruhrgebiet.[21] However, the Polish *Vereine* did not wholly disappear. When Nazi Germany officially dissolved all Polish organizations—and it did so only in September, 1939—some 250 remained, two-thirds of them religious groups.[22]

Having sketched the course of the Polish *Verein* movement in the Ruhrgebiet, one may now turn to an examination of the Bottrop *Vereine*. In addition to chronicling the origin and development of each of them, it is necessary—and more useful—to analyze them in terms of purpose and function. The *Vereine* can be grouped according to the nature of their stated goals and activities. In this way it can be shown that under the rubric of Polish nationalism a variety of forms can be discerned which varied greatly in direction and intensity.

One such grouping can be made of *Vereine* which were primarily religious in orientation. The first Polish *Verein* in Bottrop was of this kind. It was the Upper Silesian Association of St. Barbara (*Górnośląski Związek św. Barbary*) which was established in November, 1886, by forty-eight founding members.[23] The inaugural meeting was reported, though without detail, in the *Bottroper Volkszeitung*, which subsequently published Polish language announcements for the *Verein*.[24] The St. Barbara *Verein* grew steadily. Within a year it had tripled its membership, and by the time of its tenth anniversary celebration in 1896 it had enrolled more than four hundred members.[25] In 1897 two new Polish organizations appeared. In June of that year the St. Hyacinth *Verein* was founded with an initial membership of sixty-one. Six months later the St. Stanislaus Kostka *Verein* was established in Bottrop-Boy by twenty-five Poles. Both organizations seemed to represent something of a reaction against what was perceived as the conservative leadership of the St. Barbara *Verein*. In both cases the founding memberships were dominated by young people.[26] Neither of the two new *Vereine* were as successful as the St. Barbara *Vereine*. Both were often required to defend themselves against charges of radicalism leveled by Poles as well as Germans. Eight years passed before the fourth Polish religious *Verein* was established, the St. Adalbert *Verein*, in 1905. In 1907 the Cäcilia Choir was formed, a group dedicated primarily to the performance of religious music. After another two years intervened the Bottrop Poles founded a Marian Society in Eigen.[27] The following year, 1910, a second St. Stanislaus Kostka *Verein* was formed. Its membership regulations was drawn especially to attract the young. Most of its members were already affiliated with the Bottrop Youth Rosary Society (*Rosenkranzbruderschaft*), a group formed in 1903 in imitation of the long established adult organization.[28]

By 1910 then, seven religous *Vereine* and two rosary societies had been established by Bottrop's Poles. The first St. Stanislaus Kostka *Verein* and the St. Hyacinth *Verein* had not survived to that date, at least in original form. The remaining seven organizations, however, had prospered in varying degree. A government sponsored survey of 1910 credited them with a combined membership of almost two thousand.[29] Additional growth was recorded during the next decade. The number of religious organizations remained almost stable during that period—one became secular and two new ones were formed, in 1913 and 1914—but the combined membership rose to over twenty-five hundred.[30] That was the high water mark of the Polish religious *Vereine* in Bottrop. Thereafter activity declined, as it did in the rest of the Ruhrgebiet. Yet in 1927 four Polish religious organizations remained in Bottrop with a combined membership of eleven hundred.[31]

The questions remain: what were the aims of these organizations; how did they attempt to achieve them; in what ways and to what degree were either goals or activities nationalist? The goals of the religous *Vereine* were publicly stated in their by-laws. All of them save one pledged themselves to a defense of morality and a striving toward a more religious life. Political activities were expressly prohibited. The Cäcilia Choir was specifically interested in choral music of a religious nature, but it too required moral habits and unsullied reputation (*Unbescholtene Person*) of its members.[32] The purpose of the Rosary Societies was implicit in their name. The activities of the *Vereine* which were directed toward achieving those ends were also set forth in the by-laws. The most frequently required duty was attendance at Mass and reception of communion in a body by the members of the *Verein* at specified times during the year. Regular attendance at Mass on Sundays and holy days was also a common requirement. Most of the *Vereine* made provision for lectures of moral, Christian content. A few felt it important to stress the need to avoid association with Social Democrats and their propaganda in order to lead a religious life.[33]

The nationalistic aspects of the religious *Vereine* are, perhaps, not obvious, but they were nonetheless real. They were manifested in two ways. The first was the aggressive profession of Catholicism itself. The practice of that faith was considered, and not alone by Poles, an essential part of Polishness. Thus, to the extent that Poles were defending and preserving their religion they were also defending and preserving a part of the Polish ethnic character. The second is more obvious. The Poles sought to inject specifically Polish forms into their religious practice. The struggle, discussed earlier, for the right to conduct religious services in the Polish language is one example. *Verein* meetings, of course, were conducted in Polish. Further, each *Verein* strove, sometimes at considerable expense, to equip itself with a *Verein* banner. Such a banner would be adorned on one side with a representation of the patron saint and the name of the *Verein*. On the other side would be displayed something explicitly connected with Polish Catholicism. The banner of St. Barbara *Verein,* for example, depicted the Częstochowa Madonna.[34] The banners were displayed in church on the occasions of joint attendance at Mass and communion. They were also carried in religous processions, during which *Verein* members also wore caps with piping in the Polish national colors. The Polish religious *Vereine* then, did exhibit nationalistic characteristics. Theirs, however, was a nationalism which was indissolubly linked with, and predicated on, religious practice.

The primacy of religion in the above described relationship can more clearly be seen in comparison with the *Vereine* which were founded on that basis, but which later evolved into quite different organizations. The members of the Cäcilia Choir, which began dedicated to the performance of both religious and Polish folk music, soon found themselves drawn more powerfully to the latter. Within two years of its establishment its increasing emphasis on the performance of secular folk music, with the unalloyed nationalism thus implied, resulted in its recognition by both Poles and Germans as a secular organization. It later confirmed that position by merging with a *Verein* which had been founded on a purely secular basis.[35] The St. Hyacinth *Verein* and the first St. Stanilaus Kostka *Verein* had, from the dates of their respective foundings, been accused of subordinating religion to nationalism. There was a good deal of justice in the accusation. St. Hyacinth was the only religious *Verein* to function without a cleric as *Präses.* It had offered to elect a priest as honorary *Präses,* but the offer was declined.[36] Thereafter it operated without clerical leadership. St. Stanislaus Kostka tendered the same offer, but when it was also met with refusal the *Verein* relented and elected a priest as actual rather than titular leader.[37] This common position taken by the two *Vereine* was naionalistic rather than anti-clerical. They were rejecting not priests, but German priests. That the St. Stanislaus Kostka *Verein* backed down on this point was cause for repeated attacks on it by *Wiarus Polski* and St. Hyacinth. In addition, many of its own members called for the ouster of the German *Präses*.[38] Several attempts at reconciliation between the two *Vereine* and the more conservative St. Barbara *Verein* failed. In 1907 St. Stanislaus and St. Hyacinth compromised their differences and merged into a new, still nominally religious, *Verein,* Unity (*Jedność*). Three years later the Unity *Verein* changed its name to the Guard (*Straz'*) *Verein*. A new set of by-laws was drawn up and the Guard *Verein* emerged as an openly secular organization.[39] Thus, the religious *Verein* held Catholicism to be the most important consideration. Nationalism was present, but only as an adjunct. Those *Vereine* which emphasized that value eventually felt constrained to withdraw from the regligious group and pursue their ends in a completely secular manner.

Another sort of Polish organization for which nationalism was an explicit but concomitant value was that type which directed itself toward economic ends. Several of them existed in Bottrop. The most important was the ZZP, the Polish Trade Union. While the ZZP was a national organization, active throughout Germany wherever Poles lived in numbers, local leaders and members could and did speak out on issues that were important in their own communities. One of the reasons for the founding of the ZZP, it will be remembered, was the unwillingness of the *Gewerkverein* to accord to Poles positions of influence in it. The socialist oriented *Alter Verband* had never appealed greatly to Poles because of its anti-relgious bias. That position was viewed by most Poles as being incompatible with their national character. An accompanying motive for the establishment of the ZZP, vis-à-vis the *Gewerkverein,* was its denial of the ethnic character of the Ruhrgebiet Poles. A Bottrop miner complained to *Wiarus Polski* in 1901 that the local leader of the *Gewerkverein* had stated in a speech that the Poles in the Ruhrgebiet should be considered Germans.[40] However well intended as an expression of non-discrimination —if, in fact, it was such—that kind of declaration was not happily accepted by Polish miners. From that point of view the establishment of the ZZP can be seen as an affirmation of nationality as well as a practical exercise in labor politics. Another letter to *Wiarus Polski* from Bottrop in 1903 bemoaned the number of Polish miners still adhering to the *Gewerkverein.* Most particularly, the writer felt that continued membership in the *Gewerkverein* by a Pole meant, inevitably, Germanization.[41] Ethnicity was also the focal point of a regional conference of the ZZP held in Borbeck in 1907. The speakers, including one from Bottrop, extolled the indestructible national feeling of Poles, castigated the German culture and called upon Poles to refrain from practices, e.g. drunkenness, immorality and card playing, which brought disrepute to the Polish community.[42] As late as 1927 the ZZP counted six hundred members in Bottrop.[43]

Two local *Vereine* were formed in Bottrop whose ends were specifically economic. One was a group dedicated to frugality. Its members were required to deposit sums regularly in the municipal savings bank. It never aroused much interest, however. By 1910 it had enrolled only twelve members, and by the beginning of World War I it had passed out of existence.[44] The second was an association of Polish merchants and tradesmen. It was rather longer-lived. Founded in 1906, it lasted until the post-*Verein* by-laws, was to advise members in all business activities and to provide moral and, when possible, material support to them.[45] Membership in both *Vereine* was, of course, open only to Poles. They were designed to promote economic advancement among members of the Polish community, and it that way buttress feelings of self worth.

Polish economic nationalism was also manifested in the disposition of their savings. The wages paid in the Ruhrgebiet coal mines—the highest in Germany—allowed many Poles to accumulate some savings. During the early years of the in-migration period it was a common practice among Poles to send at least a part of these savings to family members at home in the East. To some extent, no doubt, those monies were used for the support of those less well off than the in-migrant miners. It was generally understood, however, that the major part of the savings were to be placed in a bank against the day when the in-migrant would return and purchase his own farm.[46] Even after the passage of laws which made the purchase of land by Poles in the East most difficult this practice continued. One reason must certainly have been the higher rate of interest on savings offered by the Polish banks in the East, but appeals to national duty were not neglected.[47] As time passed, however, more and more Poles turned their aspirations from land in the East to mobility into the middle class in the Ruhrgebiet by means of the purchase of a shop or entrance into a trade. For that purpose the accumulation of savings in Posen or Upper Silesia was not convenient. The redirection of savings from the East to the West did not, however, mean that Poles turned exclusively to the use of German banks. As the Polish banks became aware of the trend they began to open branches in Ruhrgebiet cities. By 1913 two such branches were operating in Bottrop.[48] Thus, it was possible for the Polish in-migrant both to work toward economic success in the German milieu and to make use of Polish institutions in that quest.

Finally, there were a number of *Vereine* for which Polish nationalism was, explicitly, the *raison d'etre*. However, even among these openly nationalist groups there were variations in tactics and militancy. The Polish Women's Association (*Polinnenverein*)—two were founded in Bottrop in 1914—seemed to be primarily concerned with the question of child rearing. In this case it meant not only the universal problems of infancy, puberty and the like, but also of educating, in the broadest sense, their children as Poles in a German society. Thus, great emphasis was placed on instruction on a national and Catholic basis, literacy in the Polish language and the creation of a corps of supervisors to superintend the children at play and protect them from German contamination.[49]

Several *Verein* were established which were dedicated to the preservation of Polish folk music. The Cäcilia Choir, mentioned above, began as an association devoted to religious music, but it soon developed a secular orientation. In 1913 it merged with the *Wyspiański* Choir which had been founded in 1908 entirely independent of the Church. Two others, the Lute Choir (*Lutnia*) and the Wanda Choir, were established in 1910. The last of these, the New Village Choir (*Nowowiejski*), came into being in 1913. Their common goal was the preservation of a fragment of Polish culture in a hostile, or at least indifferent, society. Although the cultivation of ethnic music seems innocuous enough the authorities were convinced that these *Verein* were nests of radical agitators.[50]

The most aggressively nationalistic of Polish organizations were the gymnastic clubs, the Falcons (*Sokół*), two of which were founded in Bottrop (1905 and 1913). Their by-laws obligated them not only to the maintenance of physical fitness but also to the cultivation of a national consciousness among the members.[51] The physical activity itself included instruction in fencing and drill in military fashion. In addition, the local Falcon groups were subordinated to district units which, in turn, were under the overall direction of the *Sokół* headquarters in Posen. Before the First World War 117 local groups existed in the Ruhrgebiet which enrolled about 6,900 members.[52] Because of their quasi-military training and vocal nationalism there was a tendency to regard the *Sokół* as a revolutionary cadre preparing for a future struggle for an independent Poland.[53] During the war many of the *Sokół* disbanded and the surviving ones pursued social activities. In 1919 the Ruhrgebiet contained 139 *Sokół* with 5,600 members. The next year the *Sokół* in Germany were disbanded and the headquarters moved to Warsaw. Later that year some of the old members began to reorganize an independent association of *Sokół* in Germany.[54]

The attitude of the German public was clearly against Polish nationalism. As early as 1898 the *Bottroper Volkszeitung* addressed itself to the question. In order to enjoy the rights of German citizens, it said, the Poles must avoid all agitation against Germany and the German movement. On this score, however, it was optimistic. The Poles of the Ruhrgebiet, if felt, were much too reasonable to exert themselves in any so quixotic activity as agitation for the resurrection of an independent Polish kingdom.[55] The opposition to Polish nationalism thus, was coupled with a conviction that the local Poles were not, for the most part, involved in it. What manifestations were demonstrated in the city were blamed on a small number of radicals. Part of the Polish community itself appeared to hold that attitude. What Polish nationalism did exist in Bottrop, this group felt, was attributable to a minority of Posen-born activists.[56] The German and conservative Polish opinion may not have been wholly wrong. During the most critical period of the existence of the Wilhelmian *Reich*, the World War, many Poles demonstrated their support for it in the most obvious way. In the first days of the war the *Bottroper Volkszeitung* reported that among the hundreds who rushed to volunteer for military duty were numbers of Poles.[57] Throughout the war the newspaper noted many Poles among the fallen and as recipients of decorations. In all, of the 292 Bottrop war dead, 143 were Poles.[58]

The government was rather more suspicious. In 1890 a special Polish section was established in the *Polizeipräsidium* in Bochum. *Kreis* authorities reported in detail the activities and behavior of Poles to provincial authorities. All public meetings of Poles were attended by police agents who were fluent in Polish. The *Verein* law of 1907, which proscribed the use of Polish in public assemblies, obviated the need for bilingual agents, but the observations continued. Occasionally meetings were dispersed, usually for technical violations. Police spent an inordinate amount of time searching out and seizing such articles as postcards with Polish nationalist themes, proscribing Polish patriotic songs and squashing attempts to celebrate the 500th anniversary of the battle of Tannenberg. The intensive and continued harassment appears to indicate that the government doubted the loyalty of the Poles and considered them, at least potentially, traitorous. That undoubtedly was the official opinion, but such treatment was not unique. The government harassed and persecuted socialists and Catholics. It suspected political parties, *Reich* deputies, bureaucrats, *Junkers* and bourgeoisie. The constituent states of the *Reich* themselves were considered inimical to it. That is, Wilhelmian Germany was a state whose leaders believed that virtually every person and institution was hostile to it. From this perspective the treatment of the Poles in the Ruhrgebiet must be considered normal, if not mild.

In the discussion of Polish nationalism to this point no mention has been made of political activity. The aims and activities of many of the Polish *Vereine* were, of course, in a broad sense political, and police registration of all but the religious *Vereine* used that designation. There was, however, a more narrowly defined area of political activity open to Poles, i.e. the election of public officials, and, at times, they involved themselves deeply in it. Elective politics and divine right monarchy are not comfortable partners. The incongruities of such a partnership were manifested in the electoral systems of Wilhelmain Germany. Each of the constituent states of the *Reich* was free to expand or limit the franchise in state elections as it wished. Prussia retained the most archaic system. The voting right was limited to male, taxpaying heads of household. Voters were then divided into three groups on the basis of the amount of tax payments. The third section, which paid the smallest per capita tax, contained the largest number of voters. The second section was made up of the middle class. The first section in any city would contain very few voters, perhaps only one. Each section was entitled to an equal number of representatives. Thus, the votes were weighed as well as counted. This system of franchise was valid in local (*Gemeinde*) and state (*Landtag*) elections. The national

(*Reichstag*) elections, thanks to Bismarck, were decided by universal (male) suffrage. This arrangement lasted until the advent of the Weimar Republic. Prior to that time then, it is impossible to directly compare the results of local and national elections.

Poles had been active in national elections and had formed a faction in the *Reichstag* since the founding of the *Reich* in 1871. In that first election they took fourteen seats, a number which varied only slightly across the succeeding years.[59] The Polish electoral success was gained entirely in the East. Through the 1870s and 1880s the in-migrant Poles in the West took no part in politics.[60] It was not until near the end of the century that the Poles resident in the Rhenish-Westphalian industrial region began to seriously consider political action. In December of 1897 a Polish assembly in Bochum called for the organization of voters' associations (*Wahlvereine*) in every district (*Wahlkreis*) that contained a considerable number of Poles.[61] In the *Reichstag* election of 1898 *Wiarus Polski* assumed leadership of the western Poles in electoral matters. The newspaper at first called for the abstention of Polish voters, but later it advocated support of the Center Party, both as a check to the anti-Polish nationalists, the *Hakatists*, and as a show of strength to gain influence in the party.[62] The call for abstention was in response to the refusal of the Center to support Polish-language church services. When that party realized that it needed Polish support in some Ruhrgebiet districts, e.g. Bochum and Mülhein, it came to terms with the Polish leadership.[63] The partnership was not an easy one. During the first years of the twentieth century cracks between the two appeared and widened. In 1902 the Center supported legislation in the Prussian *Landtag* which the Poles considered flagrantly anti-Polish. This action marked the complete break between the Center and the Poles in the West. In the *Reichstag* election of 1903 the Poles, for the first time, put forward their own candidates in the West.

The Poles enjoyed some success, although there was never any question of them carrying a constituency in the Ruhrgebiet. Table VIII-1 shows the percentage of the vote in the Ruhrgebiet districts which was claimed by the Poles in the last three *Reichstag* elections before World War I. The importance of the Polish vote was not in the absolute numbers themselves, but in what they represented. It seems reasonable to assume that while Poles may have voted for other parties, the Polish Party vote was cast entirely by Poles. That is, the Polish vote coalesced very rapidly into

TABLE VIII-1

Percentage of Polish Party Vote in Ruhrgebiet Districts in Reichstag Elections: 1903, 1907 and 1912

District	% Polish Population in 1910	% Polish Vote in 1903	% Polish Vote in 1907	% Polish Vote in 1912
Borken-Recklinghausen	15.0	8.0	9.4	9.9
Bochum-Gelsenkirchen-Hattingen	10.1	5.6	6.9	7.3
Dortmund	8.2	3.5	5.5	6.3
Essen	4.0	2.0	2.6	3.2
Mulheim/Ruhr-Stadt Duisburg	5.8	3.8	5.8	6.6
Average	8.6	4.4	5.8	6.5

Sources: "Zahlmässige Angaben . . . 1910" (RM VII—Nr. 37, Bd. 2); "Zahlmässige Angaben . . . 1912" (RM VII—Nr. 37, Bd. 1); VSDR, Ergänzungsheft zu 1903, IV; VSDR, 1907; SDR, Bd. 250, 2. Heft.

a bloc vote. In a close election Polish support could have meant the difference between victory and defeat for one of the other parties. This was most certainly felt by the Center Party. In 1903 it carried two of the five Ruhrgebiet districts. A Polish bloc vote for the Center would have thrown that party into runoff elections in the other three districts. In 1907 and 1912 the same would have been true.

In Bottrop the results of those three *Reichstag* elections were markedly different from the Ruhrgebiet as a whole. While the absolute vote of the Polish Party increased in Bottrop in each election, it decreased as a percentage of the total. For the entire Ruhrgebiet just the opposite was true with regard to the percentages. The pre-war peak for the Polish Party in the *Reichstag* elections in Bottrop came in 1903, the first election in which it put forward a condidate. It is possible that in the subsequent elections some Poles returned to the Center Party, although its percentage of the vote also declined. The SPD gained the most. Its percentage of the vote in 1907 was double that of 1903 and 1912 it was three times as great. Table VIII-2 gives the Bottrop vote in those three elections. It is unlikely, however, that much of the SPD gain came from the Poles. Catholicism was regarded by the Poles as an integral part of their national culture, and Catholicism and soical democracy were constantly at sword's point. The SPD was very slow to discern the possibility of attracting Polish voters in the German West, and its efforts in that direction were never more than halfhearted.[64] The Polish Socialist Party (*Polska Partja Socjalistyczna zaboru pruskiego*) began to work in the Ruhrgebiet about 1900, but no local PPS group existed in Bottrop until late in 1909.[65] By the following year it had attracted only twenty-five members, and by the beginning of World War I it had vanished.[66] The declining percentage of the vote gathered by the Polish Party in Bottrop was possibly the result of indifference to national politics by the local Polish community.

TABLE VIII-2

Reichstag Vote in Bottrop: 1903, 1907 and 1912

Party	1903		1907		1912	
	Nr.	%	Nr.	%	Nr.	%
Center Party	2,573	57.8	3,366	55.6	4,294	52.6
Polish Party	1,269	28.4	1,363	22.5	1,525	18.7
SPD	323	7.2	889	14.6	1,774	21.8
National Liberal	290	6.5	435	7.2	332	4.0
Christian Socialist	——	——	——	——	227	2.8
TOTAL	4,455		6,053		8,152	

Sources: VSDR, Ergänzungsheft zu 1903, IV; VSDR, 1907; *Bottroper Volkszeitung* (January 13, 1912).

The participation of the Poles in local (*Gemeinde*) elections prior to World War I evolved in a different direction. The electorate for local elections was regulated by the three class Prussian system. There were, however, additional municipal qualifications. The city council (*Gemeinderat*) was composed of eighteen members (*Gemeindeverordnete*). Eight represented the central village and two were elected from each of the five *Bauernschaften.* That is, there were six separate constituencies for local elections. A councilman elected from a district had to reside in that district. In addition, two-thirds of the councilmen elected by each voting section were required, by provincial law, to be homeowners. The first and third voting sections both elected one representative in the central village and each of the five *Bauernschaften.* The second section elected six members, all from the central village. Elections took place every two years, but only one-third of the council seats, from two districts, were filled in each election. In order to exercise the franchise one had to be male, twenty-five years of age, a Prussian subject, resident of the *Gemeinde* for at least one year and not in arrears to local taxes. Only heads of household could vote; boarders (*Kostgänger* and *Schlafgänger*) were denied the franchise as were those who received public assistance.[67]

The electoral system assured a political life dominated by a stable and relatively conservative population. Because of the confessional structure of the city the Center Party wielded unchallenged political power. Elections in the first section could, of course, be settled in a sitting room and those of the second section in a small hall. Only in the third section were elections rather than votes of confidence possible. Bottrop's Catholicism, however, effectively excluded the SPD, and the Poles were slow to organize politically. The *Gemeinde* election of 1901 was carried off without a single political editorial or advertisement in the *Bottroper Volkszeitung.* In 1903 the two candidates who were elected by the third section in the village and Eigen received 84 and 100 percent of the vote respectively. In 1905 elections were held in Fuhlenbrock and Lehmkuhle. Only 6 percent of those eligible voted, and the successful candidates each received over 90 percent of the vote. One of the new members relinquished his seat amost immediately and a special election was necessary. It was, in the context of Bottrop's elections, a contest. The winner gathered just over two-thirds of the valid ballots. Less than 4 percent of the electorate went to the polls. In 1907 the successful candidates were put forward by the (Catholic) *Gewerkverein.* Some excitement was generated, as 15 percent of eligible voters cast ballots giving each winner 99 percent of the vote. The turnout was halved two years later when the new third section councilman from the village received 97 percent of the vote and a singulary unpopular candidate in Eigen was held to 70 percent.[68]

The election of 1911 marked the beginning of partisan political contests in local Bottrop elections. For the first time other political groups mobilized to challenge the Center Party's control of *Gemeinde* politics. The SPD and a new Citizen Party (*Bürgervereinigung*) both threatened to put forward their own candidates. The Poles, too, were stirring. In April and June of 1911 they organized two Polish Voters' Leagues (*Wahlvereine*). The by-laws of the two were identical. They pledged themselves to participation in a specifically Polish sense in all local elections.[69] That could only mean Polish candidates. The Center was shocked. The headline of its organ, the *Bottroper Volkszeitung,* announced the advent of partisan politics. The Center Party was, however, the paper went on to say, willing to live with its political opponents so long as they *truly* wanted peace (". . .wenn auch die Gegner den Frieden *ehrlich* wollen." Italics in the original). The paper urged every partisan of the Center Party to cast his ballot and castigated the radicalism of the SPD and the Poles. Anticlimatically, neither the SPD nor the Poles put forward a candidate in the end.[70] Only 12 percent of the voters turned out, and both Center candidates were elected over their *Bürgervereinigung* opponents by margins of four to one.[71]

A week after the regular election a special election was held to fill a vacant seat in Eigen. A Polish candidate stood for election. After the first day's balloting he led by six votes. Alarmed, the *Bottroper Volkszeitung* informed the Center voters that their exercise of the franchise was a duty in the face of imminent danger (". . .dieses Recht is heute *Pflicht, wo Gefahr im Verzuge ist!*" Italics in the original). At the end of the second day the Polish candidate's lead increased to twenty-six votes. "The Poles are advancing!" (Die Polen sind im Vormarsch . . .") the headlines of the newspaper martially proclaimed. It called on the Center voters to repulse the assault (". . .den Ansturm der Polen abzuschlagen . . ."). The exhortation of the newspaper seems to have struck home. The final results gave the Center candidate a 51 percent majority.[72]

The narrow victory of the Center in 1911 inoculated it against overconfidence in the 1913 elections. The *Bottroper Volkszeitung* endorsed the Party's candidates early, warned its readers against a coalition of

Socialists and radical Poles and urged every advocate of the Center to vote. It favored the Center candidates, it incomprehensibly editorialized, on the basis of compensatory fairness (*auf den Boden der ausgleichenden Gerechtigkeit*). As the campaign continued the Center was pleased and relieved when the Poles announced their oppostion to coalition with the SPD. The *Bottroper Volkszeitung* praised the Poles for their reasonableness. It was understandable, the newspaper said, that the Poles should desire representation on the *Gemeinderat,* and, no doubt, some day they would have it. It would not do, however, for them to be too zealous (*eifrig*) in that pursuit.[73] After the first day's balloting the Center candidates led, followed closely by the Poles. The SPD and the *Bürgervereinigung* trailed far behind. At the end of the second day the parties held the same positions. With the Center still leading the *Bottroper Volkszeitung* grudgingly conceded the party discipline of the Poles. The next day, however, the Poles pulled into the lead and the newspaper railed against the unfounded and inexplicable hatred of the other parties which led them to attempt to replace Center councilmen with their own partisans. At the end of the fourth day the Center had cut into the Polish lead, and after the fifth and final day of balloting it regained the top position.[74] The Center, however, had not gained a majority and a runoff election was necessary.

The Poles moved into the lead on the first day and stayed there through the fourth day's voting when only about 150 votes separated the candidates in each race. At that point the *Bottroper Volkszeitung* launched a curious attack on the Poles. The extraordinarily large turnout of Polish voters, it said, was engineered by outside agitators sent in by the ZZP. It understood, the newspaper went on, the wish of the Poles for representation on the *Gemeinderat,* and would have been amenable to compromise had it not been for the treachery of the Poles in the previous election. This, apparently, was a reference to the candidacy of a Poles in the special election of 1911. There remained nothing, therefore, except an honorable passage at arms (". . . in Ehren die Waffen zu kreuzen.") Not that a Polish victory would be a misfortune; it was simply necessary to elect the German candidates, not, of course, to oppose the Poles, but rather in order to prevent the consequences of their victory. ("Siegen die polnischen Kandidaten, so betrachten wir das nicht an sich als ein Unglück, wohl wird gelegentlich über de Folgen zu reden sein.") Two days later the balloting ended and both Polish candidates were elected with 51 percent majorities.[75]

In a report of the runoff election prepared by the local police for the Polish section of the *Polizeipräsidium* in Bochum the analyst wrote that the victory of the Poles was assured by SPD voters who cast ballots for them in the runoff.[76] It is not possible to verify that assertion. The addition of the SPD vote to that of the Poles in the regular election would still have left the Center ahead. It seems somehow unlikely that the SPD would have been able to get more of its voters out in the runoff to vote for a Pole than were willing to go to the polls in the first place for their own candidate. It is more probable that the Poles simply exhorted their own eligible voters to greater efforts in the runoff. The percentage of eligible voters who went to the polls increased from 48.4 percent in the regular election to 69.8 percent in the runoff election.[77]

If a nascent coalition of Poles and SPD did exist in 1913 there was no opportunity to foster it. The era of domestic peace (*Burgfrieden*) ushered in by the First World War prevented further political contests. The *Kreis* authorities prohibited partisan campaigns in 1915, and the parties met and agreed to re-elect the sitting members without opposition. Only eighty-odd voters bothered to cast a unanimous vote for the incumbents. A year later the Minister of the Interior cancelled elections for the duration of the war.[78]

When electoral politics resumed in post-war Germany several important conditions of suffrage underwent change. On the national level the franchise was extended from the Bismarckian limits with the introduction of universal manhood suffrage for everyone above the age of twenty. In Prussia the traditional limitation of the franchise to male heads of household and the archaic three class system disappeared. The numbers of the electorate for the *Reichstag* were doubled, and even greater increases were counted in the Prussian system. This vastly increased electorate had ample opportunity to exercise the franchise in the early post-war period. During the first two years after the war, from January 1919 to February 1921, the voters of Bottrop participated in six elections. Polish Party candidates stood in three of them.

On January 19, 1919 elections were held for the National Assembly which was to create a new governmental form for the defeated Germany. The Poles put forward no candidates and were instructed by the Executive Committee to boycott the election. The *Bottroper Volkszeitung* reported that the local Poles followed that instruction, with the exception fo a few radicals who supported the SPD. The Poles, the newspaper said, were to blame for holding the turnout down to 75 percent to the eligible voters.[79] A week later a Prussian Assembly was elected. Again no Polish candidate stood, and again Poles were urged to withhold their votes. Voter participation in Bottrop dropped to 70 percent. On March 9, 1919 the first postwar *Gemeinde* elections were held. Throughout the Ruhrgebiet Poles ran and enjoyed considerable success. Before the elections Poles had held only twenty-four seats altogether in the *Gemeinderäte* of the Ruhrgebiet. The elections increased their holdings ten-fold, to 251 seats.[80]

The greatest Polish success came in Bottrop. Seventeen of the fifty-four seats fell to Poles, a greater number than in any other city of the Ruhrgebiet. The *Bottroper Volkszeitung,* bowing to the inevitable, referred to the Poles as fellow citizens (*Mitbürger*) and expressly acknowledged their right to participation in local government. At the same time it admitted its surprise at the size of the Polish vote and attributed it to almost wondrous (*geradezu bewundernswert*) party discipline.[81] The implication of the newspaper's remarks was that the Poles had, in fact, followed the instruction of their leadership and abstained in the two elections just past and then voted *en masse* in the *Gemeinde* election. An examination of the results, however, does not wholly support that position (see Table VIII-3). The number of votes cast in the *Gemeinde* election was almost the same as that cast in the election for Prussian Assembly. If the newspaper's analysis is accepted, then it must be believed that six thousand Poles voted in the *Gemeinde* election who had stayed home the month before, while an equal number of Germans who had cast ballots for the Prussian Assembly could not be bothered with local matters. An alternative thesis is that some German voters did weary of the incessant balloting—three elections in seven weeks—a number of Poles were enticed to vote for the first time for Polish candidates, but also that other Poles who had previously supported non-Polish candidates in the first two elections now switched to the Polish Party.

Another example is afforded by the elections of February 20, 1921 (see Table VIII-4). On that day there were two elections, one for the Provincial Assembly (Westphalia) and the other for the Prussian Assembly. The Polishh Party was on the ballot for the former, while it was absent from the latter. Since these elections were held simultaneously there was no question of voting in one election and staying home for the other. However, about fifteen hundred more votes were cast in the election for Provincial Assembly than in that for the Prussian Assembly. By comparison, the Polish Party

TABLE VIII-3

Results of Gemeinde and Prussian Assembly
Elections of 1919 by Party

Party	Gemeinde Nr.	%	Pr. Assembly Nr.	%
Zentrum	8,595	42.8	10,439	50.2
DVP	972	4.7	1,108	5.3
SPD	2,445	11.9	5,401	26.0
USPD	1,740	8.4	3,852	18.5
DDP	565	2.8	—	—
Polish	6,163	30.0	—	—
TOTAL	20,480		20,800	

Source: *Bottroper Volkszeitung,* January 27 and March 10, 1919.

drew over twenty-seven hundred votes in the former election.[82] If it is to be held that all Poles who voted for the Provincial Assembly abstained from voting for the Prussian Assembly some assumptions must be made.

TABLE VIII-4

Results of Provincial and Prussian Assembly
Elections of 1921 by Party

Party	Provincial Nr.	%	Prussian Nr.	%
Zentrum	11,669	41.0	12,112	44.9
SPD	4,773	16.8	4,975	18.4
USPD	944	3.3	953	3.5
KPD	5,764	20.0	6,342	23.5
DNVP, DVP, DDP	2,520	8.8	2,570	9.5
Polish	2,764	9.7	—	—
TOTAL	28,434		26,962	

Source: *Bottroper Volkszeitung,* February 21, 1921.

The first is that the Poles displayed perfect party discipline. There is no reason to doubt that they did show party discipline in great measure. That they attained perfection, however, is a proposition wich must be regarded with some skepticism. The second and corollary assumption is that voters of other parties did not possess such party discipline. That is, it must be assumed that they withheld their votes in the one election while marking their ballots in the other. It is not wholly impossible that such action did occur. However, the consequences of a proportional representation system should not be ignored. It seems must unreasonable to hold that Zentrum voters, for example, wished to see their party less well represented in the Provincial than in the Prussian Assembly.

A more plausible explanation—although an unprovable one with the information at hand—is the same as offered for the previously discussed pair of elections. It is quite possible that many Polish voters refused to mark ballots which did not list their party. However, in view of the figures shown in Table VIII-4, an inability to credit the Poles with perfect party discipline and the fact of the proportional representation system in Germany it is more reasonable to conclude that many—perhaps half—of the Polish voters chose another party when theirs was not available.

The Poles never again approached the electoral success that they achieved in the local elections of 1919. In the *Reichstag* election of June 1920 the Polish Party attracted 3200 votes and in the Provincial election of February 1921 only 2700. By the second *Reichstag* election of 1924 the party's vote stood at just over one thousand.[83] Five years later, in the local election of 1929, the Polish Party vote was just under twelve hundred, but it managed to retain one council seat.[84] It hung on tenaciously until the end. In March of 1933, after Hitler had attained power but before the Nazi grip had tightened on the city, the Poles again retained their single council seat. The eight other parties that were represented on the council coalesced into three blocs with the Poles remaining the odd man out.[85] It was, however, of small moment. By the end of the year the elected councilmen had been thrown out and the *Oberbürgermeister* empowered to administer the city with the aid of eight Councilors (*Ratsherren*), one of them Poles.[86]

Certainly much of the loss sustained by the Polish Party must have been due to the attractive power of the new Polish state. A substantial, though indeterminable, number of Poles left Bottrop to return to their homeland, as indeed happened throughout the Ruhrgebiet. (See Chapter IX.) Even without that loss, however, it is likely that the party would have declined. Certainly this would have been true in terms of percentage even had the Poles been able to maintain the absolute number of votes which they cast in the local election of 1919. Migrants continued to pour into Bottrop after the war, and most, if not all, of them would have been Germans. (See Chapter VII.) By 1930 the number of voters in Bottrop had doubled. The Polish vote, at best, could only have increased by the number of Polish children who attained their majority in those years.

The decline of the Polish Party must also be considered in terms of its function. It is clear that the party had never been in a position to gain majority power at the local, regional or national level. (Even in pre-war Posen the three-class system would have effectively prevented that.) It was a vehicle for making the collective Polish voice heard and safeguarding, insofar as it could, Polish interests. In post-war Germany much of what the party might have hoped to accomplish by cajolery or political log-rolling was achieved thrugh the general legal revisions of the Weimar government. Polish language education in an institutional setting was possible—sometimes even subsidized by the state. The language restrictions of the *Reichsvereinsgesetz* were not longer effective.

Polish nationalism in the West then, was something more than an inchoate ethnic pride and less than a concerted movement directed at the recreation of an independent national homeland or the attainment of Polish autonomy in the Ruhrgebiet. It was sustained and reinforced by formal, institutional means, the *Vereine,* which themselves differed in emphais. The church related *Vereine* manifestations of nationalism were subsumed in the context of religion, although that was itself an integral part of the Polish culture. At the other end of the scale the sole purpose of the *Straz* was to maintain in its members a commitment to Polish nationalism. The *Wahlvereine* and their fruits, the Polish election successes, represented nationalism of an ambiguous sort. It was, unquestionably, ethnic politics, but it was also conventional politics conducted within the Geman context. That is, the Poles acted as any other interest group in a system which employed representative political institutions. They attempted to place exponents of their position in places of power through orderly and legal means. In sum, while Polish nationalism did serve to perpetuate the distance between Bottrop's Poles and their German co-inhabitants, its threatening aspects existed only in the minds of officialdom. Finally, the consequences of the First World War, which at first raised Polish nationalism in the Ruhrgebiet to unprecedented heights, inevitably led to its decline.

CHAPTER IX

OUT-MIGRATION

The resurrection of the Polish national state was a consequence of the First World War that was of particular importance to the people of the Ruhrgebiet. Although its direct effect, the transfer of sovereignty over particular territories, was confined to the (pre-war) German East, the sizable minority of ethically Polish residents in the Ruhrgebiet was inevitably affected by it. The old slogan of German proponents of Polish assimilation, that there were no Poles in the Ruhrgebiet, became at once absurd. Except for the war it might, in time, have become true. German policy regarding land tenure in the East and the generally backward economic conditions in that area encouraged continued residence in the West. Thus, despite the determined efforts of many Poles to preserve their culture and pass it on to their children it is probable that the "Polish immigrant colony" (*kolonia polska na obczyznie*) would have, in the end, been absorbed by the more numerous Germans. The attempts of Polish leaders to involve all Ruhrgebiet Poles in a complex of Polish social, political and economic organizations and the incessant warnings against undue association—at worst, intermarriage—with Germans testify to the Polish awareness of this danger. However, those institutional defenses and the ethnicity that supported them were intensified by the sudden emergence of a Polish state more than a century after its disappearance from the map of Europe. In the years immediately following the end of the war the number of Polish organizations and the memberships therein reached their peaks. The local elections held in the Ruhrgebiet in early 1919 showed the political strength of the Poles which had been latent until that time.

The intensification of Polish activity was temporary. Within a few years memberships in Polish organizations declined drastically and many of them passed out of existence. The Polish political successes of 1919 were not repeated; before long the Polish Party vote was lumped together at the end of published results with "others." Still, neither Polish institutional nor political activity wholly disappeared. The assumption of Polishness by an individual had, until the end of the war, been relatively simple in spite of whatever official harassment and personal obloquy that might have ensued. It involved such things as membership in Polish organizations, endogamous marriage and the use of the language. The Treaty of Versailles required more stringest tests. For those Poles of legal German nationality (*Staatsangehörigkeit*) it meant a formal and legal declaration. For a two year period following the effective date of the Treaty (January 10, 1920) Poles living in Germany were given the option of declaring citizenship. Those who chose Polish citizenship would thereafter lose whatever rights they had previously possessed as German subjects, and further they would be required to leave Germany by the first of January 1923. This was not a popular course of action. In May 1921, at a time when the option had existed for almost eighteen months, the Bottrop authorities reported to the provincial government in Münster that there was little likelihood that many of the Poles in Bottrop would declare Polish citizenship if serious attempts were made at Polish-German conciliation.[1] After assessing reports from local authorities the provincial governor in Münster was able to assure the Minister of the Interior that only one-third to one-half of the Poles in Westphalia would exercise their option and, of that group, only a part would choose Polish citizenship.[2] Those predictions were borne out. To the end of September 1922, only about 50,000 Poles in the Ruhrgebiet declared under the option and almost 70 percent of them chose Germany.[3]

Another, and more dramatic, way of asserting one's Polishness was physical movement to Poland. The suggestion that a new Polish state be created was advanced before the end of the war. In January of 1918 in the "Fourteen Points" speech in which he outlined his scheme for a general European peace settlement Woodrow Wilson stated that "An independent Polish state should be erected which should include the territories inhabited by indisputably Polish populations . . . ."[4] That such a state would be created was made certain by the outcome of the war. All three states that had participated in the division of Poland at the end of the eighteenth century had been defeated. The German *Reich* and the Habsburg Empire sued for an armistice in November of 1918. Russia, which had submitted to the Central Powers a year earlier, now became, technically, a victor power. However the imposition of the settlement at Brest-Litovsk, the successful Bolshevik revolution and the incipient civil war effectively prevented her from participating in boundary settlements at Versailles. If the certainty of a Poland was established by mid-November 1918, its exact location and extent remained unsettled for a considerable time thereafter. The Ruhrgebiet Pole who wished, at the end of 1918, to go to Poland would have been justified in asking where, exactly, it lay.

There were several historical models to choose from. A Poland, united under the Piast kings, had emerged as a recognizable power in East-central Europe by the tenth century. Its boundaries, fluctuating with time and fortune, ran northward from the Carpathians mountains to the Baltic and eastward from the Oder to the Niemen. It was, of course not a national but a dynastic state. When, in the latter part of the fourteenth century, it was united through marriage with Lithuania it became the greatest state of Europe reaching from near the Oder in the West through European Russia and southward almost to the Black Sea. It managed to retain much of this territory through four centuries. By the latter part of the eighteenth century, however, the effects of the country's singular political organization and the emergence of powerful neighbors both East and West had drained it of vitality. The three divisions which eliminated historical Poland resembled anatomical dissection more closely than rape. For a brief time during the period of Napoleon's ascendency a quasi-state bearing the name "Grand Duchy of Warsaw" appeared under his protection. However, it lasted only as long as Napoleon himself, and any hopes of a Polish revival were quickly laid to rest at Vienna.

For the next century Poland existed only as an historical memory for most Europeans and as a goal for those advocates of the gathering force of nationalism. Twice during the nineteenth century, in the 1830s and again in the 1860s, revolts broke out in partitioned Poland, but they were put down with relative ease. Not until the First World War was a revival of Poland seriously considered by anyone with the power to accomplish it. Paradoxically, the first move in that direction was taken by Germany. Faced with a two-front war and the consequent demand for enormous numbers of troops the German General Staff advocated the limited re-creation of Poland. At base the scheme was nothing more than an extension of the widely practiced art of war propaganda. The idea was that the proclamation of a new kingdom of Poland in German occupied Russian Poland would rally Polish volunteers to the German cause. With the force of the General Staff behind the plan it was adopted, and in November of 1916 an "independent" Kingdom of Poland war proclaimed. From the Polish point of view the most serious drawbacks of the new "independent" Kingdom were that it remained under German control, had no king and was left without defined boundaries.[5]

Thus, the Council of Ten—the premiers and foreign ministers of the five principal powers at Versailles—whose duty it was to recommend boundaries for the new Polish state, was faced with a somewhat more complex task than, for example, the restoration of Belgium. The eastern boundaries were, from the perspective of Versailles, easily settled. The Poles, Russians, Lithuanians, Ruthenians and Ukranians could be left to fight it out. Settlement was not reached in that area until 1923. However, clashes between Polish and German claims regarding the western boundaries were unavoidable at Versailles. The Polish delegation demanded from Germany restoration of Poland's western boundaries to the limits of 1772 together with the *Regierungsbezirk* Allenstein in East Prussia and the whole of Upper Silesia.[6] The Germans were prepared to countenance a plebiscite in Posen.[7] When a draft treaty was presented to the German delegation in May of 1919 it provided for their cession to Poland of virtually the whole of West Prussia, Posen and Upper Silesia. Despite vehement German protest the final draft of the following month contained few concessions. The only ones of consequence were provisions for plebiscites in Upper Silesia and Allenstein rather than the uncontested transfer of those areas to Poland. The former was of considerable importance to Bottrop. Although Upper Silesians made up only a small part of the Polish community of the Ruhrgebiet, in Bottrop they were the most numerous of the Polish in-migrants.

The plebiscite area was defined in the Versailles Treaty, which was signed by the German delegation on June 28, 1919. It included almost the whole of Upper Silesia. Three *Kreise* and part of a fourth which were located in the northeast were excluded. The German census of 1910 had shown those areas to be 85 to 90 percent German speaking.[8] A part of *Landkreis* Ratibor—about 122 square miles, with a population around 48,000 and 80 percent Czech (*mährisch*) speaking—had been given without plebiscite to Czechoslovakia.[9] A small—fourty square mile—part of *Kreis* Namslau, although part of *Regierungsbezirk* Breslau, was included in the plebiscite area.[10] Upper Silesia had never formed part of the Polish state in the modern period. In medieval times it had been a fief of the Piast dynasty, but by the middle of the fourteenth century the Polish crown had renounced all claims to it and the area came under the overlordship of the Bohemian monarchy. Only in the eighteenth century did it pass into German hands as a result of the policy of territorial aggrandizement pursued by Frederick the Great.

Despite the remote connection with Poland and the long years of German control much of Upper Silesia had remained Polish in custom and language. Germanization had been most effective west of the Oder and in the cities. In the *Kreise* on the left bank of the Oder German speakers formed 85 percent of the population. In the *Kreise* through which the Oder flowed 61 percent of the population was Polish speaking, and in those *Kreise* wholly east of the river Polish speakers formed 73 percent of the population. In the five industrial cities of Upper Silesia—Gleiwitz, Beuthen, Kattowtiz, Königsütte and Zabrze—the German speaking majority ranged from 54 to 58 percent. The anti-Polish campaign of Bismarck had strengthened rather than weakened the ethnic consciousness of the Poles in Upper Silesia as elsewhere. Traditionally the Poles had voted for the Catholic Center Party in Upper Silesia. However, in 1903 a candidate of the Polish Party was, for the first time, elected. In 1907 the Polish Party gained control of five seats in Upper Silesia and gathered 30 percent of the vote.[11] It was with evidence such as this that the Poles supported their claims to Upper Silesia as a part of "...the territories inhabited by indisputably Polish populations...."

The date fixed for the plebiscite and the determination of eligible voters permitted a protracted and bitter campaign to be waged. Article 88 of the Treaty declared that the vote should take place no earlier than six months and no later than eighteen months after the assumption of authority by an allied commission in Upper Silesia, itself to assume command within two weeks of the Treaty coming into force. The date finally settled on for the plebiscite was March 20, 1921. The franchise for the plebiscite was extended to all persons above the age of twenty who had been born in the area or who had lived there since a date to be determined by the allied commission.[12] That date was ultimately fixed as January 1, 1904.[13]

The extended period between the effective date of the Treaty of Versailles and that of the plebiscite allowed large scope for those who wished to influence the vote by extra-legal means. Most of the wealth and power —industry, land and office—in the plebiscite area was in the hands of Germans. In addition, paramilitary organizations, e.g. the *Grenzschutz* and the *Heimatschutz,* were organized and trained there by former officers of the German Army. As soon as it became known that a plebiscite would occur the provincial governor declared martial law in the region. Officially sanctioned pro-German propaganda was freely distributed, while similar action by the Poles was regarded as treason.[14] Unable to influence the vote through the exercise of official power or normal campaign methods the Poles had recourse to other means. On August 18, 1919 they began an insurrection in Kattowitz and Pless, near the Polish border. Regular German troops quelled the uprising within a few days.[15] Even after the assumption of authority by the allied commission Germans were in a position to exercise great influence over the campaign and the vote. Although the higher offices in Upper Silesia passed over to the allies, most middle and lower level positions remained in German hands. With a single exception the *Landräte* and Bürgermeister were left to the German incumbents.[16] In the countryside the manorial estates (*Gutsbezirke*) were owned by Germans, who thus held considerable power over the Polish peasantry. Throughout the spring and summer of 1920 conditions in the plebiscite area became more and more heated. On the seventeenth of August trouble erupted in Kattowitz. German demonstrators clashed with French troops, and the latter were ordered back to barracks. With a free hand the mob stormed the Polish political headquarters, destroyed all Polish businesses in the city, sacked the offices of a Polish newspaper and killed a Polish doctor in the street.[17] A second Polish insurrection began almost immediately accompanied by a strike of Polish coal miners. Within a few days a Polish force estimated at fifty thousand had gained control of much of southern and eastern Upper Silesia. By September the allied commission had worked out a settlement which left the Poles with great influence in the areas that they had overrun.[18]

While provocation and counterattack of the sort mentioned above followed one another in the plebiscite area, a non-violent, but nonetheless intense, campaign was waged in Bottrop, the locus of Upper Silesian settlement in the Ruhrgebiet. Since the Versailles Treaty had extended the franchise for the plebiscite to persons born in the plebiscite area, but not necessarily resident there, thousands of Bottropers were eligible. In an earlier plebiscite (July 20, 1920) in the East Prussian district of Allenstein and the West Prussian district of Marienwerder, in which the same rules applied, the so-called out-voters had formed a considerable part of the total electorate. In Allenstein 30.2 percent of the total vote had been cast by non-residents; in Marienwerder the figure was 22.6 percent.[19] In that plebiscite the out-voters had gone almost unanimously for Germany. If a similar percentage of out-voters participated in the Upper Silesian plebiscite, however, a similar result could not be guaranteed. Polish leaders, recognizing the potential of the Ruhrgebiet diaspora, began as early as 1919 to send agents to the West to stimulate the interest of the Poles there.[20]

The plebiscite was also a source of concern for Germans in the West. Early in 1921 advertisements began to appear in the *Bottroper Volkszeitung* which stressed the importance of saving Upper Silesia for Germany. These pieces emphasized the backwardness of the Poles and predicted chaos for Upper Silesia should the Poles win. The newspaper aligned itself editorially with the advertisements. It spoke, on the one hand of the duty of all eligible voters to participate, while, on the other, bemoaned the fact that the names and addresses of the eligible voters were a matter of public record, a circumstance which would allow the Poles to discover potential voters for Poland and proselytize among them.[21] In its traditional recognition of the social, economic and political realities the newspaper was careful to direct its criticism outward. It was never applied to local Polish residents.

In the end, a mass Polish exodus from the Ruhrgebiet to the plebiscite area did not occur. About 16 percent (191,154) of the total electorate was composed of out-voters.[22] Of that number only about 13,000 voted for Poland.[23] According to the *Bottroper Volkszeitung,* five special trains carrying 1,711 *Heimattreuen,* i.e. German voters, journeyed to Upper Silesia. If any of the Bottrop's Poles made the trip the fact was not advertised by the newspaper.[24] In any case, the out-voters had little effect on the outcome. They were distributed very unevenly through the *Kreise* of the region. Most voted in the western and northern areas where Germany would have had a large majority without them. In only eighty-five of the 1,522 voting districts could the out-voters have decided the result had all of them voted for Germany, and only five of those districts had more than 5,000 voters. Altogether, almost 60 percent of the voters cast their ballots for Germany.[25]

While the votes were cast and counted in a few days' time the exact lines of partition were pondered by the allied commission for many months. The passions aroused in Bottrop as well as in the plebiscite area, thus, remained high even after the election. A leaked report of a proposed scheme of partition occasioned a third Polish insurrection in Upper Silesia in May, 1921.[26] In Bottrop efforts were made to dampen the fires of animosity. A notice warning against unrest and calling for peaceful rebuilding was placed jointly in the *Bottroper Volkszeitung* by all the political parties, not excluding the Polish Party.[27] Throughout the period of deliberations by the allied commission the newspaper published reports concerning the plebiscite area, but it refrained from attacking the Poles.

The boundary settlement was made public in October of 1921. It succeeded in outraging both sides. Poland was awarded about a quarter of the area with 46 percent of the population. It was, in general, the area in which Poland had gained a majority of the vote, the South and East of the district. This region contained most of the mineral and industrial wealth of Upper Silesia.[28] The Poles had demanded everything to the east of the Oder, and they claimed that the out-voters had unfairly influenced the voting results. The Germans, pointing to their overall majority, had claimed the whole area. A large protest meeting was held in Bottrop after the announcement of the final partition lines. Notices were taken out in the *Bottroper Volkszeitung* by the political parties, this time excluding the Polish Party, which urged attendance. Even at this assembly—which was, of course, an anti-Poland demonstration—the final speaker called for the participants to go in peace and without hate or hostility for their Polish fellow residents and workers (". . .gehen Sie jetzt wieder in Ruhe und ohne Hass und Feindseligkeit gegen unsere polnischen Mitbürger an die Arbeit.")[29]

At the same time that Polish border disputes were being settled the Ruhrgebiet experienced a mass out-migration of Poles. Contemporary observers and, subsequently, historians have written that large numbers of Poles, perhaps hundreds of thousands, left the Ruhrgebiet in the several years following the war. Estimates range from 150,000 to 225,000.[30] Many of them, perhaps fifty thousand emigrated to France. The figures cited for the migration vary widely because they are estimates. No official or unofficial count was kept. It is probable that no figure even approaching the exact will ever be discovered. Fortunately, for the purposes of this study such a figure is not necessary. It is sufficient that there is general agreement that the number of out-migrants was large. The implication is that a great part of the Ruhrgebiet Polish community was ready, when sufficient inducement was offered, to yield whatever economic or other advantage that was attendant upon German residence and citizenship. The attraction of the new Polish is obvious. That of France is less so. It has been held that the French won the political sympathy of the Poles during their military occupation of the Ruhrgebiet in the years 1923 to 1925.[31] One might speculate with equal plausibility that during that period the French coal fields offered a familiar type of employment without the disruptive effects of a foreign occupation.

Despite the impossibility of obtaining an exact count of the Poles who migrated out of the Ruhrgebiet in the years after World War I it is desirable to attempt some measure of the strength of that movement. The sample of in-migrants that has been used as the basis of analysis in other sections of this work also provides information that gives some indication of the dimensions of the migration out of Bottrop.

The figures listed in Table IX-1 represent the total out-migration from Bottrop which can be attributed to the cases drawn in the sample. The numbers include the in-migrants, their spouses and minor children and also the members of the second generation, their spouses and minor children. The category "Poles" includes all Poles, both German- and foreign-born. Germans and all other foreign born in-migrants are combined in the second category.

The average number of out-migrants per year is greater for Poles than for Germans and others during all three periods shown in the table. Of a certainty that comparison is somewhat misleading. First, native Bottropers and their progeny were not taken into account since they were not included in the sample. It would strain credulity to believe that none of them migrated out of Bottrop. Second, the sample was drawn from a listing of in-migrants who entered the city through 1920. It may be assumed that few, if any, Poles migrated into Bottrop after the war.[32] Thus,

TABLE IX-1

Out-migration of the In-migrant-generated Sample Population
1901-1933

	1901-1918		1919-1923		1924-1933		Total	
	Nr.	Avg./ Yr.	Nr.	Avg./ Yr.	Nr.	Avg./ Yr.	Nr.	Avg./ Yr.
All Poles	165	9.2	123	24.6	77	7.7	365	11.0
Germans and others	102	5.6	52	10.4	52	5.2	206	6.2
TOTAL	267	14.8	175	35.0	129	12.9	571	17.3

Source: AEB.

it is likely that the sample is a microcosm of the pool of Bottrop's Polish residents who were available to join the out-migration, even after 1918. However, Bottrop continued to receive German and foreign in-migrants, over sixty-five thousand in the five years following the end of World War I.[33] Many of them must have been temporary residents. The comparison for the period 1919-1923 then, probably displays the ranking accurately, but probably overestimates the difference between the two categories. In all likelihood, during the period 1924-1933 German and foreign-born out-migrants outnumbered Poles.

The table confirms the observations of contemporaries and historians. During the five years following the end of the war the rate of out-migra-tion of Bottrop's Polish residents increased greatly (267.4 percent) over the previous five year period. To some extent this may be attributed to the effects of the war since the rate for Germans and the foreign-born also increased (185.7 percent), though not as much as that of the Poles. From 1924 through 1933 the Polish out-migration subsided, and the average number of out-migrants per year fell below the pre-1919 figure. Since the pool of potential Polish out-migrants was non-renewable that trend is scarcely surprising. It is impossible to determine—given the information gained from the sample—what the true average was for Germans and foreigners, but it must have remained higher than the pre-1919 figure.

Since the beginning of industrialization the population of Bottrop, in common with the population of the Ruhrgebiet cities in general, had been highly unstable. Only a relatively small portion of the large annual in-migration settled permanently in the city. Most new arrivals moved on within a short time. Polish out-migration in the years after the war, then, was not an exceptional occurrence. However, the scale on which it occurred was.

Because the out-migration of Poles from the Ruhrgebiet after the First World War was not enumerated it is impossible to trace exactly its ebb and flow. The years 1919 and 1923 are generally given as the temporal boundaries of the mass out-migration.[34] The Polish section (*Polenüberwachungsstelle*) of the police of Bochum, however, reported only days after the signing of the armistice that soldiers of Polish ethnic birth (*Herkunft*) were planning to go to Poland as soon as they were demobilized. It also maintained that a mass migration from the Ruhrgebiet was planned, although it could furnish no details.[35] At the beginning of 1920 the authorities in Bottrop, in answer to an inquiry from the provincial governor in Münster, wrote that a number of Poles had already left the city. However, the report also emphasized that, to that time, the greatest part of the city's Polish community had remained in Bottrop and probably would continue to reside there.[36] Information available from the sample allows a more exact picture to be drawn of the timing of the out-migration of Bottrop's Poles. As in Table XI-1, the figures in Table IX-2 below represent the total Polish in-migrant-generated population.

A considerable part of Bottrop's post-war Polish out-migration did, in fact, occur in the last days of 1918 after the signing of the armistice. That group was composed almost exclusively of Russian-born Poles who were returning to their native area. Between 1919 and 1922 the out-migration continued at a pace nearly equal to that early rush. It slackened in 1923, and continued at a low level for the next ten years.

Before 1918 the movement of migrants had been largely intra-regional, i.e. within the Ruhrgebiet. The favorable employment situation had attracted hundreds of thousands of persons into the Ruhrgebiet, but at the same time it had allowed relatively easy movement from mine to mine and city to city. The post-war migration was directed, to a much greater extent, outside the region.

TABLE IX-2

Pos-War Out-migration from Bottrop of the Sample Group of Poles

Year	Nr.	%
1918	30	13.0
1919	32	13.9
1920	28	12.2
1921	19	8.2
1922	33	14.3
1923	11	4.8
1924-33	77	33.4
TOTAL	230	

Source: AEB.

To the end of World War I the percentages of Poles and others who migrated from Bottrop to other Ruhrgebiet cities were almost equal. A test of the null hypothesis for difference of proportion shows that the small difference is inconsequential. From the end of the war, however, a statistically significant difference between Poles and others is apparent. More than a third of Germans and foreign-born in-migrants who left Bottrop after the signing of the armistice declared as destination another city of the Ruhrgebiet. Fewer than twenty Poles in a hundred who chose to leave the city did the same.

The political unrest, strikes and food shortages extant in the Ruhrgebiet during the immediate post-war years must certainly have contributed to the increase of out-migration from that region. However, it is unlikely that the consequences of the war fell more heavily on Poles than other Ruhrgebiet residents. An explanation for the discrepancy must be sought, first, in the promise, and then, in the reality of a sovereign Polish state. What emotions or resolve its creation roused among Ruhrgebiet Poles cannot, of course, be measured. Nonetheless, its effects were apparent to contemporaries. The authorities in Bottrop reported to their provincial supervisors at the beginning of 1920 that the local Poles were unanimous in their desire to see the formation of the long dreamed of national state

TABLE IX-3

Direction of Out-migration (In-migrants and Second Generation), 1901-1933

	1901-11.11.18				11.12.18-1933				Total	
	All Poles		Others		All Poles		Others			
	Nr.	%	Nr.	%	Nr.	%	Nr.	%	Nr.	%
Ruhrgebiet	32	43.2	29	39.7	18	17.0	20	33.8	99	31.7
Elsewhere	42	56.8	44	60.2	88	83.0	39	66.1	213	68.2
TOTAL	74		73		106		59		312	

Source: AEB.

Poles-Others to the end of World War I: $H_0 : P_1 - P_2 = 0$ $Z = 0.43$.

Poles-Others after World War I: $H_0 : P_1 - P_2 = 0$ $Z = 2.48$.

("... , das erträumte Polen-Reich erstehen zu sehen . . . .")[37] Very shortly after the signing of the armistice the Executive Committee, which had
been set up by the Polish Congress in 1913, opened an emigration office in
Bochum to facilitate migration to the, still unborn, Polish state. In 1920 a
Polish consulate was set up in Essen which assumed that responsibility.[38]
Apparently those steps were necessary. The annual report of the provincial
government to the Interior Ministry for the year 1920 claimed that immediately after the creation of the new Polish state a wild, mass emigration
of Poles from the Ruhrgebiet to Posen took place.[39]

A measurement of the dimensions of that emigration, even for the Polish population of Bottrop, is not simple. A resolution of the question may
be attempted by means of an analysis of the sample of in-migrants, since
the forms of the *Einwohnermeldeamt* recorded the declared destination
of out-migrants. However, the interpretation of that information is not
straightforward. The problem of determining who among the post-war
out-migrants were bound for Poland is formidable. The dicussion at the
beginning of this chapter illustrates the difficulty. If a person left Bottrop
on June 29, 1919 bound for Krotoschin (Posen) did he arrive in Poland
or Germany? The Treaty was signed the day before, but the area was formally transferred to Poland only on January 10, 1920. A similar question
may be asked concerning the plebiscite areas. Did rail passage to Kattowitz ental a foreign journey only after June 19, 1922? The question
only becomes more complex if the destination was east of the Vistula.
That area was in dispute until the end of the Russo-Polish war. It should
also be necessary—though impossible—to take intentions into account.
Were persons bound for Posen or Warsaw a few days or weeks after the
end of the war journeying to those places because they expected them to
come under Polish sovereignty? Should such persons be considered as having emigrated to Poland? Ultimately, of course, those places did become a
part of Poland. If positive answers were given to the two questions above,
what is to be done with the plebiscite areas? German language statistics in
the census of 1910 had led the Poles to be very optimistic concerning the
acquisition of the Allenstein district of East Prussia and most of Upper
Silesia. In the former, *Kreis* Ortelsburg's school population in 1911 was
70.9 percent Polish-speaking.[40] In the latter, in 1911, 89.2 percent of the
school children of Gross Strehlitz were Polish speakers.[41] Yet, in the end,
both Ortelsburg and Gross Strehlitz remained German. These are the

problems which make impossible an unequivocal answer to the question of who emigrated to Poland.

An imperfect solution was reached by considering persons to have emigrated to Poland who could be placed in either of the following two categories.

1) All persons who migrated at any date following the signing of the armistice in 1918 to any territory which became part of the Polish state.
2) All persons who migrated to the plebiscite areas, whether or not those territories became part of Poland, if the date of migration was prior to the boundary settlement.

Table IX-4 was constructed on that basis.

TABLE IX-4

Post-War Migration of Sample Group of Poles* from Bottrop, 11.12.18-1933

	Nr.	%
To Poland	36	11.6
Elsewhere	70	22.6
Remained in Bottrop	204	65.8
TOTAL	310	

Source: AEB.

*First and second generation of German- and foreign-born Poles.

The confidence interval for those who emigrated to Poland is:
$C(8.1 \leqslant p \leqslant 15.1) = .95.$

Of those adult Poles who were resident in Bottrop between the end of World War I and 1933 less than 12 percent emigrated to Poland. Nor did France claim a large portion of the city's post-war out-migrants. Just over 1 percent of them emigrated to that country while 6.4 percent emigrated to the Netherlands. In this respect the post-war migration pattern of Botrop's Poles was considerably different from that exhibited in the Ruhrgebiet as a whole. Altogether almost 23 percent of eligible Poles migrated from Bottrop to other parts of Germany or migrated to other countries. Two-thirds of the eligible sample-generated Polish population remained in the city at the end of 1933. Thus, the findings of the sample appear anomalous in view of the widely accepted positions that a larger portion of the Ruhrgebiet's Polish population left that region after the war, and that the greater part of it emigrated to Poland. When the out-migration is examined more closely the contradiction is partially resolved.

The rates of out-migration in the pre- and post-war periods are very similar (see Table IX-5). To the date of the armistice just over two-thirds

TABLE IX-5

Pre-War and Post-War Out-migration of Sample Group of Poles

	Pre-War		Post-War	
	Nr.	%	Nr.	%
To Poland (the East)	15	6.6	36	11.6
Elsewhere	59	25.8	70	22.6
Remained in Bottrop	155	67.6	204	65.8
Total eligible*	229		310	

Source: AEB.
*In-migrants and children eighteen by the end of the war.

of the eligible Polish population, i.e. in-migrants and adults of the second generation, remained in Bottrop. After the end of the war just under two-thirds stayed in the city to the end of 1933. However, the direction of the out-migration does show a significant difference, particularly with respect to movement eastward. In Table IX-5 the East is that area of heavily Polish population which has been previously defined. (See footnote 1 of Chapter II.) Not all of that area was absorbed by Poland after the war. A comparison of Poles who migrated out of Bottrop shows that to the end of the war a fifth of them returned to the East, while after the end of the war over a third of those who left the city emigrated to Poland. That difference in percentage is a statistically significant one. (H0: $P_1 - P_2 = 0$

yields $Z = 2.01$.) The total percentages of eligible Poles who left Bottrop to the end of the war and after it were very close, but the direction of that out-migration had been significantly altered. The attraction of an independent Polish homeland is thus clear.

It is also necessary to take into account the whole of the migration that is represented by the figures for the in-migrants and the second generation. Briefly, the out-migration of an unmarried in-migrant involved only one person, but the same movement by a married in-migrant meant that at least two and possibly more people left the city (see Table IX-6). The

TABLE IX-6

Total Persons Represented by Post-War Out-migration of Sample Groups of Poles

	To Poland		Elsewhere		Total	
	Nr.	%	Nr.	%	Nr.	%
Single	16	14.5	47	39.2	63	27.4
Married	40	36.4	46	38.3	86	37.4
Minor Children	54	49.0	27	22.5	81	35.2
TOTAL	110	47.8	120	52.2	230	

Source: AEB.
For single out-migrants: $H_0 : P_1 - P_2 = 0$ $Z = 4.18$.

total number of persons represented by the emigrants to Poland, i.e. including spouses and minor children, was almost equal to the total number represented by those who migrated out of Bottrop to other cities in Germany or to other countries. The percentage of single persons who emigrated to Poland was only about a third of that of the other in-migrants while the percentage of minor children among them was double that of the others. Indeed, minor children made up almost half of the group bound for Poland. The difference in median age between those who emigrated to Poland (31.0 years) and the others (23.5 years) shows why the latter

group was composed so largely of single persons and childless couples.
The median age at marriage for in-migrants and the second generation was
24.4 years.

Those figures suggest a difference between the generations in direction
of out-migration, and a striking contrast is found when the sample group
is divided in that way (see Table IX-7).

TABLE IX-7

Generational Difference in Post-War Migration of Poles from Bottrop

	In-Migrants		Second Generation		Total	
	Nr.	%	Nr.	%	Nr.	%
To Poland	30	62.5	6	10.3	36	34.0
Elsewhere	18	37.5	52	89.6	70	66.0
TOTAL	48		58		106	

Source: AEB.
$x^2 = 31.86, df = 1, p \leqslant .001.$

Almost two-thirds of the first generation of Poles who left Bottrop
after the First World War emigrated to Poland. Only 10 percent of the second generation did so. The pattern shown in the table is a statistically
significant one, and the association between generation and direction of
out-migration is one of considerable strength. Leaving aside for the moment the question of the direction of out-migration, the members of the
second generation showed a lesser tendency than the in-migrants to leave
Bottrop at all. During the period covered by the study 63 percent of Polish
in-migrants left the city. Only 30 percent of the second generation did so.
The difference in percentage between the sample group of in-migrants and
the second generation is statistically significant. There is less than one
chance in a thousand that it does not reflect a real difference in the total
in-migrant-generated population in Bottrop.[42] Nor was that contrast unique to the Poles. The comparable figures for all other in-migrants and

members of the second generation are very close to those of the Poles —72.8 percent and 30.6 percent respectively.[43] No doubt more members of the second generation of Poles migrated from Bottrop after the date at which this study ends, 1933. However, it is not certain that they ever did so at a rate equal to that of their parents. By 1933 all members of the second generation who were included in the sample, i.e. those born through 1910, were at least twenty-three years old. The median age for those who migrated out of Bottrop by the end of 1933—in-migrants and members of the second generation alike—was 21.6 years.

The attraction of the new Polish state for Bottrop's Poles then, varied in intensity. For Polish in-migrants it was clearly a strong one. They left the city in large numbers, taking their wives and minor children with them. However, for the second generation, which had either been born or had grown to maturity in Bottrop, the force of Polish nationalism was not nearly as strong. Not only did a greater percentage of them than of their parents tend to remain in Bottrop, but if they did leave the city it was not likely that they emigrated to Poland. Their associations with that country were secondhand, while their own experiences, personal relationships and institutional ties were products of a German environment. In sum, it is clear that a great migration out of the Ruhrgebiet to Poland did take place in the years after Wold War I. However, that migration was composed, at least in Bottrop, largely of in-migrants and their dependents. During their years of residence in the city many of them had married and raised children to maturity. Great efforts had been made to inculcate a sense of Polish ethnicity in that second generation. If the pattern of post-war emigration from Bottrop to Poland can be accepted as credible evidence, however, that effort yielded mixed results. Emigration to the new Polish state—the ultimate display of Polish nationalism—was chosen only by a small minority of the second generation. Nor did the migrants remove themselves en masse to the renascent Poland. Thus, a large number of Poles continued to live and work in post-war Germany. A specifically Polish institutional and political life then existed throughout the tenure of the Weimar Republic.

CHAPTER X

CONCLUSION

To speak of an integrated society at all in Wilhelmian Germany is to risk ridicule. A social, political or economic description of the country would show at once the cleavages and centrifugal forces. Wilhelmian Germany was a country in which class divisions were real and visible. Working class children did not take the high school diploma (*Abitur*) or study at a university. Children of the middle class, of course, did, but they did not join the student corps (*Studentenkorps*). They were destined for careers in business, government bureaucracy or the professions, callings which left them quite without the sense of honor necessary to engage in the formalized student duels, the *Mensur*. The scions of the hereditary nobility, who did bear the scars of honor, aimed at the diplomatic service, the executive arm of the government, the management of family estates or, above all, the army. Mobility between classes was neither frequent nor expected. The most advanced system of social insurance in the world existed side by side with patriarchal relationships in the factories and almost feudal ones on the agricultural estates of the East.

In political terms, a unified nation had been thrust upon an unwilling king by an avowed opponent of most of its constituent states. The upper house of the country's legislature, the *Bundesrat,* was a council of delegated civil servants. The lower house, the *Reichstag,* was a popularly elected parliament, but a government was not formed from its majority party, nor was it responsible to the *Reichstag.* Its strongest political party was never a part of the government and achieved a position of leadership only in time to accept the responsibility for the defeat of the nation whose policies it had never set. Commitment of German business leadership to technological progress and the rational exploitation of productive forces through the cartel system was as strong as its opposition to the modern form of labor organization, the trade union. The clash between the interests of Rhenish industrialists and East-Elbian Junkers required all the political acumen of Bismarck to bridge. In brief, if a model for a modern nation state were constructed on the basis of the realities of Wilhelmian Germany it would be universally derided as impossibly self-contradictory and unworkable.

Yet Imperial Germany not only survived but rose to a position of world power. It crumbled, finally, not as a result of irreconcilable internal contradictions, but as a consequence of defeat in total war, a war which it had been able to sustain for four years against numerically superior enemies on two fronts. Clearly, on some levels and in some ways social compromises and accommodations had been reached which allowed this incongruous state to function. This study has been an effort to explain the workings of one such system of accommodations—those involving Polish in-migrants in the Ruhrgebiet, in particular the Polish coal miners of Bottrop.

Theirs was a success story of American dimensions. It begins with the migration of thousands from the rural East into an expanding industrial city of the Ruhrgebiet. The migrants were probably illiterate, very likely poor and certainly ethnically foreign. Yet they steadily adapted to the urban society and worked assiduously to secure a satisfactory place in it. Employed chiefly in the mines, many of the Polish migrants rose to the skilled positions which were among the best paid of all industrial jobs. They sought and attained places of influence in councils that wielded significant economic, social and political power. All the time they fought tenaciously to preserve their ethnic identity and inculcate it in their children.

These general observations are neither particularly new nor insightful. Contemporaries saw and noted Polish behavior; there is an extensive pre-World War I literature. Historians have subsequently interested themselves in the western Polish colony and investigated many of its aspects. Both contemporaries and historians, however, have failed to grasp the implications.

In particular, they heave viewed the strongly defended ethnic sensibility of the Poles as merely a reflex stimulated by the crude harassment of the political authorities. Ill conceived policies only postponed the inevitable absorption of the Poles into the German milieu. The characteristic chauvinism of Imperial Germany, reenforced by overt government policy, would permit no other end. Perversely, the Poles continued to remain Polish throughout the Imperial era and into the Nazi miasma. This has been ignored, but it cannot be denied.

Since the Polish community in the Ruhrgebiet cannot be casually committed to the inexorable process of Germanization, how is one to interpret it? One alternative is the melting pot theory. It is possible that this has some validity for a later period but, at least until 1933, the evidence shows that the pot has scarcely begun to simmer. Thus the Poles, neither absorbed nor transmuted, appear to have been an anomaly in Imperial and even Weimar Germany. However, if the story of their success may be said to be American, the society which they helped to build and of which they formed a major part may also be viewed in an American perspective. It was, in short, a pluralist society.

Cultural pluralism is a theory which was designed to explain the immigrant-built American society, but there is no reason that it cannot be put to work elsewhere. The theory has been most clearly defined by the American sociologist, Milton M. Gordon. His definition is based on an explication of the concept of assimilation, a word that has been defined in myriad ways and frequently used as a synonym for amalgamation, acculturation and integration. Gordon, however, eschews a uni-dimensional definition; instead he postulates several types or stages of assimilation which may occur indepedently or in various patterns and in differing degree.[1] Each type of assimilation deals with an aspect of the relationship between an immigrant group and the core society, that group whose ". . .way of life is dominant by virtue of original settlement, the preemption of power, or overwhelming numbers."[2]

Structural assimilation, the large-scale entrance of immigrants into the primary level organizations and institutions of the core society, is the key to the understanding of a plural society. In such a society it will be wholly or largely absent. An immigrant group will maintain its own network of clubs and organizations which affirm and reenforce its separate, distinguishable ethnic existence. Identification, the sense of ethnic peoplehood, will continue to grow out of that carefully fostered cultural group. Close associations, friendships and, most importantly, marriages will be achieved largely within the homogeneous groups. On the other hand, the immigrant groups must not be so closed as to preclude all intercourse with the wider society. The language of the core society, for example, must be learned for use in a variety of social institutions. Cooperation between groups and individuals is vital in such areas as secondary relationships as political action, economic activity and civic responsibility. Those relationships create the basis for mutual respect between the cultural groups which, in turn, will reduce prejudice and discrimination to a minimum. Any value or power conflicts which do arise can be settled in the arena of public opinion or by the ballot box.[3] That model is, of course, an ideal type. However, I believe that a review of the evidence will show that Bottrop between 1891 and 1933 very nearly approached it.

For hundreds of years Bottrop had remained a small and unremarkable market village, a backwater of some thousand or so souls. From the beginning of the nineteenth century it experienced a growth of population. During the first sixty years of that century it doubled its size but still held only about four thousand inhabitants. When coal mining began in the city in the early 1870s the pace quickened. In the decade of the 1870s the population increased by over 40 percent. In the 1880s the gain exceeded 60 percent. From 1890 to 1900 the population doubled, and from 1900 to 1910 it doubled again. As has been shown, that spectacular growth was due chiefly to the large-scale in-migration which Bottrop experienced, especially in the years after 1890. Further, in order for Bottrop to have net migration gains an enormous number of in-migrants had to enter the city. Many of them must be termed transients. Almost a third left the city within a year of registration. About 43 percent remained there as long as a decade. In order for in-migration to add, say, ten thousand to Bottrop's population, it is probable that double that number had to enter the city. Thus the doubling and redoubling of the population in the decades after 1890, while impressive, does not accurately show the full extent of the in-migration.

These facts had important implications for in-migrants in Bottrop. By 1900 at the latest Bottropers of old, native stock had become a minority, and their proportion of the total population continued to decrease over the years.[4] The Poles, and indeed all the in-migrants, did not enter a society in which the social structure was fixed and rigid but rather one that was made and continued to be in flux. Bottrop was changing from village to city and from market town to industrial center. Large numbers of persons entered and left it every year. Those who did remain in Bottrop for a period of five or ten years constituted, comparatively, the stable core of the population. In that group of long term residents the Poles were well represented. While only about half of the in-migrants were Poles, more than 60 percent of those who stayed in Bottrop for at least ten years were. More than half of the Poles remained there that long but less than a third of the other in-migrants did so. It was that group persistence that made possible the extensive and vital institutional network that supported the Polish community in Bottrop.

Economic activity and the relationships which flowed from it were of great importance to the Polish community. In the late nineteenth and early twentieth century Bottrop was predominantly a working class city, one which was almost solely dependent on a single industry, coal mining. Therefore, it was in terms of the gradations of skill in employment and wages among working men that an examination of the Polish economic position had to be conducted. The material supplied by the city's regis-tration forms showed that a larger percentage of Poles than of Germans or foreigners entered the city as skilled workers. The occupational level listed by the Polish in-migrants at registration, it is true, may not have been accurate, but that possibility must also be admitted of the other in-migrants. If that initial listing may be accepted as true for most of the Poles, then it is clear that, as a group, they achieved a rate of upward mobility which was not significantly different from that of ethnically Ger-man in-migrants. If large numbers of Poles exaggerated the level of occupa-tional skill at registration, then the rate of upward mobility for them might well have been higher than for the Germans. By 1930 the Polish in-mi-grants were concentrated almost exclusively in the ranks of skilled workers. Just over half of the Germans were to be found there. The contrast was likely the result of the longer periods of residence that the Poles, in gen-eral, enjoyed in Bottrop. That situation allowed the second generation of Germans to achieve a rate of upward mobility, vis-à-vis their parents, which was more than twice as great as that of the Polish second genera-tion. In real terms, however, this only meant that the German second gen-eration was able to move into skilled occupations, thus advancing beyond ing. 193

their un- or semi-skilled parents, while the Poles of the second generation who occupied similar positions simply achieved an economic status equal to their parents. In sum, the evidence shows that Poles did not, as a group, suffer from discrimination in their attempt to reach an acceptable level of economic status which, in Bottrop, most often meant the acquisition of a skilled trade.

Those skilled positions were most commonly as experienced coal cutters (*Vollhauer*) in the mines. Poles had been an important source of manpower for the mines almost from the beginning of large-scale mining operations in Bottrop. Although some difficulty in language had been experienced in the pits many Poles had risen to *Vollhauer*. With the exception of a small number of skilled engineering positions and a very few management jobs the *Vollhauer* was the highest paid employee in the mining operation. That the Poles were able to gain these jobs shows that economic discrimination was not practiced against them in the mines. The question of whether or not native Bottropers or German in-migrants approved of the Polish success in the mines is not important. What is certain is that the Ruhrgebiet, lightly populated when industrial and mining expansion began, was dependent on large-scale in-migration to supply its labor needs. Since the Poles formed a large part of that in-migration, job discrimination against them in the mines undoubtedly would have made it difficult to continue to attract migrants from the East. Nor would that practice have helped the employers in their attempt to control the huge labor turnover which the mines experienced. Thus it is possible to view the Polish success in the mines as simply the result of circumstances and expedience.

However, the several ramifications of work in the coal mines are not to be ignored. Miners had long banded together in organizations (*Knappschaften*) which attempted to provide a measure of security for the men —and their families—who were injured or killed in the mines. By the time that Poles began to enter the Ruhrgebiet and the mines in large numbers the *Knappschaft* had been formally recognized by the government and recast into a legal agency of social security. Administration of the *Knappschaft* was shared by the miners themselves. Individual mines chose officers (*Knappschaftälteste*) who heard grievances and from whose midst were chosen half the members of the Executive Board of the Combined *Knappschaft* of the *Oberbergamt* Dortmund. They were thus positions of some considerable responsibility and status. Another group of representatives chosen by the miners were the security officers (*Sicherheitsmänner*) who were charged with the oversight of safety conditions in the mines. From this body of men were chosen members of the Workers' Committees (*Arbeiterausschüsse*) which were intended to mediate between the miners and the employers somewhat in the fashion of modern labor unions. If Poles were not represented in these bodies, and in more than a token way, it could easily be argued that while they were not discriminated against in a purely financial way, equally they were not allowed to participate in the range of activities that were intimately connected with their economic function. Certainly it appeard that this was the case early on. The offer of the *Gewerkverein* to allow the Poles two represenatives among the *Knappschaftältesten* in the whole of the *Oberbergamt* Dortmund in the election of 1898 cannot be interpreted as anything other than a token gesture. Polish resentment over this treatment was clearly shown in the action of Bottrop Poles when they chose two candidates for the election from their district alone. Although successfully excluded from equitable participation on that occasion, the Poles soon were able to force their way into positions of responsibility and power within miners' organizations. The tool which they used was the ZZP, the Polish Trade Union.

Organized in 1892 in response to the cavalier attitude of the *Gewerkverein*—and to a less extent, the *Alter Verbund*—the ZZP soon enrolled a large number of Polish miners. There is no question but that the ZZP split labor organization in the Ruhrgebiet along ethnic lines. However at the same time it increased significant Polish economic participation. Poles were selected in representative numbers as *Knappschaftälteste* and *Sicherheitsmänner* wherever they were numerous—and thus the ZZP strong. Similarly the ZZP made it possible for the Poles to play important roles in strike actions. Therefore the ZZP, while an ethnically exclusive organization, must be counted as a factor of first importance in the participation of Polish coal miners in the economic life of the Ruhrgebiet.

The relationship of religion and ethnicity was more problematic. The fact that the overwhelming majority of Poles were Catholic might have been expected to promote their acceptance in heavily Catholic Bottrop. In fact, it proved a major source of friction. The insistence of the Poles on pastoral care in their own language was heartily denounced by Bottrop's German inhabitants. It was clearly true, as they claimed, that the Poles were not being denied the comforts of religion. It was equally true that German Bottropers were adamantly opposed to Catholicism clad in Polish garb. The German position may simply have been the result of prejudice—conscious or unconscious—against Poles. On the part of the Poles it is clear that the goal was twofold: pastoral care in familiar and totally comprehensible form and the maintenance of ethnic identity. The inter-ethnic religious question took institutional form in the dispute over Polish control of the governing bodies of Herz Jesu parish. The bitter German opposition to that control was, in the end, fruitless, and within a short time Polish domination of the governing bodies was calmly accepted. On balance, the religious difficulties experienced by the Poles in Bottrop did not obstruct their integration into the city's social structure in any important way. The animosity was fairly rapidly dissipated and the Poles had made an important point. Their insistence on Polish language religious services and control of a parish which was very largely Polish in composition did hinder their assimilation, but it did not place them outside religious society in Bottrop. Rather, their successful prosecution of these demands allowed them to gain a position, in religious terms, in Bottrop's social order that placed them in an equitable position vis-à-vis the Germans. They were able, as were the Germans, to practice their religion in the manner in which they wished, and they were able to exercise the control suitable to the laity over the affairs of a parish in which they were numerically superior.

Education was not an area of critical importance to the question of integration. Some schools in Bottrop were predominantly Polish. However, no legal or coercive action fixed that pattern. It came about as a result of the Polish preponderance in the population of Lehmkuhle and Batenbrock. Many Polish children lived and went to school in other parts of the city. Nor was there a significant educational segregation through class. Bottrop was very largely a working class city, Few children pursued an academic education beyond the legal term. The city did not even boast a Gymnasium until 1910.[5] All children—Germans, Poles and foreigners—went to German schools, took subjects in German and studied the German language. The curriculum was beyond the control of the municipality, set by higher authority. This was not a point of dispute between Gemans and Poles in Bottrop. Formal education then was not a real question; Polish education was.

The necessity to educate children as Poles was a constant theme of *Wiarus Polski,* the Polish-language newspaper. Since it was forbidden to accomplish this by means of formal educational institutions—an exception was made for religious education—the burden lay on the parents and the Polish community in general. The use of the Polish language in the home, the celebration of Polish holidays and membership in the numerous Polish clubs and organizations were the instruments of an ethnic education. After the end of World War I Polish schools were made a legal alternative for formal education, but they enjoyed only temporary success. However, the Polish community and its institutional manifestations, which had always been the primary tutors of ethnicity, remained realities in Bottrop. Thus Polish children received both a formal education, which equipped them for a life in an urban, industrial setting, and a knowledge of their ethnic heritage which arose from their familiar milieu.

An examination of marriage patterns among in-migrants and their children provided evidence for the strength and durability of Polish ethnic awareness in Bottrop. Endogamous marriage—from several points of view—was the rule in the city. Less than 8 percent of marriages took place between partners of working class and middle class background. If a distinction between skilled and un- or semi-skilled workers in permitted, then an additional 27 percent of the marriages may be said to have been inter-class marriages. Even so, two-thirds of all marriages contracted in Bottrop by in-migrants and their children over a period of forty-three years were within class limits. A religious constraint was also apparent. Only about 15 percent of the marriages of in-migrants and their children were between partners of different faiths. Until the end of World War I inter-faith marriage was almost unknown; from 1919 about one marriage in five was of this kind. Still, through 1933 religious endogamy was an observable phenomenon in the city.

Marriage within the ethnic group—a practice crucial to the survival of the Polish community—was also the norm in Bottrop. Only one in ten of the Polish in-migrants (most of whom married before the end of the war) married across ethnic lines. The second generation contracted inter-ethnic marriages at three times that rate. (Doubtful cases were considered to have contracted inter-ethnic marriages, so the rate for the Polish children may be an exaggeration.) It is clear therefore that ethnic boundaries suffered some erosion over the years. However, it is important to note that 70 percent of the children of the Polish in-migrants chose to marry within the ethnic community. Those facts are testimony to both the strong ethnic sense of the Polish in-migrants and its continued existence among the members of the second generation.

An analysis of in-migrant residential patterns in Bottrop in the first thirty years of the twentieth century also contributed to an understanding of the city's Polish community. Some of the findings pointed to the very recent development of Bottrop from a rural to an urban society. Those implications were at least as important for the city as a whole as for the Poles in particular. The growth of the city after the beginning of large-scale mining operations had produced an urban structure which, to a great extent, mirrored that of the historical central village and surrounding *Bauernschaften*. Each of the mines with its adjacent workers' quarters (*Arbeiterkolonie*) was a focus of economic and social life. If that development were not opposed by contravailing centripetal forces the city, as a urban unit would have remained a fiction, purely an administrative entity. This was not a specifically Polish problem but one which bore on the whole city and its total population, and it is thus outside the scope of this study.

Within that divided framework there existed areas—Lehmkuhle and Batenbrock—which were inhabited predominately by Poles. There were several factors, however, which prevent the labelling of Lehmkuhle and Batenbrock as Polish ghettoes. The concentration of Poles there was voluntary; they were not denied housing in other parts of the city. The availability of cheap company housing, proximity to the place of employment and the company of ethnic fellows made residence in the two districts attractive to many Poles. Still, they were not inhabited exclusively by Poles. The residential pattern of the sample group of in-migrants in 1910 showed that 85 percent of the population of the two was Polish, but since the sample excluded the old, native population that figure was almost certainly an exaggeration. The same is true for the pattern displayed in 1920. After that date the ethnic ratio in Lehmkuhle and Batenbrock must have altered considerably although that change is only hinted at in the analysis of the city's in-migrants. Nor did Poles live only in Lehmkuhle and Batenbrock. In 1910 a third of the Polish in-migrant population was resident in other sections of the city. By 1920 that percentage had increased marginally, and it remained about the same in 1930. Changes in the composition of the Polish enclave were not the result of in and out-migration alone. To some extent they occurred because of the maturation of the second generation. However, there was also a considerable movement among the city's districts. The Polish enclave in Bottrop then was created not by a policy of housing discrimination but by choice and economic advantage. Further, it never contained the whole of the city's Polish population, and that part that it did hold decreased over the years. Finally, the enclave did not represent a static population. Its composition changed over time both by the process of migration and through movement within the city

Polish nationalism, the overt display of ethnicity, was most clearly manifest in the intricate network of organizations that was created by the in-migrants. Those institutional forms of Polish nationalism, *Vereine,* were not in themselves foreign to German society. The ancient saw, that two Germans shake hands and three form a *Verein,* is not without a measure of truth. Associations dedicated to sport, choral music, pigeon raising, *ad infinitum* abounded in Germany. It was the primacy of ethnicity in the Polish *Vereine* that distinguished them from other social groupings. and clearly stated their goal—the maintenance of the Polish community. However, not all of them were of equal strength in promoting Polish separation. The variety of organizations, directed to almost every public aspect of life, guaranteed that. Some were church related organizations that must be considered primarily religous in orientation and only secondarily of nationalist import. The practice of Catholicism was itself a part of the Polish national character, but it was an aspect of culture that was shared with the majority of Bottrop's German inhabitants. The Polish religious *Vereine* always insisted that political questions not be permitted to intrude themselves and that Polish nationalism be admitted only insofar as it constituted an expression of traditional religious practice. The difficulties surrounding the practice of a particularly Polish form of Catholicism had been settled in fairly rapid order and without lasting rancor. Thus it is likely that such organizations were viewed, on both sides, strictly in a religious context rather than as specific instruments of ethnicity. This position is supported by the fact that the religious *Vereine*—alone among the Polish organizations—were listed as nonpolitical in government reports. In sum, the religious *Vereine* did contribute to the institutional maintenance of Polish ethnicity, but that function was co-incident with the preservation of the faith in the Polish community.

The Ruhrgebiet Poles created a number of organizations that were directed toward economic ends. Of these only the ZZP enjoyed any great degree of success. Membership in the ZZP did separate Poles from Germans in the area of economic life, which is not normally a matter of ethnic concern. However, it is also true that before its establishment the German trade unions had effectively excluded Poles from the important positions of influence and leadership. After the emergence of the ZZP the Poles gained significant representation in bodies with important economic functions, and the Polish voice was heard and respected in the organization of the most critical of labor actions, strikes. On balance, it must be concluded that the exclusiveness of Polish organization in an area not usually of ethnic concern was offset by the position which that organization won for them.

tion. The choral societies, women's clubs, theater groups and athletic organizations had as their sole object the preservation of the city's Polish community. The last, the *Sokół,* were nervously viewed by some Germans as a para-military cadre that was preparing for a war of national liberation. In the event that fear proved unjustified. What those Polish *Vereine* did do was to provide an ethnic context for the avocations of the members of the community. In performing that function they reenforced the sense of ethnicity and helped to assure that one's circle of associates and intimate friends would likely be chosen from the ranks of Bottrop's Polish inhabitants.

The Polish role in the political life of the city is a classic example of the functioning of a plural society. Poles only became active in local politics a short time before the outbreak of World War I. Their entry, in the form of a Polish Party, surprised and dismayed the city's German inhabitants. In the first local election after the end of the war the Polish Party captured almost a third of the seats on the city council, a percentage that approximated the Polish representation in the general population. The wide support given to the party by Bottrop's Poles clearly indicated a political consciousness that was based on ethnic rather than religous or class interest. They pursued those interests by means of the conventional political instruments that were available to them. However, the Poles were not inextricably wed to ethnic politics. Within five years after the end of the war the Polish Party has shrivelled to a rump group. It is certain that a major cause was the out-migration of Polish voters. However, it is also true that the Weimar Republic had satisfied many of the Polish desires with regard to the safeguarding of ethnicity. Thus it is probable that many Poles simply began to vote along religious or class lines.

The creation of an independent Polish national state after the First World War occasioned a severe test for Bottrop's Polish community. Had the city's Poles become indistinguishable from their German neighbors by that time no problem would have existed. However, that was not the case as has been made clear by the post-war burgeoning of the Polish *Vereine,* the continued high rate of ethnic inter-marriage and the Polish political success in the local election of 1919. Thus the plebiscite that was intended to settle the boundary question in Upper Silesia became a center of controversy in Bottrop. The separation of a part of Upper Silesia from Germany was bitterly resented in Bottrop as it was in all of Germany. Many of the Polish inhabitants of the city were natives of that area, eligible to vote in the election, and it might have been expected that they sould have had to bear the brunt of the German outrage. The local newspaper, the trade unions and the political parties all damned the Treaty, the partition, the plebiscite and the Poles. However, the Poles who received that condemnation were a nebulous "them." Either a long acquaintance with the local Poles prevented such execration for reasons of comradeship or respect, or a discreet silence was maintained in the knowledge of the strength of Poles in the local social, economic and political order. For their part, Bottrop's Poles appear not to have taken any great part in the plebiscite. This may have been due to the cost of the necessary journey, apathy or fear of German retaliation. It is also possible that by the time of the plebiscite those Poles who felt themselves irrevocably committed to Poland had already gone there. This critical period came to a close after the announcement of the partition line with a call by local German leadership for peace and toleration among the city's inhabitants of both ethnic groups.

The revival of the Polish national state also raised the possibility of the collapse of the city's Polish community through emigration. There is indeed evidence that it was a considerable attraction. Before the end of the war only a fifth of the Poles who left the city returned to their eastern homeland. After the end of the war more than a third of those who left emigrated to Poland. However, the emigrants accounted for only a little over 11 percent of Polish adults among both the in-migrants and the members of the second generation. Double that precentage migrated else-where, and almost two-thirds of the total remained in Bottrop. If so power-ful an attraction as the revived Polish national state could not tempt them from the city *en masse* they must certainly have been well established. That is, the attraction of a sovereign Polish homeland could only have been offset by strong personal and institutional ties which bound the Poles to Bottrop.

The foregoing chapters have not attempted to show that no anti-Polish prejudice existed in Bottrop. There is every reason to believe that it did. *Wiarus Polski* constantly railed against it. The attitudes of the trade unions and of the leading organ of Bottrop German opinion, the *Bottroper Volks-zeitung,* have been described. The Poles were accused of being filthy, drunken and immoral, and terms of ethnic abuse were freely used.[6] How-ever, the circumstances of the city's growth, the employment pattern and the manner in which housing was provided made it difficult for persons of anti-Polish bent to translate their prejudice into effective action. For their part the Poles were equally determined to preserve their cultural unique-ness and to enter into active participation in important areas of the city's life. That determination, manifested in discipline and organization, result-ed in the creation of a plural society in the nascent urban structure that was Bottrop.

APPENDIX A

CROSSTABULATIONS OF THE SAMPLE GROUP OF IN-MIGRANTS AND DEMOGRAPHIC CHARACTERISTICS AT THE TIME OF REGISTRATION

TABLE A-1

Ethnic/National Group and Date of Registration

Years	German		Pole		Foreign		Total —	
	Nr.	%	Nr.	%	Nr.	%	Nr.	%
1891-1900	6	6.0	27	16.6	—	—	33	10.2
1901-1910	41	41.0	73	44.8	9	15.2	123	38.2
1911-1920	53	53.0	63	38.6	50	84.7	166	51.6
TOTAL	100	31.0	163	50.6	59	18.3	322	—

Source: AEB.

x^2 = 42.24, df = 4, p $\leqslant$ .001, Cramer's V = .256.

TABLE A-2

Ethnic Group* and Last Residence

Last Residence	German		Pole		Total	
	Nr.	%	Nr.	%	Nr.	%
Kreis of birth	50	50.0	81	49.7	131	49.8
Other	50	50.0	82	50.3	132	50.2
TOTAL	100	38.0	163	62.0	263	—

Source: AEB.

* This information available for German-born only.

x^2 = .006, df = 1, p $\leqslant$ .95.

TABLE A-3

Ethnic/National Group and Age at Registration

Age	German		Pole		Foreign		Total —	
	Nr.	%	Nr.	%	Nr.	%	Nr.	%
To 25 years	54	54.0	90	55.2	33	56.8	177	55.1
26 years +	46	46.0	73	44.8	25	43.1	144	44.8
TOTAL	100	31.2	163	50.8	58	18.0	321	—

Source: AEB.

x^2 = .12, df = 2, pf ≤ .95.

TABLE A-4

Ethnic/National Group and Marital Status

Status	German		Pole		Foreign		Total	
	Nr.	%	Nr.	%	Nr.	%	Nr.	%
Single	67	67.0	97	59.5	38	64.4	202	62.7
Married	11	11.0	19	11.7	10	16.9	40	12.4
Family	22	22.0	47	28.8	11	18.6	80	24.8
TOTAL	100	31.0	163	50.6	59	18.3	322	—

Source: AEB.

x^2 = 4.08, df = 4, p = .39.

TABLE A-5

Ethnic/National Group and Religion

Religion	German		Pole		Foreign		Total	
	Nr.	%	Nr.	%	Nr.	%	Nr.	%
Catholic	65	65.0	132	81.0	44	74.6	241	74.8
Protestant	35	35.0	31	19.0	15	25.4	81	25.2
TOTAL	100	31.0	163	50.6	59	18.3	322	——

Source: AEB.

x^2 = 8.47, df = 2, p = .01.

APPENDIX B

CROSSTABULATIONS OF LENGTH OF RESIDENCE AND DEMOGRAPHIC CHARACTERISTICS OF IN-MIGRANTS AT THE TIME OF REGISTRATION

TABLE B-1

Length of Residence (One Year) and Marital Status

Length of Residence	Single		Married		Married/ Children		Total	
	Nr.	%	Nr.	%	Nr.	%	Nr.	%
—— 1 year	88	43.6	15	37.5	3	3.8	106	32.9
1 year +	114	56.4	25	62.5	77	96.2	216	67.1
TOTAL	202	62.7	40	12.4	80	24.8	322	——

Source: AEB.
x^2 = 41.57, df = 2, p $\leqslant$ .001, Cramer's V = .359.

TABLE B-2

Length of Residence (Ten Years) and Marital Status

Length of Residence	Single		Married		Married/ Children		Total	
	Nr.	%	Nr.	%	Nr.	%	Nr.	%
—— 10 years	145	71.8	20	50.0	19	23.8	184	57.1
10 years +	57	28.2	20	50.0	61	76.2	138	42.9
TOTAL	204	62.7	40	12.4	80	24.8	322	——

Source: AEB.
x^2 = 55.19, df = 2, p $\leqslant$ .001, Cramer's V = .413.

TABLE B-3

Length of Residence (One Year) and Place of Birth

Length of Residence	German-Poland		Germany		Foreign		Total	
	Nr.	%	Nr.	%	Nr.	%	Nr.	%
—— 1 year	33	20.2	44	44.0	29	49.2	106	32.9
1 year +	130	79.8	56	56.0	30	50.8	216	67.1
TOTAL	163	50.6	100	31.1	59	18.3	322	——

Source: AEB.

$x^2 = 24.46$, df = 2, p $\leq$ .001, Cramer's V = .275.

TABLE B-4

Length of Residence (Ten Years) and Place of Birth

Length of Residence	German-Poland		Germany		Foreign		Total	
	Nr.	%	Nr.	%	Nr.	%	Nr.	%
—— 10 years	75	46.0	61	61.0	48	81.4	184	57.1
10 years +	88	54.0	39	39.0	11	18.6	138	42.9
TOTAL	163	50.6	100	31.1	59	18.3	322	——

Source: AEB.

$x^2 = 22.79$, df = 2, p $\leq$ .001, Cramer's V = .266.

TABLE B-5

Length of Residence (One Year) and Date of Registration

Length of Residence	1891-1900		1910-1910		1911-1920		Total	
	Nr.	%	Nr.	%	Nr.	%	Nr.	%
—— 1 year	——	——	36	29.3	70	42.2	106	32.9
1 year +	33	100.0	87	70.7	96	57.8	216	67.1
TOTAL	33	10.2	123	38.2	166	51.6	322	——

Source: AEB.

x^2 = 23.36, df = 2, p ⩽ .001, Cramer's V = .269.

TABLE B-6

Length of Residence (Ten Years) and Date of Registration

Length of Residence	1891-1900		1901-1910		1911-1920		Total	
	Nr.	%	Nr.	%	Nr.	%	Nr.	%
—— 10 years	2	6.0	69	56.0	113	68.0	184	57.1
10 years +	31	93.9	54	43.9	53	31.9	138	42.9
TOTAL	33	10.2	123	38.2	166	51.6	322	——

Source: AEB.

x^2 = 43.57, df = 2, p ⩽ .001, Cramer's V = .368.

TABLE B-7

Length of Residence (One Year) and Age of Registration

Length of Residence	— 25 yrs.		26 yrs. +		Total	
	Nr.	%	Nr.	%	Nr.	%
— 1 year	74	41.8	32	22.2	106	33.0
1 year +	103	58.2	112	77.7	215	67.0
TOTAL	177	55.1	144	44.9	321	—

Source: AEB.
x^2 = 12.90, df = 1, p $\leqslant$ .001, Phi = .207.

TABLE B-8

Length of Residence (Ten Years) and Age at Registration

Length of Residence	— 25 yrs.		26 yrs. +		Total	
	Nr.	%	Nr.	%	Nr.	%
— 10 years	119	67.2	64	44.4	183	57.0
10 years +	58	32.8	80	55.6	138	43.0
TOTAL	177	55.1	144	44.9	321	—

Source: AEB.
x^2 = 16.83, df = 1, p $\leqslant$ .001, Phi = .229.

TABLE B-9

Length of Residence (One Year) and Last Residence*

Length of Residence	Kreis of Birth		Other		Total	
	Nr.	%	Nr.	%	Nr.	%
—— 1 year	27	20.6	49	37.1	76	28.9
1 year +	104	79.4	83	62.8	187	71.1
TOTAL	131	49.8	132	50.2	263	——

Source: AEB.

* German-born only.

x^2 = 8.79, df = 1, p $\leqslant$ .01, Phi = .183.

TABLE B-10

Length of Residence (Ten Years) and Last Residence*

Length of Residence	Kreis of Birth		Other		Total	
	Nr.	%	Nr.	%	Nr.	%
—— 10 years	56	42.7	80	60.6	136	51.7
10 years +	75	57.2	52	39.4	127	48.3
TOTAL	131	49.8	132	50.2	263	——

Source: AEB.

* German-born only.

x^2 = 8.34, df = 1, p $\leqslant$ .01, Phi = .178.

TABLE B-11

Length of Residence (One Year) and Religion

Length of Residence	Catholic		Protestant		Total	
	Nr.	%	Nr.	%	Nr.	%
—— 1 year	73	30.3	33	40.7	106	32.9
1 year +	168	69.7	48	59.2	216	67.1
TOTAL	241	74.8	81	25.2	322	——

Source: AEB.

$x^2 = 2.54$, df $= 1$, p $\leqslant .11$, Phi $= .096$.

TABLE B-12

Length of Residence (Ten Years) and Religion

Length of Residence	Catholic		Protestant		Total	
	Nr.	%	Nr.	%	Nr.	%
—— 10 years	130	53.9	54	66.6	184	57.1
10 years +	111	46.0	27	33.3	138	42.9
TOTAL	241	74.8	81	25.2	322	——

Source: AEB.

$x^2 = 3.99$, df $= 1$, p $\leqslant .05$, Phi $= .112$.

APPENDIX C

CLASSIFIED LIST OF OCCUPATIONS OF THE
SAMPLE GROUP OF IN-MIGRANTS

Coding: The number to the left of the dash indicates a particular economic sector, e.g. 1 = Agriculture. The number to the right of the dash is a socio-economic rank: 1 = un- or semi-skilled; 2 = skilled; 3 = non-manual. The rankings are intended to be comparable between economic sectors. The non-manual category is undifferentiated.

UNCLASSIFIABLE (99)

Privatier
Invalide
Witwe (r)
Ehefrau
Militär
Student

AGRICULTURE (1)

1-1	1-2	1-3
Landarbeiter	————	————
Landhelfer		
Melker		
Häusler		
Kötter		
Einlieger		
Halbbauer		

COAL MINING (2)

2-1	2-2	2-3
Seilbahnarbeiter	Schiessmeister	Steiger
Lehrhauer	Bergmann	Forderaufsteiger
Platzarbeiter	Vollhauer	Schachtaufseher
Schlepper	Zechenschmied	Aufseher
Kokereiarbeiter	Zechenmaurer	Fahrsteiger
Bergtagelöhner	Vorarbeiter	
Schichtlöhner		
Berglehrling		

MANUFACTURING AND PROCESSING (3)

3-1	3-2	3-3
Packer	Ziegler	Müller
Molkereigehilfe	Mälzer	Maschinenbauteck-niker
Hilfsmaschinist	Maschinist	Werkmeister
Heizer	Mechaniker	
Zuschlager	Klempner	
Fabrikarbeiter	Schmied	
Lagerarbeiter	Dreher	
Munitionsarbeiter	Schlosser	
Stellmacherlehrling	Former	
Brennereilehrling	Maschinenbauschlosser	
Holzschuhmacher	Monteur	
Weber	Kesselmeister	
Bäckergehilfe	Metzger	
Magazinarbeiter	Hufschmied	
	Buchdrucker	
	Glasmacher	
	Bäcker	
	Schneider	
	Schuhmacher	
	Schuster	
	Konditor	
	Bildhauer (Grabmalkunst)	
	Bauschlosser	

CONSTRUCTION AND CASUAL LABOR (4)

4-1	4-2	4-3
Erdarbeiter	Maurer	Bauführer
Arbeiter	Schreiner	Unternehmer
Wegebauer	Fuger	
Rottenarbeiter	Schieferdecker	
Tagearbeitar	Zimmerer	
Tagelöhner	Dachdecker	
Handlanger	Anstreicher	
Bauarbeiter	Tapezierer	

(3) - Continued

4-1	4-2	4-3
Hallenarbeiter	Maler	
Tischlergihilfe	Elektriker	
	Bauhandwerker	

TRANSPORTATION AND COMMUNICATION (5)

5-1	5-2	5-3
Eisenbahner	Lokomotivführer	Postschaffner
Fuhrmann		Postebote
Guterbodenarbeiter		Bahnbeamter
Bahnarbeiter		Oberpostschaffner
Telegrafenarbeiter		Rangiermeister
Kraftwagenführer		Kuttermeister
Strassenbahner		Eisenbahnunter- assistent
Brotkutscher		Eisenbahnbetriebs- assistent
Weichensteller		
Kutscher		

COMMERCIAL AND SERVICE (6)

6-1	6-2	6-3
Bote	Verkäuferin	Kaufmann
Hausierer	Handlungsgehilfe	Büroangestellter
Düsternwächter	Bürogehilfe	Kaufmannischer Angestellter
Versorgungsanstalt- wärter	Bürolehrling	Rohprodukthändler
Haushälterin	Friseur	Gemüsehändler
Dienstmädchen		Milchhändler
Magd		Viehhändler
Stütze		Händler
Hausdiener		Buchhalter
Knecht		Schneidermeister
Köchin		Schuhmachermeister
Hausmeister		Bäckermeister

Appendix C   217

(6) - Continued
  6-1   6-2   6-3
Schulwärter
Masseur

        PROFESSIONAL AND GOVERNMENT (7)
  7-3
Amtssekretär   Ingenier
Oberpostbeamter   Kaplan
Amtsassistent   Architekt
Postassistent   Gymnasiumoberlehrer
Standesamtbeamter   Steuer Inspektor
Bürobeamter   Stadtsekretär
Polizeiwachmeister   Bergassesor
Polizeioberwachmann Artz
Ordenschwester

NOTES

Notes to Introduction

1. Richard W. Tims, *Germanizing Prussian Poland* (New York, 1941), is the historian of the *Hakatist* struggles in Posen.

2. JSB, Vol. VIII, 1933.

3. Wilhelm Brepoh, *Der Aufbau des Ruhrvolkes im Zuge der Ost-West-Wanderung* (Recklinghausen, 1948).

4. Ibid., p. 206.

5. Hans-Ulrich Wehler, "Die Polen im Ruhrgebiet bis 1918," pp. 452-454. In *Moderne deutsche Sozialgeschichte,* ed. Hans-Ulrich Wehler (Köln, 1966), pp. 437-455.

6. Ibid., p. 455.

7. Chirstoph Klessmann, *Polnische Bergarbeiter im Ruhrgebiet, 1870-1945* (Göttingen, 1978), perhaps the most comprehensive work on Ruhr Poles places particular emphasis on their institutional network.

8. The registration forms for Bottrop for the years 1891 through 1920 have been placed on microfilm. There are 168 spools with a varying number (average, about 1300) of frames per spool. The forms are arranged in alphabetical order from the first through the last spool. Seventeen spools were selected with the aid of a table of random numbers. From each of the seventeen a frame between the first and fiftieth was randomly selected, and thereafter every fiftieth frame was taken for the sample. The resulting sample contained 437 cases of which 115 were either blank or outside the desired population, i.e. registrations before or after the period 1891-1920 or registrations of native born. A sample of 322 cases was thus obtained. In addition, a subsidiary sample population was selected. It consists of the 311 children of the persons in the initial sample population. In order that inter-generational comparisons might fruitfully be made no child was selected who was born after 1910.

9. The data yielded by the sample were, for the most part, nominal level data. Such data can neither be placed in rank order nor be the object of mathematical computation. The nature of nominal level data greatly

restricts their statistical manipulation. However, it does permit the testing of the so-called "null hypothesis". That hypothesis states that there is no difference between groups or no relationship between variables. Extensive use was made of two methods of testing the null hypothesis. One is the chi-square (X^2) test. The second involves the computation of the "Z score". An excellent reference source for these and other statistical techniques is Hubert M. Blalock, Jr., *Social Statistics,* 2d ed. (New York, 1972). Recently two techniques—MNA and THAID—have been developed which permit multivariate analysis of nominal level data. Those techniques were employed in the analysis of persistence. Descriptions of them may be found in Frank M. Andrews and Robert C. Messenger, *Multivariate Nominal Scale Analysis: A Report on a New Analysis Technique and a Computer Program* (Ann Arbor, 1973); and James N. Morgan and Robert C. Messenger, *THAID: A Sequential Analysis Program for the Analysis of Nominal Scale Dependent Variables* (Ann Arbor, 1973).

Notes to Chapter I

1. Wilhelm Brepohl, *Der Aufbau des Ruhrvolkes im Zuge der Ost-West-Wanderung* (Recklinghausen, 1948), pp. 34-35. See Helmut Croon, "Vom Werden des Ruhrgebiets," in Walter Först, ed., *Rheinische West-fälische Rückblende* (Köln und Berlin, 1967), Bd. I, pp. 201-202, for the opposing view.

2. Norman Pounds, *The Ruhr: A Study in Historical and Economic Geography* (London, 1952), p. 19.

3. Ibid., pp. 218-219.

4. Bochum, Bottrop, Castrop-Rauxel, Dortmund, Duisburg, Essen, Gelsenkirchen, Gladbeck, Herne, Mülheim/Ruhr, Oberhausen, Recklinghausen, Wanne-Eickel, Wattenscheid and Witten.

5. William O. Henderson, *The State and the Industrial Revolution in Prussia, 1740-1870* (Liverpool, 1967), p. 23.

6. Ibid., p. 28. See also Georg Schreiber, *Der Bergbau* in *Geschichte, Ethos und Sakralkultur* (Köln und Opladen, 1962), p. 516.

7. Pounds, *The Ruhr*, p. 49; and Henderson, *State and Industrial Revolution*, pp. 28-29.

8. Pounds, *The Ruhr*, p. 43.

9. David S. Landes, *The Unbound Prometheus* (London, 1969), p. 178.

10. Ibid., pp. 89-93, gives a good, short description of these innovations.

11. E. A. Wrigley, *Industrial Growth and Population Change* (Cambridge, England, 1961), pp. 6-8.

12. Landes, *The Unbound Promethus,* p. 178.

13. Pounds, *The Ruhr,* p. 80.

14. Pounds, *The Ruhr,* pp. 105-107, and Landes, *The Unbound Prometheus,* pp. 258-259, both emphasize the importance of the Gilchrist-Thomas process.

15. Pounds, *The Ruhr,* p. 65.

16. Ibid., pp. 97-98.

17. Johann Victor Bredt, *Die Polenfrage im Ruhrkohlengebiet* (Leipzig, 1909), p. 91, gives a figure of more than 50 percent.

18. Pounds, *The Ruhr,* p. 147.

19. Ibid., p. 43.

20. Croon, "Vom Werden," p. 181.

21. Quoted in Pound's, *The Ruhr,* p. 91.

22. Croon, "Vom Werden, " pp. 223-225; and Pounds, *The Ruhr,* p. 228.

23. Croom, "Vom Werden," pp. 224-225; and Pounds, *The Ruhr,* pp. 229-230.

24. The population growth of the cities of the Ruhrgebiet as shown in the census figures reflects not only growth by natural increase and in-migration, but also by the process of annexation (*Eingemeindung*). The patchwork of *Gemeinde, Kreisfreie Städte* and *Landkreise* was only gradually simplified into the contemporary picture of the Ruhrgebiet.

25. Robert Müller, *Die Bevölkerungsentwicklung des rheinischewestfälischen Industriegebiets von 1895 bis 1919* (Dissertation, Münster, 1921), Zahlentafel 6. The figures given are for areas which encompassed respectively only 42 percent and 61 percent of the total population.

26. VSDR, 6. Jg. (1897); and SDR, Bd. 240, II.

27. Croon, "Vom Werden," p. 196.

28. Gerhard Adelmann, *Die soziale Betriebsverfassung des Ruhrbergbaus vom Anfang des 19. Jahrhunderts bis zum Erstern Weltkrieg* (Bonn, 1962), p. 29.

29. Ibid., p. 22.

30. Ibid., p. 52.

31.   Ibid., p. 56; and August Heinrichsbauer, *Industrielle Siedlung im Ruhrgebiet in Vergangenheit, Gegenwart und Zukunft* (Essen, 1936), p. 18.

32.   Franz Schulze, *Die polnische Zuwanderung im Ruhrrevier und irhe Wirkungen* (Dissertation, München, 1909), p. 44; and Stanislaus Wachowiak, *Die Polen in Rheinland-Westfalen* (Dissertation, München, 1916), p. 4.

33.   John H. Clapham, *The Economic Development of France and Germany,* 3rd ed. (Cambridge, England, 1961), p. 278; and SJDR, 35. Jg. (1914), pp. 4-5.

34.   SJDR, 53. Jg. (1934), p. 12 and pp. 30-31; and Stanislaus Chmielecki, *Die Bevölkerungs-Entwicklung im Stadt-und Landreis Recklinghausen in den Jahren 1975 bis 1910* (Dissertation, Freiburg, 1914), p. 50.

35.   Müller, *Die Bevölkerungsentwicklung, Zahlentafel 9.*

36.   SJDR, 53. Jg. (1934), p. 12; and Chmielekci, *Die Bevölkerungs-Entwicklung,* p. 37 and pp. 44-45.

37.   Adelmann, *Die soziale Betriebsverfassung,* p. 156; and Brepohl, *Der Aufbau,* p. 140.

38.   Adelmann, *Die soziale Betriebsverfassung,* p. 157.

39.   Max Jürgen Koch, *Die Bergarbeiterbewegung im Ruhrgebiet zur Zeit Wilhelms II.* (1889-1914) (Düsseldorf, 1954), p. 24.

40.   The difficulties involved in arriving at satisfactory population figgures are discussed in Hans-Ulrich Wehler, "Die Polen im Ruhrgebiet bis 1918," in Hans-Ulrich Wehler, ed., *Moderne deutsche Sozialgeschichte* (Köln, 1966), pp. 439-444.

41.   Ibid., p. 440.

42.   Müller, *Die Bevölkerungsentwicklung, Zahlentafel* 15.

43.   Brepohl, *Der Aufbau,* divides the Ruhrgebiet into five zones—the Ruhr valley, the Hellweg, the southern Emscher valley, the Recklinghausen *Vest* and the Lippe. This study follows the scheme of Croon, "Vom Werden," which distinguishes between the historic cities of the Hellweg and the more recently developed industrial cities of the Emscher valley.

44.   Rudolf Schetter, "Von Bottrop's Werden und Geschichte," in *Festschrift zur Grossstadtwerdung Bottrops* (Bottrop, 1953), pp. 8-10.

45.   Ilse Vogel, *Bottrop: Eine Bergbaustadt in der Emscherzone des Ruhrgebiets* (Remagen/Rhein, 1959), pp. 15-16.

46.   Schetter, "Von Bottrops Werden," p. 10.

47.   Ibid., pp. 18-21.

48. Ibid., p. 22.

49. Ibid., pp. 22-25.

50. Vogel, *Bottrop,* p. 18.

51. Ibid., p. 28.

52. Paul Ronge, "Bottrop–fast eine Stadt der Oberschlesier," *Unser Oberschlesien,* nr. 10 (May 11, 1961), unpaginated.

53. JSB, Nr. 6, p. 6.

54. According to Koch, *Die Bergarbeiterbewegung,* p. 10, the Emscher Zone experienced such great in-migration that it lost entirely its Westphalian character. Chmielecki, *Die Bevölkerungs-Entwicklung,* p. 10, points out that *Kreis* Recklinghausen had the greatest growth of all Prussian *Kreise* in the period 1875 to 1910.

55. Compiled from figures in JSB, Nr. 2 and Nr. 8.

56. It is, of course, possible that most or all of the in-migrants who entered during this period remained in Bottrop while the out-migration was made up of natives of the city. Such a pattern, however, would have been unusual enough to have aroused comment, and none was discovered.

Notes to Chapter II

1. Since the political map of Germany during this period retained some of its historical fragmentation, I have simplified the provincial structure for purposes of analysis. The references in the body of the text are to the list given below.

Upper Silesia–*Regierungsbezirk* Oppeln of Provinz Schlesien

Posen–pre-WWI boundaries

East Prussia–pre-WWI boundaries

West Prussia–pre-WWI boundaries

Lower Silesia–*Regierungsbezirke* Breslau and Liegnitz of *Provinz* Schlesien

Pomerania–pre-WWI boundaries

(The six above are referred to in the Test and the German East.)

Rhineprovince-Westphalia–*Rheinprovinz* (includes Malmedy and Eupen) *Provinz* Westfalen and *Land* Lippe

Saxony–*Provinz* Sachsen, *Land* Sachsen, Thüringen, Anhalt and the *Herrschaft* Schmalkalden

Hannover—Hannover, Braunschweig, Schaumburg-Lippe, Bremen and Oldenburg

Palatinate—Saarland and the *bayrische* Pfalz

Hessia—Hessen-Nassau except the *Herrschaft* Schmalkalden and *Land* Hessen

Bavaria—Bayern except the *bayrische* Pfalz

Brandenburg—Brandenburg, Mecklingburg and Berlin

Baden-Württemburg—Baden, Württemberg and the *Hohenzollerische Lande*

Schleswig-Holstein—Schleswig-Holstein and Hamburg

Alsace-Lorraine—Elsass-Lothringen

2.   Transcript of *Alte und Neue Heimat: Oberschlesiersiedlung Bottrop, Westdeutscher Rundfunk Sendung;* (April 29, 1961), p. 6. According to Dr. Paul Ronge in that transcript and in conversation with the author (interview of February 26, 1973) surnames are, at best, no real clue to the ethnicity of Upper Silesians, and, at worst, can be misleading. The assertion that in-migrants from the East were Polish is ultimately unprovable since the registration forms did not ask for *Nationalität*. However, one knows that the city contained large numbers of Poles and that first generation Polish in-migrants were not natives of Trier or München. The assumption is made because, quite simply, without it further work is impossible.

3.   Wachowiak, *Die Polen,* pp. 5-8.

4.   Tims, *Germanizing Prussian Poland,* p. 166.

5.   Koch, *Die Bergarbeiterbewegung,* p. 21. See also Ludwig Bernhard, *Das polnische Gemernwesen im preussischen staat: Die Polenfrage* (Leipzig, 1907), p. 182.

6.   Wachowiak, *Die Polen,* p. 5.

7.   Eberhard Franke, *Die Polnische Volksgruppe im Ruhrgebiet (1870-1940)* (Essen, 1940), MS, pp. 20-22.

8.   Wachowiak, *Die Polen,* pp. 11-13, gives a list of inducements offered by a labor recruiter working among the Masurians.

1) the countryside around the mine is pastoral

2) excellent housing with stalls for livestock and gardens

3) the mine will pay DM 1/mo. for any boarder taken in

4) good streets, water, sewers and electric street lights

5) consumer co-operative

6) schools will be built

7) only ten minutes to work

8) no holiday work, but plenty of overtime
9) Masurians can all live in the same area
10) moving expenses paid

9.   According to Vogel, *Bottrop,* p. 67, the same pattern was evident after WW II. Of the 5,000 eastern refugees who entered Bottrop after the war more than 4,000 were from Upper Silesia.

10.   *Kirche und Religion im Revier, Teil I: Geschichte einer polinischen Kolonie in der Fremde* (Essen, 1968), p. 3—a translation of *Dzieje Kolonii Polskiej na obeyżnic* (Bottrop, 1911).

11.   Ibid., pp. 3-4.

12.   Ibid., p. 4.

13.   *Bottroper Volkszeitung,* various issues, the first February 16, 1884.

14.   Interview with Paul Ronge by the author, February 26, 1973.

15.   Johannes Kaczmarek, *Die polnischen Arbeiter im rheinischwestfälischen Industriegebiet,* (Dissertation, Köln, 1922), pp. 9-10.

16.   *Westdeutscher Rundfunk,* p. 6.

17.   Paul Ronge, "Die Oberschlesiersiedlung Bottrop i. W.," in: *Schlesien,* Heft IV (1960), p. 246.

18.   Vogel, *Bottrop,* p. 28.

19.   Kurt Degen, *Die Herkunft der Arbeiter in den Industrien Rheinland-Westfalens bis zur Grunderzeit,* (Dissertation, Bonn, 1915), pp. 28-35.

20.   Norman Pounds, *The Upper Silesian Industrial Region* (Bloomington, Indiana, 1958), p. 11 and p. 15, and Otto Stoltenberg, *Herkunftsgebiet und Zuwanderung Bottroper Zechenbelegschaften am Ende des 19. Jahrhunderts,* (MS) *Hausarbeit der Fachprüfung für das Lehramt an Gymnasien,* (Bochum, 1970), *Tafel* 6, p. 45.

21.   Alexander Raabe, *Die Abwanderungsbewegung in den östlichen Provinzen Preussens,* (Dissertation, Berlin, 1910), p. 48.

22.   JSB, Nr. 3, p. 12.

23.   AbB, 1911, *Abteilung* I.

24.   For the purposes of this study a permanent resident is defined as one who was resident in Bottrop at the end of 1933. This means a residence period of from thirteen to forty-three years. A long time resident must have remained in the city for at least ten years.

25.   The MNA program was used. Andrews and Messenger, *Multivarrate Nominal Scale Analysis.*

26. *Kirche und Religion im Revier, Teil I,* p. 10, estimated Bottrop's Polish population in 1898 at 10,000 or 46.2 percent. Calculations from my sample indicated a Polish population in 1900 of about 11,000 or 44.5 percent.

27. Ronge, "Bottrop–fast eine Stadt der Obschlesier."

28. Stoltenberg, *Herkunftsgebiet und Zuwanderung, Tafel* 6, p. 45. These figures, however, are not strictly comparable to those calculated from the sample. Stoltenberg's study begins in 1870 and ends in 1899, covers only coal miners and includes Ebel.

Notes to Chapter III

1.   Vogel, *Bottrop,* pp. 22 and p. 18.

2.   Ibid., pp. 20-21.

3.   Ibid., p. 20.

4.   Ibid., p. 20.

5.   Ibid., p. 23.

6.   Ibid., p. 20.

7.   Ibid.

8.   Ibid., p. 25.

9.   Ibid., p. 26.

10. Chmielecki, *Die Bevölkersungs-Entwicklung,* p. 2.

11. The *Berufszählung* did not list Bottrop separately until its report of 1925.

12. Chmielecki, *Die Bevölkerungs-Entwicklung, Tabelle* 9, p. 18.

13. Vogel, *Bottrop,* pp. 39-40.

14. Ibid., p. 36. In 1938 54.0 percent and in 1953 52.3 percent of all employed persons in Bottrop worked for the mines.

15. See Appendix C for a classification of occupations.

16. *Denkschrift zur Erinnerung an das 50 jährige Bestehen der Arenberg'schen AG. zu Essen* (Düsseldorf, 1906), p. 60.

17. The same conclusion was reached by Stephan Thernstrom, *The Other Bostonians,* pp. 38-44; and David Crew, "Definitions of Modernity: Social Mobility in a German Town, 1880-1901," *Journal of Social History* (Fall, 1973), pp. 59-60.

18. See for example Harmut Kaelble, "Sozialer Aufstieg in Deutschland 1850-1914," *Vierteljahrschrift für Sozial- und Wirtschaftsgeschichte,* 60. Bd., *Heft* 1, 1973. David Crew's article was recently translated and published in *Geschichte und Gesellschaft,* 1, Jg., *Heft* 1, 1975.

19. No attempt is made here even to summarize the vast literature. The notes of Stephan Thernstrom, *The Other Bostonians,* provide the basis for an excellent background in the subject.

20. The decreasing numbers in each cohort over the years are the result of deaths and out-migration.

21. No unequivocal statement can be made since the absolute numbers of non-manual employees yielded by the sample were too few to test.

22. While over 40 percent of the total in-migrantion did so, only 20 percent of those who remained in the city for at least a year fell into the un- or semi-skilled category.

23. See Thernstrom, *The Other Bostonians,* the chapter "Yankees and Immigrants."

24. If the parent was retired or dead by 1930, the last occupation before retirement or death was used.

25. These figures do not appear in the same form in the studies of the authors which are cited as sources for the table. Their published data were used to make the calculations, the results of which are shown in the table.

26. Bottrop's commercial sector was particularly small. For the most part, only daily supplies were sold in the city. Most durable goods were bought in neighboring cities, especially Essen. See Vogel, *Bottrop,* pp. 43-48 for a fuller exposition.

27. It would have been at least unusual had the percentage of people in the white collar occupations surpassed the percentage of those in the tertiary sector altogether.

28. Thus, this study tends to confirm—for an earlier period—the similarity of mobility in industrial societies which was found by Lipset and Bendix. Seymour Martin Lipset and Reinhard Bendix, *Social Mobility in Industrial Society* (Berkeley, 1959).

Notes to Chapter IV

1. "Zahlenmässige Angaben über das Polentum in rheinisch-westfälischen Industriebezirke, 1912" (RM VII-Nr. 37, Bd. 1).

2. "Zahlenmässige Angaben über das Polentum in der Provinz Westfalen, 1904" (RA I Pa-Nr. 91).

3. "Nachweisung über die in der Gemeinde Bottrop vorhandenen

Polen, 14. Februar 1911" (RM VII-Nr. 37, Bd. 3). According to Vogel, *Bottrop,* p. 36, the figure in 1953 was still 90 percent.

4. "Nachweisung über die in der Gemeinde Bottrop vorhandenen Polen, 6. Februar 1905" (RM VII-Nr. 35b); and "Nachweisung. . . Bottrop, 14. Februar 1911" (RM VII-Nr. 37, Bd. 3).

5. *Kirche und Religion im Revier, Teil II,* p. 42; and "Aufnahme der im Landkreis Recklinghausen vorhandenen polnischen Firma" (RM VII-Nr. 33).

6. Bredt, *Die Polenfrage,* p. 91.

7. Vogel, *Bottrop,* p. 32.

8. After World War I a formal training program was instituted in some mines. The course lasted almost two years. There was one and a half years of practical training and five months of classroom work. A written examination followed each section. Rudolf Schwenger, *Die betriebliche Sozialpolitik im Ruhrkohlenbergbau* (München, 1932), pp. 52-55.

9. Pounds, *The Ruhr,* p. 147.

10. Bredt, *Die Polenfrage,* p. 91.

11. Koch, *Die Bergarbeiterbewegung,* pp. 79 and 141.

12. Wachowiak, *Die Polen,* p. 10.

13. See, for example, Vogel, *Bottrop,* p. 69; Ronge, "Bottrop—fast eine Stadt der Oberschlesier"; and Karl Kosterhalfen, "Die polnische Bevölkerung in Rheinland und Westfalen," *Deutsche Erde,* 10. Jg. (Gotha, 1911).

14. SDR, Bd. 111.

15. Stoltenberg, *Herkunftsgebiet und Zuwanderung,* pp. 28-29.

16. *Kirche und Religion im Revier, Teil I,* p. 24.

17. Max Metzner, *Die soziale Fürsorge im Bergbau unter besonderer Berücksichtigung Preussens, Sachsens, Bayerns und Oesterreichs* (Jena, 1911), p. 56.

18. G. Mehler, "Probleme der Poleneinwanderung im rheinisch-westfälischen Industriebezirk," *Caritas,* 18. Jg., Nr. 7/8, (April/Mai, 1913), p. 193.

19. Bredt, *Die Polenfrage,* pp. 91-93.

20. Heinrich Imbusch, *Arbeitsverhältnis und Arbeiterorganisationen im deutschen Bergbau* (Essen, 1909), p. 506.

21. Wehler, "Die Polen im Ruhrgebiet," p. 453.

22. "Die Polen in Rheinland und Westfalen," *Gau "Ruhr und Lippe" des Alldeutschen Verbandes,* 10. Jg. (1900), p. 492.

228 GUESTWORKERS IN THE *REICH*

23. Hans Georg Kirchhoff, *Die staatliche Sozialpolitik im Ruhrbergbau, 1871-1914* (Köln, 1958), p. 128.

24. See Koch, *Die Bergarbeiterbewegung*, for a good, concise account of the origins of the various unions. My narrative is based on Koch unless otherwise indicated.

25. Imbusch, *Arbeitsverhältnis*, pp. 504-505, discusses the problems of a Polish-language jounral.

26. Josef Hoeffner, *Sozialpolitik im deutschen Bergbau* (Münster, 1956), p. 48.

27. "Landrat Recklinghausen an den Regierungspräsidenten, Münster," June 2, 1898 (RM Nr. 1046).

28. *Bottroper Volkszeitung*, June 25, 1898 and July 27, 1898.

29. See Wachowiak, *Die Polen*, for a detailed account of the founding of the ZZP.

30. Koch, *Die Bergarbeiterbewegung*, p. 72, and Wehler, "Die Polen im Ruhrgebiet," p. 447.

31. Wachowiak, *Die Polen*, p. 77.

32. Wehler, "Die Polen im Ruhrgebiet," p. 449. According to Metzner, *Die soziale Fürsorge*, p. 114, some Poles remained active in the *Alter Verband* and the *Gewerkverein*. Bredt, *Die Polenfrage*, p. 53, estimated the numbers as about 7,000 and 8,000 respectively.

33. *Die Polen im Rheinisch-westfälischen Steinkohlenbezirke* (München, 1901), *Tafel 3*, pp. 120-121.

34. For a thorough discussion of the *Arbeiterausschüsse* and *Sicherheitsmänner* see Adelmann, *Die soziale Betriebsverfassung*, pp. 134-152.

35. Wachowiak, *Die Polen*, p. 82, and Hans Schäfer, *Die Polenfrage im rheinisch-westfälischen Industrierevier während des Krieges und nach dem Kriege* (Dissertation, Würzburg, 1921), p. 143.

36. Adelmann, *Die soziale Betribesverfassung*, p. 147. The percentage of Poles is taken from Schulze, *Die polnische Zuwanderung*, pp. 100-103, and is for the year 1909.

37. Ronge, "Die Oberschlesiersiedlung Bottrop," p. 246; Wachowiak, *Die Polen*, pp. 38-41; Bredt, *Die Polenfrage*, p. 45.

38. Kirchhoff, *Die staatliche Sozialpolitik*, p. 51.

39. *Kirche und Religion im Revier, Teil I*, pp. 26-27.

40. Koch, *Die Bergarbeiterbewegung*, p. 72.

41. "Nachweisung. . . Bottrop, 6. Februar 1905" (RM VII-Nr. 35b).

42. This account is based on Koch, *Die Bergarbeiterbewegung,* which has made good use of the extensive sources.

43. The formal exchange of correspondence is found in Engel, "Der Bergarbeiterausstand im Ruhrbezirk im Jahre 1905," *Glückauf,* Nr. 8 (Februar, 1905), pp. 213-232.

44. "Statistik des Bergarbeiterausstand im Ruhrrevier," *Glückauf,* Nr. 20 (Mai, 1905), pp. 641-643.

45. "Landrat Recklinghausen an den RegierungsPräsidenten, Münster," February 28, 1905 (RM VII-Nr. 35b).

46. *Bottroper Volkszeitung,* February 3, 1905.

47. "Landrat Recklinghausen an den RegierungsPräsidenten, Münster," February 28, 1905 (RM VII-Nr. 35b).

48. Wachowiak, *Die Polen,* p. 71.

49. "Nachweisung. . . . Bottrop, 6. Februar 1905" (RM VII-Nr. 35b).

50. Again, see Koch, *Die Bergarbeiterbewegung,* for an account of the strike of 1912.

51. Kirchhoff, *Die staatliche Sozialpolitik,* p. 174, stresses the different nature of this strike.

52. Ibid., p. 158.

53. *Bottroper Volkszeitung,* throughout the month, but especially on March 13 and March 16, 1912.

Notes to Chapter V

1. It is assumed in this argument that the several confessions are varieties of a single general metaphysical system—specifically, in the Ruhrgebiet, Christianity.

2. Croon, "Vom Werden," p. 206, maintains that in the villages of *Kreis* Recklinghausen at the turn of the century there was a great degree of religious solidarity. For example, Catholic shopkeepers would not sell to Protestants.

3. *Kirche und Religion im Revier, Teil I,* p. 5.

4. Ibid., p. 6.

5. Ibid., pp. 6-7; and Paul Ronge, "Die polnischen Zuwanderer in das Ruhrgebiet: Stammestreue einer Minderheit," *Westfälischer Heimatkalender,* Nr. 25 (1971), unpaginated.

6. *Kirche und Religion im Revier, Teil I,* p. 37.

7. Ibid., p. 7.

8. Ibid., p. 7.

9. *Bottroper Volkszeitung,* July 18, 1885.

10. Ibid., October 7, 1886; *Kirche und Religion im Revier, Teil I,* pp. 8-9. Irregular reports from the *Landrat* Recklinghausen to the *Regierungspräsident* in Münster mentioned the absence of Polish priests in the *Kreis* and commented whenever a visiting priest made an appearance. (RM-Nr. 1043 and RM VII-Nr. 35).

11. "Landrat Recklinghausen an den Herrn RegierungsPräsident, Münster," March 24, 1898 (RM-Nr. 1046).

12. Ibid., May 2, 1898 (RM-Nr. 1046).

13. Ibid., May 15, 1898 (RM-Nr. 1046).

14. *Bottroper Volkszeitung,* May 17, 1898.

15. "Übersetzungen aus *Wiarus Polski* zu Bochum, 1898-1900," May 21, 24, and 28, 1898 (RA I-Nr. 149).

16. Ibid., July 9, 1898 (RA I-Nr. 149).

17. Rufolf Schetter, "50 Jahre Herz-Jesu-Kirche, Bottrop; 50 Jahre Kirchenchor St. Cäcilia," in *Bottroper Festschriften,* Nr. 3, 1926-1953 (Bottrop, 1952), p. 5.

18. Ibid., pp. 5-6.

19. Ibid., p. 6.

20. Ibid., pp. 6-7.

21. *Kirche und Religion im Revier, Teil I,* p. 18.

22. Ibid., pp. 30-31; "Landrat Recklinghausen an den Herrn RegierungsPräsident, Münster," May 27, 1904 (RM VII-Nr. 35b).

23. "Zahlenmässige Angaben . . . , 1904" (RA I Pa-Nr. 91).

24. Schetter, "Herz-Jesu," pp. 8-9.

25. "Uebersetzungen aus *Wiarus Polski* zu Bochum, 1902-1903," December 13 and 25, 1902 (RA I-Nr. 151).

26. "Uebersetzungen aus *Wiarus Polski* zu Bochum, 1904-1905," September 12, 1905 (RA I-Nr. 153).

27. Schetter, "Herz-Jesu," p. 26; "Zahlenmässige Angaben über das Polentum in den zum rheinisch-westfälischen Industriegebiet gehörigen Kreisen der Provinz Westfalen, 1906" (RA I Pa-Nr. 93).

28. *Bottroper Volkszeitung,* November 16, 1905.

29. "Nachweisung . . . Bottrop, 14. Februar 1911" (RM VII-Nr. 37, Bd. 3).

30. *Bottroper Volkszeitung,* November 16, 1905.

31. "Landrate Recklinghausen an den Herrn RegierungsPräsident, Münster," March 12, 1909 (RM VII-Nr. 24, Bd. 1); and February 27, 1913 (RM VII-Nr. 24, Bd. 1).

32. "Polen- und Masurenaufnahme (Umfang der Seelsorge in polnischer Sprache), 3. Januar 1913" (RM VII-Nr. 37, Bd. 1).

33. Schäfer, *Die Polenfrage. . . während des Krieges,* p. 69.

34. Ibid., p. 63.

35. Ibid., p. 69.

36. Wachowiak, *Die Polen,* p. 61.

37. Ronge, "Die polnischen Zuwanderer."

38. Schetter, "Herz-Jesu," pp. 26-28.

39. See, for example, "Uebersetzungen aus *Wiarus Polski* zu Bochum, 1898-1900," August 4, 1898 and October 20, 1900 (RA I-Nr. 149); June 1, 1901 (RA I-Nr. 150); and October 24, 1903 (RA I-Nr. 152).

40. Bredt, *Die Polenfrage,* p. 33.

41. *Bottroper Volkszeitung,* November 30, 1911.

42. These and the following figures from : "Zahlenmässige Angaben . . . , 1912" (RM VII-Nr. 37, Bd. 1).

43. W. H. Bruford, *Germany in the Eighteenth Century: The Social Background of the Literary Revival* (Cambridge, England, 1965), p. 123.

44. Landes, *The Unbound Prometheus,* p. 342.

45. Tims, *Germanizing Prussian Poland,* pp. 77-78.

46. Ibid., pp. 83-84.

47. Ibid., p. 91.

48. "Landrat Recklinghausen an den Herrn RegierungsPräsident, Münster," October 25, 1894 (RM-Nr. 1042).

49. Ibid., February 28, 1895 (RM-Nr. 1042); September 16, 1897 (RM-Nr. 1043); and July 19, 1909 (RM VII-Nr. 35a, Bd. 1).

50. "Uebersetzungen aus *Wiarus Polski* zu Bochum, 1898-1900," November 3, 1898 (RA I-Nr. 149).

51. "Uebersetzungen aus *Wiarus Polski* zu Bochum, 1902-1903," August 1902 (RA I-Nr. 151). Freely translated from the German by the author.

52. Bredt, *Die Polenfrage,* p. 75.

53. Ronge, "Die polnischen Zuwanderer."

54. This account is based on "Der Königliche Polizei-Präsident in Bochum an den Herrn Minister des Innern, Betrifft: den Winterswijk in Holland, 9. November 1913" (RM VII-Nr. 35a, Bd. 1).

55. "Landrat Recklinghausen an den Herrn RegierungsPräsident, Münster," April 20, 1914 and June 12, 1914 (RM VII-Nr. 29).
56. Ibid., June 27, 1914 (RM VII-Nr. 229).
57. Schäfer, *Die Polenfrage... während des Krieges*, p. 70.
58. Martin Dachselt, *Die Lage der fremden Minderheiten in Deutschland* (Berlin, 1929), p. 8.
59. *Bottroper Volkszeitung*, May 19, 1919.
60. "Jahresbericht des Landrates Recklinghausen an den Herrn RegierungsPräsident, Münster, 1919" (RM VII-Nr. 35).
61. Dachselt, *Die Lage der fremden Minderheiten*, pp. 8-9.
62. Ibid., pp. 9-10.
63. "Jahresbericht des Landrates Recklinghausen an den Herrn RegierungsPräsident, Münster, 1929" (RM VII-Nr. 35a, Bd. 2).
64. "Nachweisung... Bottrop, 14. Februar 1911" (RM VII-Nr. 37, Bd. 3).

Notes to Chapter VI

1. Milton M. Gordon, *Assimilation in American Life: The Role of Race, Religion and National Origins* (New York, 1964), pp. 31-32.
2. Ronge, "Bottrop—fast eine Stadt der Oberschlesier"; Bredt, *Die Polenfrage*, p. 72.
3. Chmielecki, *Die Bevölkerungs-Entwicklung, Tabelle* 30, p. 50.
4. SDR, Bd. 150 II; SDR, Bd. 240 II.
5. Ronge, "Bottrop—fast eine Stadt der Obderschlesier."
6. Chmielecki, *Die Bevölkerungs-Entwicklung, Tabelle* 30, p. 50.
7. Ibid., *Tabelle* 33, p. 53.
8. Ibid.
9. $H_0 : P_1 - P_2 = 0; Z$ 2.77.
10. $H_0 : P_1 - P_2 = 0; Z$ 2.20.
11. The confidence interval for inter-faith marriage is: $C(10.5 \leqslant p \leqslant 19.9) = .95$.
12. Helmut Croon and Kurt Utermann, *Zeche und Gemeinde: Untersuchungen über Strukturwandel einer Zechengemeinde im nördlichen Ruhrgebiet* (Tübingen, 1958), pp. 80-81.
13. See, for example, Croon and Utermann, *Zeche und Gemeinde*, pp. 80-81; and Ronge, "Die Oberschlesiersiedlung Bottrop i. W.," p. 246.

14. The confidence interval for native-in-migrant inter-marriage is:
$C(3.05 \leqslant p \leqslant 9.45) = .95$.

Notes to Chapter VII

1. Koch, *Die Bergarbeiterbewegung, Tabelle* 1, p. 139.
2. Adelmann, *Die soziale Betriebsverfassung*, p. 76.
3. Schwenger, *Die betriebliche Sozialpolitik*, p. 201.
4. Koch, *Die Bergarbeiterbewegung, Tabelle* 1, p. 139.
5. Kirchhoff, *Die staatliche Sozialpolitik*, pp. 22-24.
6. Schwenger, *Die betriebliche Sozialpolitik*, p. 202.
7. Adelmann, *Die soziale Betriebsverfassung*, pp. 162-163.
8. Kirchhoff, *Die staatliche Sozialpolitik*, p. 126.
9. Ibid.
10. Adelmann, *Die soziale Betriebsverfassung*, p. 155.
11. Ibid., pp. 156-157.
12. Kirchhoff, *Die staatliche Sozialpolitik*, pp. 160-161.
13. Adelmann, *Die soziale Betriebsverfassung*, p. 158.
14. Ibid., p. 160.
15. Kirchhoff, *Die staatliche Sozialpolitik*, pp. 164-166.
16. Ewald Oberschuir, *Die Heranziehung und Sesshaftmachung von Bergarbeitern im Ruhrkohlenbecken* (Dissertation, Aachen, 1910), p. 150.
17. Schwenger, *Die betriebliche Sozialpolitik*, p. 203.
18. Robert Hunt, *Bergarbeiter-Wohnungen im Ruhrrevier* (Dortmund, 1902), p. 4.
19. Adelmann, *Die soziale Betriebsverfassung*, p. 162.
20. Heinrichsbauer, *Industrielle Siedlung*, p. 82.
21. Schwenger, *Die betriebliche Sozialpolitik*, pp. 203-204.
22. Heinrichsbauer, *Industrielle Siedlung*, p. 82.
23. Schwenger, *Die betriebliche Sozialpolitik*, pp. 204-205.
24. Adelmann, *Die soziale Betriebsverfassung*, p. 172.
25. Heinrich Münz, *Die Lage der Bergarbeiter im Ruhrrevier* (Essen, 1909), p. 131; Heinrichsbauer, *Industrielle Siedlung*, p. 50; and Adelmann, *Die soziale Betriebsverfassung*, p. 166.
26. Heinrichsbauer, *Industrielle Siedlung*, p. 40.
27. Hundt, *Bergarbeiter-Wohnungen*, p. 25.
28. Adelmann, *Die soziale Betriebsverfassung*, p. 166.

29.   Ibid., pp. 167-169.
30.   Mehler, "Probleme der Poleneinwanderung," p. 186.
31.   Croon and Utermann, *Zeche und Gemeinde*, p. 221.
32.   Vogel, *Bottrop*, pp. 56-57.
33.   Ibid., p. 37.
34.   Adelmann, *Die soziale Betriebsverfassung*, p. 162.
35.   Vogel, *Bottrop*, p. 73.
36.   Ibid., p. 74.
37.   Ibid., pp. 75-76.
38.   Ibid., p. 84.
39.   Ibid., pp. 80-81.
40.   Ibid., pp. 85-88.
41.   ˙ The following tables include the in-migrants from the sample, their adult children (20 yrs. or older), and the spouses of both generations. This group is the in-migrant-generated population.
42.   Vogel, *Bottrop, Karte* 14.
43.   *Bottroper Volkszeitung*, February 3, 1905.
44. $H_0 : P_1 - P_2 = 0$; for out-migration $Z = 2.18$
           for inter-district movement $Z = .062$.
           for intra-district movement $Z = 0.68$
           for stability $Z = 2.01$.
45. $H_0 : P_1 - P_2 = 0$; $Z = 2.33$.
46.   *Adressbuch* Bottrop 1930.
47. $H_0 : P_1 - P_2 = 0$; for out-migration $Z = 0.28$.
           for inter-district movement $Z = 0.80$.
           for intra-district movement $Z = 1.04$.
           for stability $Z = 1.4$.
48. $H_0 : P_1 - P_2 = 0$; for out-migration $Z = 2.07$.
           for inter-district movement $Z = 3.7$.
           for intra-district movement $Z = 4.24$.
           for stability $Z = 7.65$.

Notes to Chapter VIII

1.   Wachowiak, *Die Polen*, p. 61.
2.   Koch, *Die Bergarbeiterbewegung*, pp. 68-69.
3.   Ibid., pp. 69-70; and Wehler, "Die Polen im Ruhrgebiet," pp. 445-447.
4.   Wachowiak, *Die Polen*, p. 64.
5.   Koch, *Die Bergarbeiterbewegung*, p. 71; and Wehler, "Die Polen

im Ruhrgebiet," p. 447.

6. Ronge, "Die polnischen Zuwanderer."

7. Koch, *Die Bergarbeiterbewegung,* p. 71.

8. Bredt, *Die Polenfrage,* pp. 30-31; Kaczmarek, *Die polnischen Arbeiter,* p. 37; and Koch, *Die Bergarbeiterbewegung,* p. 71.

9. Wachowiak, *Die Polen,* pp. 61-62. A police report of a meeting of religious *Vereine* in *Amt* Recklinghausen in October of 1906 makes clear the orientation of this group. "Bericht über die 7.10.06 Polenversammlung der Vorsitzenden der in der Diözese Münster bestehenden polnischen Kirchenverein" (AR–Nr. 1722).

10. "Zahlenmässige Angaben . . . , 1912" (RM VII-Nr. 37, Bd. 1).

11. Ludwig Bernhard, *Das polnische Gemeinwesen,* p. 183.

12. Wehler, "Die Polen im Ruhrgebiet," footnote, p. 557.

13. "Wir wollen uns verständigen, um alle dem gemeinsam Ziel entgegenzustreben, nämlich der Erhaltung des Glaubens, der Sprache unser Väter, sowie der Hebung der ganzen polnischen Gemeinwesens in der Fremde in moralischer und materieller Beziehung durch Arbeit und Aufklärung." "Der Königlich Polizei-Präsident im Bochum an den Herrn Minister des Innern, Berlin, den 9. November, 1913. Betrifft: den *Polentag* in Winterswijk in Holland" (RM VII-Nr. 35a, Bd. 1).

14. *"Polentag".*

15. Schäfer, *Die Polenfrage . . . während des Krieges,* p. 6.

16. *Kirche und Religion im Revier, Teil II,* p. 45.

17. Ibid., pp. 43-45.

18. Ibid., pp. 50-52.

19. Franke, *Die polnische Volksgruppe,* pp. 50-51.

20. Ibid., p. 52.

21. Ibid., p. 162.

22. Ibid., p. 163.

23. *Kirche und Religion im Revier, Teil I,* pp. 12-14.

24. *Bottroper Volkszeitung,* November 30, 1886 and December 25, 1886.

25. *Kirche und Religion im Revier, Teil I,* pp. 14-15.

26. "Amtmann Bottrop an den Landrat Recklinghausen," June 28, 1897 (RM-Nr. 1043); "Landrat Recklinghausen an den Herrn Regierungs-Präsident, Münster," June 30, 1897 (RM-Nr. 1043); "Amtmann Bottrop an den Landrat Recklinghausen," November 7, 1897 (RM-Nr. 1043); and "Landrat Recklinghausen an den Herrn RegierungsPräsident, Münster," November 13, 1897 (RM-Nr. 1043).

27. *Kirche und Religion im Revier, Teil I*, p. 27.

28. Ibid., p. 20.

29. "Nachweisung . . . Bottrop, 14. Februar 1911" (RM-Nr. 37, Bd. 3).

30. "Nachweisung über die vorhandenen polnisches Vereine, Amtsbezirk Bottrop, o.J." (RM VII-Nr. 340, Bd. 2).

31. "Nachwisung über die vorhandenen polnischen Vereine, Amtsbezirk Bottrop, 30. März 1927" (RM VII-Nr. 35a, Bd. 2).

32. "den polnischen St. Barbara Knappenverein zu Bottrop" (RM VII-Nr. 248); "den katholischen St. Hyacinth Polenverein zu Bottrop" (RM VII-Nr. 228); "den polnischen Knappenverein St. Stanislaus-Kostka zu Boyer, Amt Bottrop" (RM VII-Nr. 247); "den Polenverein St. Adalbert in Bottrop" (RM VII-Nr. 231); "den polnischen Gesangsverein Cäcilia in Bottrop" (RM VII-Nr. 242); "den St. Marien Polenverein in Bottrop" (RM VII-Nr. 244); "den polnischen Verein St. Stanislaus-Kostka in Bottrop" (RM VII-Nr. 246); "polnisch-katholischer St. Josefs Verein zu Bottrop" (RM VII-Nr. 234); "den polnischen St. Barbara Knappenverein im Bezirk der St. Michaelskirche in Bottrop" (RM VII-Nr. 230).

33. Ibid.

34. "Landrat Recklinghausen an den Herrn RegierungsPräsident Münster," December 14, 1894 (RM-Nr. 1042).

35. *Kirche und Religion im Revier, Teil I*, p. 21; and Ronge, "Die polnischen Zuwanderer".

36. "Amtmann Bottrop an den Landrat Recklinghausen," June 28, 1897 (RM VII-Nr. 1042).

37. "Landrat Recklinghausen an den Herrn RegierungsPräsident, Münster," November 13, 1897 (RM VII-Nr. 1043).

38. See, for example, "Knappenverein St. Stanislaus-Kostka"; and "Uebersetzungen aus *Wiarus Polski* zu Bochum, 1900-1902," February 7, 1901 (RA I-Nr. 150).

39. *Kirche und Religion im Revier, Teil I*, pp. 18-20.

40. "Uebersetzungen aus *Wiarus Polski* zu Bochum, 1900-1902," November 7, 1901 (RA I-Nr. 150).

41. "Uebersetzungen aus *Wiarus Polski* zu Bochum, 1903-1904," December 29, 1903 (RA I-Nr. 152).

42. "Polizeibericht über eine Versammlung des polnischen Berufsvereins zu Borbeck am 28.4.1907" (RD-Nr. 15911, Bl. 81-84).

43. "Nachweisung . . . , Amtsbezirk Bottrop, 30, März 1927" (RM VII-Nr. 35a, Bd. 2).

44. "den polnischen Verein Sparsamkeit in Bottrop" (RM VII-Nr. 226); "Nachweisung... Bottrop, 14. Februar 1911" (RM VII-Nr. 37, Bd. 3).

45. "Verein polnischer Kaufleute und Industrieller in Bottrop" (RM VII-Nr. 240).

46. "Königlich Polizei-Präsident in Bochum an den Herrn Regierungs-Präsident, Arnsberg, 25. November 1913" (RM VII-Nr. 33).

47. Ibid., "1. December 1909" (RM VII-Nr. 33).

48. Ibid., "25. November 1913" (RM VII-Nr. 33).

49. "den Polenverein Maria Königin der Polnischer Krone in Bottrop" (RM VII-Nr. 229); "Polinnenverein in Bottrop Eigen" (RM VII-Nr. 233).

50. "den polnischen Gesangsverein Wanda in Bottrop" (RM VII-Nr. 237); "den polnischen Verein Wyspiański zu Bottrop" (RM VII-Nr. 241); "den polnischen Musikverein Lutnia in Bottrop" (RM VII-Nr. 245); and "polnischen Gesangsverein Nowowiejski (Neudorf) Bottrop" (RM VII-Nr. 252).

51. "den polnischen Sokółverein in Bottrop" (RM VII-Nr. 238); and "Turnverein Sokół (Falke) II in Bottrop-Eigen" (RM VII-Nr. 251).

52. "Zahlenmässige Angaben..., 1912" (RM VII-Nr. 37, Bd. 1).

53. Wehler, "Die Polen im Ruhrgebiet," p. 446. A police report from Wanne in 1905 characterized them as the "erste polnische Armee". Koch, *Die Bergarbeiterbewegung*, footnote, p. 74.

54. Schäfer, *Die Polenfrage... während des Krieges*, p. 91.

55. *Bottroper Volkszeitung*, July 29, 1898.

56. *Kirche und Religion im Revier, Teil II*, p. 49.

57. *Bottroper Volkszeitung*, August 3, 1914.

58. Schetter, "Herz-Jesu," pp. 45-46.

59. Fritz Specht and Paul Schwabe, *Die Reichstags-Wahlen von 1867 bis 1903* (Berlin, 1904), pp. 319-322.

60. Bredt, *Die Polenfrage*, p. 30.

61. Bernhard, *Das polnische Gemeinwesen*, pp. 186-187.

62. "Uebersetzungen aus *Wiarus Polski* zu Bochum, 1898-1900," June 7, 14 and 21, 1898 (RA I-Nr. 149).

63. Bredt, *Die Polenfrage*, pp. 38-39.

64. Wehler, *Sozialdemokratie und Nationalstaat*, p. 184.

65. "Verein der polnisch-Sozialistischen Partei für Bottrop und Umgegend" (RM VII-Nr. 27).

66. "Nachweisung...Bottrop, 14. Februar 1911" (RM VII-Nr. 37, Bd. 3); and "Nachweisung der polnischen Vereine im Landkreis Recklinghausen, 1920" (RM VII-Nr. 340, Bd. 3).

67. "Bekanntmachung von 18.11.1902—der Amtmann, Bottrop" (AAB AI2-Nr. 13); "Bekanntmachung von 25.9.1909—der Amtmann, Bottrop" (AAB A12-Nr. 14); "Wahl der Gemeindeverordneten, 1903" (AAB AI2-Nr. 14).

68. *Bottroper Volkszeitung*, November, 1901; "Wahl der Gemeindeverordneten, 1903, 1905, 1906, 1907 and 1909" (AAB AI2-Nr. 14).

69. "den polnischen Wahlverein in Bottrop-Eigne" (RM VII-Nr. 249); and "den polnischen Wahlverein Bottrop" (RM VII-Nr. 250).

70. *Bottroper Volkszeitung*, November 23 and 24, 1911.

71. "Wahl der Gemeinderverordneten, 1911" (AAB AI2-Nr. 14).

72. *Bottroper Volkszeitung*, November 28, 29 and 30, 1911 and December 1, 1911.

73. Ibid., November 11, 15 and 18, 1913.

74. Ibid., November 18, 20, 22 and 24, 1913.

75. Ibid., December 10, 12, 13 and 15, 1913.

76. "Bottrop Polizeiverwaltung an die Polizei-Direktion, Bochum, 16. Dezember 1913" (AAB AI2-Nr. 14).

77. "Wahl der Gemeinderverordneten, 1913" (AAB AI2-Nr. 14).

78. "Landrat Recklinghausen an den Amtmann Bottrop," October 5, 1915 (AAB AI2-Nr. 14); *Bottroper Volkszeitung*, November 18, 1915; "Wahl der Gemeindeverordneten, 1915" (AAB AI2-Nr. 14); "Minister des Innern an den Landrat Recklinghausen," November 6, 1916 (AAB AI2-Nr. 14).

79. *Bottroper Volkszeitung*, January 20, 1919.

80. Schäfer, *Die Polenfrage... während des Krieges*, pp. 59-61.

81. *Bottroper Volkszeitung*, March, 1919.

82. Ibid., February 21, 1921.

83. *Bottroper Anzeiger*, May 6, 1924.

84. *Bottroper Volkszeitung*, May 5, 1924 and November 18, 1929.

85. Ibid., March 13, 1933; and Hans Nocon, "Die Ereignisse in Bottrop vom Tage der Machtübernahme bis zur Einführung der neuen Gemeindeordnung," in *Vestisches Jahrbuch*, 60. Band (1958), p. 122.

86. "Sitzung der Gemeinderat vom 15.1.1934" (AAB CI1-Nr. 15).

Notes to Chapter IX

1. "Polizei-Verwaltung/Bürgermeister, Bottrop an den Herrn RegierungsPräsident, Münster, 14. Mai 1921" (RM VII-Nr. 35a, Bd.1).

2. "RegierungsPräsident Münster an den Herrn Minister des Innern, 23. Mai 1921" (RM VII-Nr. 35a, Bd. 1).

3. Franke, *Die polnische Volksgruppe,* pp. 16-17.

4. Sarah Wambaugh, *Plebiscites Since the World War with a Collection of Official Documents,* Vol. I (Washington, 1933), quotation in footnote, p. 16.

5. An account of the General Staff's involvement in the scheme is found in Gordon A. Craig, *The Politics of the Prussian Army* (New York, 1964), pp. 313-316.

6. Wambaugh, *Plebiscites,* p. 103 and pp. 212-213.

7. The German reaction to the draft is narrated in S. William Halperin, *Germany Tried Democracy* (New York, 1946), pp. 137-153.

8. Wambaugh, *Plebiscites,* pp. 216-217.

9. SR, "Wirtschaft und Statistik, Sonderheft 2," 5. Jg. (Berlin, 1925), p. 71.

10. PSL, "Schlesien nach der Teilung" (Berlin, 1924), p. 15.

11. Wambaugh, *Plebiscites,* pp. 211-212.

12. Article 88 Section 2 and Section 4 are quoted in "Schlesien nach der Teilung," pp. 10-11.

13. Wambaugh, *Plebiscites,* p. 241.

14. Ibid., p. 219.

15. Ibid., pp. 219-220.

16. Ibid., p. 222.

17. Ibid., p. 236.

18. Ibid., pp. 236-238.

19. Ibid., pp. 133-134.

20. "Die Polenbewegung, 1919/1920" (RM VII-Nr. 35).

21. *Bottroper Volkszeitung,* January 28, 1921 and February 8, 1921.

22. Wambaugh, *Plebiscites,* p. 250.

23. *Für ein ungeteiltes Oberschlesien* (Kattowitz, 1921), p. 21.

24. *Bottroper Volkszeitung,* March 18, 1921.

25. Wambaugh, *Plebiscites,* pp. 258-259.

26. Ibid., pp. 253-254.

27. *Bottroper Volkszeitung,* April 8, 1921.

28.   Wambaugh, *Plebiscites,* pp. 258-259.

29.   *Bottroper Volkszeitung,* October 17 and 19, 1921.

30.   Franke, *Die polnische Volksgruppe,* pp. 15-16; Schäfer, *Die Polen-frage . . . während des Krieges,* p. 56; SDR, Bd. 401, p. 537.

31.   Brepohl, *Der Aufbau,* p. 143.

32.   "Polizei-Verwaltung Bottrop an den Landrat Recklinghausen," July 17, 1920 (RM VII-Nr. 35a, Bd. 1) mentions some in-migration by foreigners, but does not mention Poles. Its report of October 27, 1920 notes that a few Poles have entered the city, probably to avoid the Russo-Polish war.

33.   AbB, 1920; JSB, Br. 2 and Nr. 3.

34.   See, for example, Croon and Utermann, *Zeche und Gemeinde,* pp. 35-36; and Eberhard Franke, "Einbürgerungen und Namenänderungen im Ruhrgebiet," in *Westfälische Forschungen,* 2. Bd. (1939), footnote, p. 24.

35.   Wolfgang Schumann, *Oberschlesien, 1918/19,* (Berlin, DDR, 1961), footnote, p. 150.

36.   "Polizei-Verwaltung/Bürgermeister, Bottrop an den Regierungs-Präsident, Münster," January 26, 1920 (RM VII-Nr. 35a, Bd. 1).

37.   Ibid.

38.   Schäfer, *Die Polenfrage . . . während des Krieges,* p. 55.

39.   "Die Polenbewegung, 1919/1920".

40.   Wambaugh, *Plebiscites,* p. 134.

41.   Ibid., p. 250.

42. $H_0 : P_1 - P_2 = 0 \quad Z = 6.54$.

43. $H_0 : P_1 - P_2 = 0 \quad Z = 6.49$.

Notes to Chapter X

1.   Gordon, *Assimilation in American Life,* p. 71.

2.   Ibid., pp. 71-72.

3.   Ibid., pp. 158-159.

4.   Croon and Utermann, *Zeche und Gemeinde,* pp. 96-99, noted that in the community that was the subject of their study the "old families" had almost all disappeared by the 1950s.

5.   Vogel, *Bottrop,* pp. 51-52.

6.   By way of comparison, Brepohl, *Der Aufbau,* pp. 42-43, writes that in the Ruhr valley in the eighteenth century in-migrant miners from Saxony and Thuringia were viewed as "foreigners" by natives of the area, and that—at least in the beginning—relations between the two groups were not good.

BIBLIOGRAPHY

Unpublished Archival Material

Staatsarchiv, Münster

Regierung Münster (RM)

VII – Nr. 17, Bd. 1–betreffend: Streiks während des Krieges, 18.8.16-14.11.17.

VII – Nr. 17, Bd. 2–betreffend: Streiks während des Krieges, 10.1.18-11.3.19.

VII – Nr. 23, Bd. 1–betreffend: polnische Vereine, Teilnahme der Polen an Versammlungen, öffentlichen Aufzügen und kirchlichen Prozessionen, 1892-1918.

VII – Nr. 23, Bd. 2–betreffend: polnische Vereine, Teilnahme der Polen an Versammlungen öffentlich Aufzügen und kirchlichen Porzessionen, o. J.

VII – Nr. 24, Bd. 1–betreffend: polnische Geistliche, Seelsorge und Gottesdienst, 1893-1909.

VII – Nr. 24, Bd. 2–betreffend: polnische Geistliche, Seelsorge und Gottsdienst, 1903-1914.

VII – Nr. 26–betreffend: polnisch-sozialdemokratische Partei für Rheinland und Westfalen, 1908-1914.

VII – Nr. 27–betreffend: polnisch-sozialdemokratische Partei im Regierungsberzirk Münster, 1908-1912.

VII – Nr. 29–betreffend: polnische Agitation unter den Frauen, 1.1.14.

VII – Nr. 30–betreffend: Polen-Bibliothekwesen, 1914.

VII – Nr. 33–betreffend: polnische finanzielle und sonstige gewerbliche Unternehmungen, o. J.

VII   — Nr. 340, Bd. 2—betreffend: Nachwisung der polnischen Vereine, ohne Jahrgang.

VII   — Nr. 340, Bd. 3—betreffend: Nachweisung der polnischen Vereine im Landkreis Recklinghausen, 1920.

VII   — Nr. 35—betreffend: Polen-Allgemeines, 1890-1931.

VII   — Nr. 35a, Bd. 1—betreffend: Polenbewegung, 1908-1921.

VII   — Nr. 35a, Bd. 2—betreffend: Polen, 1924-1935.

VII   — Nr. 35b—betreffend: Polen, 1904-1905.

VII   — Nr. 36, Bd. 3—betreffend: polnische Zeitungen, Druckschriften und Gegenagitationsschriften, o. J.

VII   — Nr. 36b—betreffend: angebliche Verfolgung und Misslandlung von Polen, 1921.

VII   — Nr. 37, Bd. 1—betreffend: Polenstatistik, 1908-1920.

VII   — Nr. 37, Bd. 2—betreffend: Polenstatistik, 1902-1921.

VII   — Nr. 37, Bd. 3—betreffend: Polenstatistik, 1910.

VII   — Nr. 225—betreffend: polnische Jugund-bezw. Jünglingsvereine in Bottrop-Eigen, 21.8.17.

VII   — Nr. 226—betreffend: den polnischen Verein "Sparsamkeit-Polenverein" in Bottrop, 13.5.10.

VII   — Nr. 227—betreffend: den polnisch-katholischen Verein "Einigkeit" in Bottrop, 1907.

VII   — Nr. 228—betreffend: den katholischen St. Hayacinth Polenverein zu Bottrop, 1901.

VII   — Nr. 229—betreffend: den Polenverein "Maria Königin der Polnischen Krone" in Bottrop, 11.4.14.

VII   — Nr. 230—betreffend: den polnischen St. Barbara Knappenverein im Bezirk der St. Michaelskirche in Bottrop, 1914.

VII   — Nr. 231—betreffend: den Polenverein "St. Adalbert"—"Wojcziecha" in Bottrop, 1906.

VII   — Nr. 232—betreffend: den polnischen Dilettantenklub "Polonia" in Bottrop-Eigen, 1.1.10.

VII   — Nr. 233—betreffend: Polinnenverein in Bottrop-Eigen, 26.3.14.

VII   — Nr. 234—betreffend: polnisch-katholischen "St. Josefs Verein" zu Bottrop, 14.3.14.

VII   — Nr. 235—betreffend: den polnischen Killettantenverein "Gwiazda" (Stern) in Bottrop, 1907.

VII   — Nr. 236—betreffend: den polnischen Verein "Straż" in Bottrop.

VII — Nr. 237–betreffend: den polnischen Gesangsverein "Wanda" in Bottrop, 1.6.10.

VII — Nr. 238–betreffend: den polnischen Sokółverein in Bottrop, 1906.

VII — Nr. 239–betreffend: Polenverein "Wyzwolenie" (Bekämpfung des Alkoholismus) Bottrop, 1906.

VII — Nr. 240–betreffend: Verein polnischer Kaufleute und Industrieller in Bottrop, 1906.

VII — Nr. 241–betreffend: den polnischen Verein "Wyspiański" zu Bottrop, 1908.

VII — Nr. 242–betreffend: den polnischen Gesangsverein "Cäcilia" in Bottrop, 12.7.08.

VII — Nr. 243–betreffend: den polnischen Verein "Komitee zur Einrichtung eines Vereinshauses" in Bottrop, 1907.

VII — Nr. 244–betreffend: den St. Marien Polenverein in Bottrop, 1909.

VII — Nr. 245–betreffend: den polnischen Musikverein "Lutnia" in Bottrop, 1910.

VII — Nr. 246–betreffend: den polnischen Verein St. Stanislaus-Kostka in Bottrop, 1910.

VII — Nr. 247–betreffend: den polnischen Knappenverein St. Stanislaus-Kostka zu Boyer, Amt Bottrop, 1901-1903.

VII — Nr. 248–betreffend: den polnischen St. Barbara Knappenverein zu Bottrop, 1901-1911.

VII — Nr. 249–betreffend: den polnischen Wahlverein in Bottrop-Eigen.

VII — Nr. 250–betreffend: den polnischen Wahlverein in Bottrop, 4.7.11.

VII — Nr. 251–betreffend: Turnverein "Sokół" (Falke) II in Bottrop-Eigen, 16.10.13.

VII — Nr. 252–betreffend: polnischen Gesangsverein "Nowowiejski" (Neudorf) Bottrop, 26.2.14.

VII — Nr. 288–betreffend: politisch unsichere Personen deutscher Staatsangehörigkeit, 1913-1914.

Nr. 1042–betreffend: Auflösung der polnischen Studentenvereine, Bund der Polen, 1886-1895.

Nr. 1043–betreffend: Auflösung der polnischen Studentenvereine, Bund der Polen, 1895-1897.

Nr. 1046–betreffend: Auflösung der polnischen Studentenvereine, Bund der Polen, 1898-1899.

Regierung Arnsberg (RA)

I Pa — Nr. 91—betreffend: die im Regierungsbezirke Arnsberg vorhandenen Polenvereine und die in anderen Regierungsbezirken vorhandenen Polenvereine, 1905-1907.

I Pa — Nr. 93—betreffend: die im Regierungsbezirke Arnsberg vorhandenen Polenvereine und die in anderen Regierungsbezirken vorhandenen Polenvereine, 1908.

I — Nr. 149—betreffend: Uebersetzungen aus "Wiarus Polski" zu Bochum, 1898-1900.

I — Nr. 150—betreffend: Uebersetzungen aus "Wiarus Polski" zu Bochum, 1900-1902.

I — Nr. 151—betreffend: Uebersetzungen aus "Wiarus Polski" zu Bochum, 1902-1903.

I — Nr. 152—betreffend: Uebersetzungen aus "Wiarus Polski" zu Bochum, 1903-1904.

I — Nr. 153—betreffend: Uebersetzungen aus "Wiarus Polski" zu Bochum, 1904-1905.

I — Nr. 154—betreffend: Uebersetzungen aus "Wiarus Polski" zu Bochuj, 1906-1907.

Acta des Amtes Bottrop (AAB)

AI1 — Nr. 21—betreffend: Wahlen für das Haus der Abgeordneten, Angefangen 1913.

AI1 — Nr. 22—über Wahlen zur National Landesversammlung, Angefangen, 1918.

AI2 — Nr. 13—betreffend: Gemeindewahlen im Allgemeines, Angefangen 1900—Geschlossen 1920.

AI2 — Nr. 14—betreffend: Wahl der Gemeindeverordneten, Angefangen 1903—Geschlossen 1920.

CI1 — Nr. 13—Protokollbuch der Stadtverordnetenversammlung von 17. 12.29 bis 14.12.33.

CI1 — Nr. 15—Sitzungen der Gemeinderäte vom 15.1.1934 bis 9.12.1935.

Polizeibericht über eine Versammlung des polnischen Berufsvereins zu Borbeck am 28.4.1907. Reproduced from Staatsarchiv Düsseldorf (Nr. 15911—Bl. 81-84).

Akten des Einwohnermeldeamtes, Bottrop: 1891-1920 (microfilm), (AEB).

Akten des Standesamtes, Bottrop: Eheregister, 1874-1939, (ASB).

Amt Recklinghausen (AR)
Nr. 1719—betreffend: Staatsangehörigkeit, Ein- und Auswanderung, Consulate und Verkehr mit denselben Impfwesen, 1895-1925.
Nr. 1720—betreffend: Staatsangehörigkeit, Ein- und Auswanderung. Auswanderungsagenten, 1918-1923.
Nr. 1722—betreffend: Polenbewegung, 1902-1907.
Nr. 1723—betreffend: Polenbewegung, 1907-1912.

Government Publications

Adressbuch für die Gemeinde Bottrop, 1911 (AbB). Bottrop. Gebr. Klanten, 1911.
Adressbuch der Stadt Bottrop, 1920 (AbB). Bottrop: Gebr. Klanten, 1920.
Adressbuch der Stadt Bottrop, 1930/31 (AbB). Bottrop: Wilhelm Postberg, 1930.
Adressbuch der Stadt Bottrop, 1953 (AbB). Bottrop: Wilhelm Postberg, 1953.
Jahrbuch der Stadt Bottrop, I-XI, 1920-1937 (JSB). Bottrop: Wilhelm Postberg, 1920-1937.
Königliches Statistischen Landesamt. "Die Polen im Westlichen Preussen 1905," by Max Broesike. Zeitschrift des Königlich Preussischen Statistischen Landesamts, 48er Jahrgang (1908): 251-274.
_____. "Die oberschlesien Polen 1905," by Max Broesike. Zeitschrift des Königlich Preussischen Statistischen Landesamts, 49er Jahrgang (1909): 25-62.
Preussisches Statistisches Landesmat. Schlesien nach der Teilung. Berlin: Verlag des Preussischen Statistischen Landesamt, 1924.
Statistisches Reichsamt. Statistik des Deutschen Reichs.
_____. Statistisches Jahrbuch für das Deutsche Reich.
_____. Vierteljahrsheft zur Statistik des Deutschen Reichs.
_____. Wirtschaft und Statistik, Sonderheft, 2. 5. Jg. (Berlin, 1925).

Secondary Sources

Books

Adelmann, Gerhard. Die soziale Betriebsverfassung des Ruhrbergbaus vom Anfang des 19. Jahrhunderts bis zum Ersten Weltkrieg unter besonderer Berücksichtigung des Industrie- und Handelskammerbezirks Essen. Bonn: Ludwig Röhrscheid Verlag, 1962.

Andrews, Frank M., and Messenger, Robert C. Multivariate Nominal Scale Analysis: A Report on a New Analysis Technique and a Computer Program. Ann Arbor, 1973.

Aurand, Harold W. From the Molly Maguires to the United Mine Workers: The Social Ecoology of an Industrial Union, 1869-1897. Philadelphia: Temple University Press, 1971.

Bernhard, Ludwig. Das polnische Gemeinwesen im preussischen Staat: Die Polenfrage. Leipzig: Duncker und Humbolt, 1907.

Berry, Brewton. Race Relations. Boston: Houghton Mifflin Co., 1951.

Beusch, Paul. Wanderungen und Stadtkultur: Eine bevölkerungpolitische und sozial-ethische Studie. München-Gladbach: Volksvereins Verlag GmbH, 1916.

Blalock, Hubert M. Jr. Social Statistics, 2nd ed. New York: McGraw-Hill, 1972.

Bredt, Johann Victor. Die Polenfrage im Ruhrkohlengebiet. Leipzig: Duncker und Humbolt, 1909.

Brepohl, Wilhelm. Der Aufbau des Ruhrvolkes im Zuge der Ost-West- Wanderung. Recklinghausen: Verlag Bitter und Co., 1948.

—————. Industrievolk im Wandel von agraren zur industriellen Daseinfrom dargestellt am Ruhrgebiet. Tübingen: J.C.B. Mohr, 1957.

Bruford, W. H. Germany in the Eighteenth Century: The Social Background of the Literary Revival. Cambridge: Cambridge University Press; paperback, 1965.

Clapham, John H. The Economic Development of France and Germany, 1815-1914. 3rd ed. Cambridge: Cambridge University Press, 1961.

Craig, Gordon A. The Politics of the Prussian Army, 1640-1945. New York: Oxford University Press; Galaxy Books, 1964.

Croon, Helmuth. "Vom Werden des Ruhrgebiets." In Rheinisch Westfälische Rückblende, Bd. I. Edited by Walter Först. Köln und Berlin: Beiträge zur neueren Landesgeschichte des Rheinlands und Westfalens, 1967.

Croon, Helmuth and Utermann, Kurt. Zeche und Gemeinde: Untersuchungen über den Strukturwandel einer Zechengemeinde im nördlichen Ruhrgebiet. Tübingen: J.C.B. Mohr, 1958.

Dachselt, Martin. Die Lage der fremden Minderheiten in Deutschland. Berlin: Carl Heymanns Verlag, 1929.

Dahrendorf, Ralf. Society and Democracy in Germany. New York; Doubleday and Company, Inc.; Anchor Books, 1969.

Denkschrift zur Erinnerung an das 50 jährige Bestehen der Arenberg'schen Actien-Gesellschaft für Bergbau und Hüttenbetrieb zu Essen (Ruhr). Düsseldorf: August Bagel, 1906.

Dolan, Jay P. The Immigrant Church: New York's Irish and German Catholics, 1815-1865. Batlimore: Johns Hopkins University Press, 1975.

Esslingen, Dean R. Immigrants and the City: Ethnicity and Mobility in a Nineteenth Century Midwestern Community. Port Washington, New York: Kennikat Press, 1975.

Franke, Eberhard. "Einbürgerungen und Namenänderungen im Ruhrgebiet." In Westfälische Forschungen, pp. 19-28. Münster: Aschendorffische Verlagsbuchhandlung, 1939.

——————. Die polnische Volksgruppe im Ruhrgebiet, 1870-1940. Essen: By the author, 1940.

Gau "Ruhr und Lippe" des Alldeutschen Verbandes. Die Polen im Rheinisch-Westfälischen Steinkohlen-Bezirk. München: Gau "Ruhr und Lippe" des Alldeutschen Verbandes, 1901.

Gordon, Milton M. Assimilation in American Life: The Role of Race, Religion, and National Origins. New York: Oxford University Press, 1964.

Green, Arnold. Sociology, An Analysis of Life In Modern Society. New York: McGraw-Hill Book Co., 1952.

Greene, Victor R. The Slavic Community on Strike: Immigrant Labor in Pennsylvania Anthracite. Notre Dame, Indiana: University of Notre Dame University Press, 1968.

Halperin, S. William. Germany Tried Democracy: A Political History of the Reich from 1918 to 1933. New York: W. W. Norton and Company, Inc.; The Norton Library, 1946.

Heinrichsbauer, August. Industrielle Siedlung im Ruhrgebiet im Vergangenheit, Gegenwart und Zukunft. Essen: Verlag Glückauf GmbH, 1936.

Henderson, William O. The State and the Industrial Revolution in Prussia, 1740-1870. Liverpool: Liverpool University Press, 1967.

Hoeffner, Josef. Sozialpolitik im deutschen Bergbau. Münster, 1956.

Hue, Otto. Die Bergarbeiter: Historische Darstellung der Bergarbeiter Verhältnisse von der ältesten bis in der neusten Zeit. Bd. 2. Stuttgart: Verlag J.H.W. Dietz Nachf. GmbH, 1913.

Hundt, Robert. Bergarbeiter-Wohnungen im Ruhrrevier. Dortmund: Verein für die bergbaulichen Interessen im Oberbergamtsbezirk Dortmund, 1902.

Imbusch, Heinrich. Arbeitsverhältnis und Arbeiterorganisationen im deutschen Bergbau. Essen: Verlag des Gewerkvereins christlicher Bergarbeiter, 1909.

Jantke, Carl. Bergmann und Zeche: Die sozialen Arbeitsverhältnisse einer Schachtanlage des nördlichen Ruhrgebiets in der Sicht der Bergleute. Tübingen: J.C.B. Mohr, 1953.

Kantowicz, Edward R. Polish-American Politics in Chicago, 1888-1940. Chicago: University of Chicago Press, 1975.

Kitchhoff, Hans Georg. Die staatliche Sozialpolitik im Ruhrbergbau, 1871-1914. Köln und Opladen, 1958.

Kirchliche Sozialforschung im Sozialinstitut des Bistums Essen. Kirche und Religion im Revier: Beiträge und Quellen zur Geschichte religiöser und kirchlicher Verhältnisse im Werden und Wandel des Ruhrgebiets. Essen: Kirchliche Sozialforschung im Sozialinstitut des Bistums Essen, 1968.

Kleßmann, Christoph. Polnische Bergarbeiter im Ruhrgebiet, 1870-1954. Soziale Integration und nationale subkultur einer Minderheit in der deutschen Industriegesellschaft. Göttingen: Vandenhoeck and Ruprecht, 1978.

Koch, Max Jürgen. Die Bergarbeiterbewegung im Ruhrgebiet zur Zeit Wilhelms II., 1889-1914. Düsseldorf: Droste Verlag, 1954.

Landes, David S. The Unbound Prometheus. Cambridge: Cambridge University Press; paperback, 1969.

Leonhard, Rudolf. Zur Soziologie des Polentums. Stuttgart: Verlag von Ferdinand Enke, 1911.

Lipset, Seymour Martin and Bendix, Reinhard. Social Mobility in Industrial Society. Berkeley: University of California Press, 1959.

Metzner, Max. Die soziale Fürsorge im Bergbau unter besonderer Berücksichtigung Preussins, Sachsens, Bayerns und Oesterreichs. Jena: Verlag von Gustav Fischer, 1911.

Münz, Heinrich. Die Lage der Bergarbeiter im Ruhrrevier. Essen: G. D. Baedeker, 1909.

Nocon, Hans. "Die Ereignisse im Bottrop vom Tage der Machtübernahme bis zur Einführung der neuen Gemeinderordnung." In Vestisches Jahrbuch, 60. Bd. Recklinghausen: Verlagsdruckerei Bongers, 1958.

Pounds, Norman. The Ruhr: A Study in Historical and Economic Geography. London: Faber and Faber, 1952.

————. The Upper Silesian Industrial Region. Bloomington, Indiana: Indiana University Publications, 1958.

Pressestelle des Verbandes heimattreuer Oberschlesier. Für ein ungeteiltes Oberschlesien: Oberschlesien muss bei Deutschland bleiben. Kattowitz: Selbstverlag, 1921.

Reekers, Stephanie. Westfalens Bevölkerung, 1818-1955. Münster: Aschendorffische Verlagsbuchhandlung, 1956.

Rosenblum, Gerald. Immigrant Workers: Their Impact on American Labor Radicalism. New York: Basic Books, 1973.

Schetter, Rudolf. "Von Bottrops Werden und Geschichte." In Festschrift zur Großstadtwerdung Bottrops. Edited by Dr. Rudolf Schetter. Bottrop: Herausgegeben und bearbeitet im Auftrage des Rates der Stadt von Dr. Rudolf Schetter, 1953.

————. "50 Jahre Herz-Jesu-Kirche Bottrop." In Bottroper Festschriften, Nr. 3, 1926-1953. Edited by Dr. Rudolf Schetter. Bottrop: Wilhelm Postberg, 1952.

Schmidt-Breilmann, A. "Der Einfluss der Industrialisierung auf das Handwerk, Untersuchung über die Auswirkung des Kohlenbergbaus im Raum Recklinghausen." In Vestiches Jahrbuch, 55. Bd. Recklinghausen: Verlagsdruckerei Bonges, 1953.

Schreiber, Georg. Der Bergbau in Geschichte, Ethos und Sakrakkultur. Köln und Opladen: Westdeutscher Verlag, 1962.

Schriften für politische Aufklärung. Der Abstimmungskampf in Oberschlesien. Berlin-Steglitz: Zentral-Europäischer Verlag GmbH, 1921.

Schumann, Wolfgang. Oberschlesien, 1918-1919: Vom gemeinsamen Kampf deutscher und polnischer Arbeiter. Berlin, DDR: Rütten und Leoning, 1961.

Schwenger, Rudolf. Die betriebliche Sozialpolitik im Ruhrkohlenbergbau. München und Leipzig: Verlag von Duncker und Humbolt, 1932.

Sprecht, Fritz and Schwabe, Paul. Die Reichstags-Wahlen von 1867 bis 1903. Berlin: Carl Heymanns Verlag, 1904.

Thernstrom, Stephan. The Other Bostonians: Poverty and Progress in the American Metropolis, 188-1970. Cambridge: Harvard University Press, 1973.

Tims, Richard W. Germanizing Prussian Poland. New York: Columbia University Press, 1941.

Vogel, Ilse. Bottrop: Eine Bergbaustadt in der Emscherzone des Ruhrgebiets. Remagen/Rhein: Bundesanstalt für Landeskunde, 1959.

Walter, Hubert. Untersuchungen zur Sozialanthropologie der Ruhrbevölkerung. Münster, Aschendorffische Verlagsbuchhandlung, 1962.

Wambaugh, Sarah. Plebiscites Since the World War with a Collection of Official Documents. 2 vols. Washington, D.C. Carnegie Endowment for International Peace, 1933.

Wehler, Hans-Ulrich. "Die Polen im Ruhrgebiet bis 1918." In Moderne deutsche Sozialgeschichte, pp. 437-455. Edited by Hans-Ulrich Wehler. Köln: Westdeutscher Verlag, 1966.

—————. Sozialdemokratie und Nationalstaat: Die deutsche Sozialdemokratie und die Nationalitätfragen in Deutschland von Karl Marx bis zum Ausbruch des Ersten Weltkrieges. Würzburg, Holzner Verlag, 1962.

Wrigley, E. A. Industrial Growth and Population Change. Cambridge: Cambridge University Press, 1961.

Periodicals

Bottroper Anzeiger. 1929-1933.

Bottroper Volkszeitung. 1885-1933.

Closterhalfern, Karl. "Die polnische Bevölkerung in Rheinland und Westfalen." Deutsche Erde, 10. Jg. (Gotha, 1911): 114-120.

Crew, David. "Definitions of Modernity: Social Mobility in a German town, 1880-1901." Journal of Social History, Vol. 7, Nr. 1 (Fall, 1973): 51-74.

Croon, Helmuth. "Die Einwirkung der Industrialisierung auf die gesellschaftliche Schichtung der Bevölkerung im rheinisch-westfälischen Industriegebiet." Rheinische Vierteljahresblätter, Nr. 20 (1955).

Engel. "Der Berarbeiterausstand im Ruhrbezirk im Jahre 1905." Glückauf, Nr. 8 (Februar 1905): 213-232.

Greely, Andrew M. "The Ethnic Miracle." The Public Interest, Nr. 45 (Fall, 1976): 20-36.

Hopkins, Richard J. "Occupational and Geographical Mobility in Atlanta, 1870-1896." Journal of Southern History, Nr. 2 (May, 1968): 200-213.

Kaelble, Harmut. "Sozialer Aufstieg in Deutschland, 1850-1914." Vierteljahrschrift für Sozial- und Wirtschaftsgeschichte, 60. Bd., Heft 1 (1973): 41-71.

Mehler, G. "Probleme der Poleneinwarderung im rheinisch-westfälischen Industriebezirk." Caritas, Nr. 7/8 (April/Mai, 1913): 193-198.

Perlick, Alfons. "Volkskunde der oberschlesischen Industriearbeiter." Der Oberschlesier, 17. Jg., 3. Heft (März, 1935): 123-142.

"Die Polen in Rheinland und Westfalen." Gau "Ruhr und Lippe" des Alldeutschen Verbandes, 10. Jg. (1900): 490-492.

Rochlitz, Walter. "Oberschlesiens Abstimmungssieg und Gesamtdeutschlands Schicksalsgemeinschaft." Deutsche Grenzland, Nr. 5/6 (März, 1931): 69-70.

Ronge, Paul. "Bottrop—fast eine Stadt der Oberschlesier." Unser Oberschlesien, Nr. 10 (1961).

—————. "Die Oberschlesiersiedlung Bottrop i. W." Schlesien, Heft IV (1960): 246-247.

—————. "Die polnischen Zuwanderer in das Ruhrgebiet: Stammestreue einer Minderheit." Westfälischer Heimatkalender (1971).

"Rücksiedlung aus dem Ruhrgebiet." Deutsche Werkmeister-Zeitung, Nr. 4 (January, 1932): 39-40.

Schauff, Johannes. "Die Ostsiedler aus dem Rheingebiet." Deutsche Grenzland, Nr. 3 (Februar, 1931): 30-32.

Schmidt, H. Th. "Belegschaftsbildung im Ruhrgebiet im Zeichen der Industrialisierung." Tradition, 3. Heft (August, 1957): 265-273.

"Statistik des Bergarbeiterausstand im Ruhrrevier." Glückauf, Nr. 20 (Mai, 1905): 641-643.

Dissertations

Chmielecki, Stanislaus. Die Bevölkerungs-Entwicklung im Stadt- und Landkreis Recklinghausen in den Jahren 1875 bis 1910. Freiburg, 1914.

Degen, Kurt. Die Herkunft der Arbeiter in den Industrien Rheinland-Westfalens bis zur Gründerzeit. Bonn, 1915.

Kaczmarek, Johannes. Die polnischen Arbeiter im rheinisch-westfälischen Industriegebiet. Köln, 1922.

Knirim, Ewald. Die Verschiebungen der Volksdichte im engeren westfälischen Ruhrgebiet von 1818 bis 1925 und ihre geographischen Grundlagen. Münster, 1928.

Metzner, Maria. Grenznot und Kommunalpolitik in Oberschlesien mit besonderer Berücksichtung von Beuthen, Gleiwitz, Hindenburg und Ratibor. Köln, 1935.

Müller, Robert. Die Bevölkerungsentwicklung des rheinisch-westfälischen Industriegebiets von 1895 bis 1919. Münster, 1921.

Oberschuir, Ewald. Die Heranziehung und Seßhaftmachung von Bergarbeitern im Ruhrkohlenbecken: Kritik der bisher getroffenen Massnahmen und Vorschläge zur Gewinnung eines sesshaften Arbeiterstammes. Aschen, 1910.

Raabe, Alexander. Die Abwanderungsbewegung in den östlichen Provinzen Preussens. Berlin, 1910.

Schäfer, Hans. Die Polenfrage im rheinisch-westfälischen Industrierevier während des Krieges und nach dem Kriege. Würzburg, 1921.

Schulze, Franz. Die polnische Zuwanderung im Ruhrrevier und ihre Wirkungen. München, 1909.

Stoltenberg, Otto. Herkunftsgebiet und Zuwanderung Bottroper Zechenbelegschaften am Ende des 19. Jahrhunderts. Bochum, 1970.

Wachowiak, Stanislaus. Die Polen in Rheinland-Westfalen. München, 1916.

miscellaneous

Ronge, Dr. Paul. Interview, 26 February 1973.

Westdeutscher Rundfunk. Oberschlesiersiedlung Bottrop: Was die Bergleute-Kartei von Paul Ronge erzählt. 29. April 1961.

INDEX

Alliance of Poles in Germany, 71, 146

Alter Verband, 69, 70, 75, 77, 78

Arenberg Bergbau, 46, 47, 130, 131, 134

Bergbaulicher Verein, 75, 123

Bottrop:
  archives, 7
  early economy, 41-3, 21-2
  effect of strikes on, 76, 77-8
  employment in, 41, 43, 46, 63-4
  growth of population in, 22-5, 31
  location, 21
  Polish dialect in, 95
  Polish population of, 29, 31, 83, 99, 135ff
  religious affiliation in 80-1

Bottroper Volkszeitung:
  and church board elections, 87, 89
  first mention of Poles, 29
  and local elections, 161-62, 163-64
  and plebiscites, 175, 176
  and Polish clerics, 82, 84
  and Polish *Vereine,* 155
  and strikes, 76, 78

Center Party (*Zentrum*), 145, 157, 158, 160, 161

Citizenship Option, 170

Coal Mining:
  development in Bottrop, 31
  employment in, 15, 46, 63, 120
  job variety in, 64
  production in, 15

Co-ownership Law (*Miteigentümergesetz*), 19

Elections:
  local (*Gemeinde*), 159ff
  Reichstag, 157-59, 166

Emigration from Ruhrgebiet:
  estimate of post-WWI, 177
  to France, 177, 183
  to the Netherlands, 183

Executive Committee (*Komitet Wykonowczy*), 147, 148, 182

Freedom of Movement Law (*Freizügigkeitgesetz*), 19, 123

Freedom of Occupation (*Gewerbefreiheit*), 65

General Mine Law, 70
  amended, 73

Germanization, 4, 5, 6, 28, 169, 190

Gewerkverein christlicher Bergarbeiter, 69, 70-71, 75, 77, 78

Hirsch-Duncker Union, 75

Home ownership, 124-25

Housing:
  colonies, 120, 126, 129
  company, 125ff
  and ethnicity, 133ff
  slum conditions in, 121

Knappschaft, 193
  election of officers, 70-71, 73
  reform of, 70

Kulturkampf, 4, 6, 82, 83

253

Labor:
migration, 19, 37-39
recruitment, 19, 28
turnover, 20, 122, 127-28
Liss, Dr.:
and Polish organizations, 145-6
and *Wiarus Polski,* 146

Marriage:
inter-class, 112-16
inter-ethnic, 116-18
"mail order", 106-7, 113-4
and out-migration, 185
outside Bottrop, 101-2
Mine Inspection Decree (*Bergpolizeiverordnung*), 67-68

Nationality (Legal and Cultural), 8, 20-21, 97-98

Oberbergamt Dortmund, 13, 65, 193, 194
Occupational mobility, 48ff
German and American rates compared, 54-58
inter-generational, 53-54, 59-60, 61
Occupations, distribution of, 46-47

Pan German League, 68
Persistence:
defined, 8-9
and demographic characteristics, 34-39
and housing, 127-28
and marriage, 103-105
and occupation, 48-49, 51, 58-9
Plebiscites:
in East Prussia, 172, 175
reaction to in Bottrop, 175-76
in Upper Silesia, 173-76
Pluralism, 6-7, 190-91, 199, 201
Polish Associations and clubs (*Vereine*), 145ff, 198

Polish language:
education, 4, 93ff, 195
religious services, 82-84, 88
Polish national state, 171-72
Polish parish:
elections in, 86-7, 88-9
founding of, 85-7
Polish Party, 3, 157ff, 170, 199
in Upper Silesia, 173
Polish Savings Bank, 153-54
Polish schools, 92-94, 97-99
Polish war dead, 155
Posen:
migration to, post-WWI, 182
school strike, 93-94
Settlement Law, 28
PPS (Polish Socialist Party), 159

Reich Law Concerning Organizations (*Reichsvereingesetz*) 5, 156, 167
Ruhrgebiet:
church board elections in, 90-91
coal mining in, 13-15
defined, 10-11
internal migration, 26, 179
as "Melting pot", 4-5, 190
population growth, 15-18
Polish population, 3, 20-21
sovereignty over, 11-12
wages in, 66

Sex ratio:
in Bottrop, 106-7
of in-migrants, 32, 106
in Prussia, 19-20, 106-107
in the Ruhrgebiet, 20, 106-7

Social Democrats (SPD), 150, 159ff
Sokół, 154-55
Strikes:
and company housing, 128-9
and lockouts, 122-3
of 1889, 74